Prince Albert;

at the age of four.

From a picture by Döll. Engraved by William Holl.

HARPER & BROTHERS.

THE EARLY YEARS

OF

HIS ROYAL HIGHNESS

THE PRINCE CONSORT.

COMPILED,

UNDER THE DIRECTION OF HER MAJESTY

THE QUEEN,

BY

LIEUT.-GENERAL THE HON. C. GREY.

NEW YORK:

HARPER & BROTHERS, PUBLISHERS,

FRANKLIN SQUARE.

1867.

CONTENTS.

CHAPTER V.

1832–1833.

CHAPTER VI.

1832–1835.

CHAPTER VII.

1835–1837.

CHAPTER VIII.

April, 1837, *to the close of* 1838.

CHAPTER IX.

1838–1839.

CHAPTER X.

1839.

CHAPTER XI.

1839.

CHAPTER XII.

1840.

CHAPTER XIII.

1840.

CHAPTER XIV.

1840.

FIRST YEAR OF MARRIAGE.

APPENDICES.

APPENDIX A.

APPENDIX B.

APPENDIX C.

APPENDIX D.

APPENDIX E.

APPENDIX F.

Directions to the Binder.

PREFACE.

This volume was originally compiled, under the Queen's direction, solely for private circulation among the members of her own family, or such other persons as, from the relations in which they had stood to her Majesty or to the Prince Consort himself, would naturally be interested in the story of his early days.

As, however, notwithstanding the limited circulation to which it was intended to confine the volume, there was felt to be considerable danger of a copy being surreptitiously obtained and published, possibly in a garbled form, the question arose whether it might not be expedient to avert this danger by publishing it in substantially the same form as that in which it was first printed for private circulation.

Acting upon the opinion of several persons in whose judgment she had the greatest confidence; believing also that the free and unreserved expression which the volume contains of her own feelings, as well as of those of the Prince, is such as, if made public (however unusual such publicity may be), will command the entire sympathy of every one whose sympathy or good opinion is to be desired; and, above all, feeling that there is not one word coming from the Prince himself which will not tend to a better and higher appreciation of his great character, the Queen has not hesitated to give her consent to the present publication.

"In regard to the effect of the volume upon the people of England," writes one of the oldest, most devoted, and most honored of the Prince's friends,* "should her Majesty hereafter resolve to publish it, there can not, I think, be the shadow of a doubt, should it ever come before them, that it would exact the loyalty and love of all true-hearted Englishmen. . . . . Where every thing is so pure, so lovely, and so true, why should not our honored and beloved Queen lay open the innermost recesses of her heart, and thereby fix forever the loyal sympathy of all who have faith in what is good, and hold true Christian allegiance to their God and to their country?"

Then speaking of the impression produced on himself by a perusal of the volume, he proceeds: "You will forgive me for noting down one or two thoughts which struck me while reading your volume. We now see, from first to last, the beautiful consistency of the Prince's character. He was a lovely boy with a gentle temper; yet even then he had a mental strength above his years, which gave him the mastery over his elder brother. And so it was in after life. Those gentler qualities, which made him the purest pattern of domestic love, never, for a moment, degenerated into feebleness or effeminacy, but were carried out into a noble purpose by their unbroken union with the firm will of his great and unselfish heart. From his earliest years he seems never to have flinched from labor, and he had amassed vast treasures of exact knowledge, which he did not for a moment exhibit for ostentation, but he made them bear,

* Professor Sedgwick. He was Secretary to the Prince as Chancellor of the University of Cambridge.

at every turn of life, upon some intellectual aim or some plan that would tell upon the moral and physical good of his fellow-creatures.

"If it be good for man, as is taught by the poet Goethe, daily to see and to feast upon objects of great beauty in art and nature, surely the contemplation of a character at once so great and so beautiful as that of the Prince Consort should be a sublime and touching lesson to our countrymen."

Thus wrote Professor Sedgwick on the 27th of May, 1867, to the editor of this volume, and it would be vain to try and add a syllable to the beautiful picture here given of the Prince's character; the more so, as in the introductory remarks to the volume as first printed, and which are here reproduced, will be found an attempt to describe that character at some length; and a still fuller and more comprehensive estimate of it will naturally fall to be given when the whole story of the Prince's life is placed before the world in the volumes by which this is to be succeeded.

The task of preparing those volumes will be executed by other and abler hands. His own occupations making it impossible for him to undertake it, the present editor is happy to think that Mr. Theodore Martin has, at the request of the Queen, consented to go on with, and has for some time been engaged upon, the work, for the prosecution of which he will have the same advantages as to information from authentic sources that have been enjoyed in the preparation of the present volume.

June, 1867.

LETTER TO THE QUEEN

ON COMPLETING THE

VOLUME FOR PRIVATE CIRCULATION.

MADAM,—I have now the honor to submit to your Majesty the various Letters and Memoranda intrusted to me by your Majesty, as, in obedience to your Majesty's commands, I have arranged and connected them to the best of my ability.

I am well aware how far my execution of the work falls short of what your Majesty had a right to expect, of what I myself could have wished, and of what the subject demands. It is, however, a satisfaction to me to feel that no failure on my part in the performance of the portion of the task allotted to me can detract from the simple beauty of many of the letters that will be found in the following pages, or from the interest in the picture of a happy domestic life, as drawn in your Majesty's own Memoranda.

As I believe your Majesty intends to limit the circulation of this volume to your Majesty's own children and family, or, if it goes beyond them, to a very small circle of personal friends, I have not thought it necessary to omit any of the very interesting and private details contained in your Majesty's Memoranda, or to withhold the touching expression of your Majesty's feelings, as given in your Majesty's own words. Some of these details, particularly those relating to your Majesty's marriage, it might seem unusual to include in a work intended for more general perusal, though even in that case, judging of others' feeling by my own, I can not doubt that they would meet with the warmest and most heartfelt sympathy.

The translations of the Prince's letters, as they appear in the text, are for the most part, and with a few merely verbal corrections, by Princess Helena. They are made, as it appears to me, with surprising fidelity; but the originals of most of them will be found in an Appendix, for the benefit of those who may wish to read them in the language in which they were written.

The present volume closes with the end of the first year of your Majesty's married life. The farther prosecution of the work will be a matter of greater difficulty.

From the Prince's constantly increasing connection with the political events of the day (so many of the principal actors in which are still living), it will be impossible to do full justice to his character without a reference to those events, and to the influence which he brought to bear upon them. Moreover, the Prince's occupations were so varied and multifarious—he gave himself with such energy and persevering activity to whatever could benefit his fellow-man, that to follow him, even through one branch of his useful and unintermitted labors for the good of his adopted country, would afford ample work to a single pen.

The early days, however, to which this volume relates, speak the promise so nobly realized of his future years.

I have felt it to be a great privilege to have been allowed to assist in your Majesty's work of love; and it will be a source of lasting gratification to me if the result shall be to make more generally known—at least as far as the limited circulation which your Majesty intends for this volume shall allow—the virtues and great qualities of one to whom I was bound by the strongest ties of gratitude and affection.

I remain, with the most heartfelt devotion, your Majesty's very humble and obedient subject and servant,

C. GREY.

Windsor Castle, March, 1866.

INTRODUCTORY REMARKS.

Albert — using only the name by which he was known and endeared to the British people—second son of Ernest I., Duke of Saxe-Coburg-Gotha, and husband of our beloved Queen, was lineally descended from those great Saxon princes whose names are immortalized in European history by the stand they made in defense of their country's liberties against the encroaching power of the German Emperors, as well as by the leading part they took in the struggle for the emancipation of the human mind from the trammels of Romish bigotry and superstition.

The names of Frederick the Warlike, first Prince Elector of Saxony; of Frederick the Wise, the friend and protector of Luther; and of John Frederick the Magnanimous, selected from a long list of rulers scarcely inferior to them in fame, sufficiently attest the by-gone glories of the race.

But to none of those great ancestors can the present descendants of that illustrious house turn with more just pride than to him whose loss the world finds every day more cause to mourn.

If goodness and virtue are inseparable from true greatness, where shall we find in history a more perfect combination of all the qualities that make a man truly great?

Eminent ability joined with the purest virtue—unremitting attention to the multifarious duties of a position all but the highest, combined with the most watchful and active benevolence—power and influence only valued as the means of advancing the best interests of mankind!

To him our leading statesmen loved to repair in all questions of doubt and difficulty, sure to find in his grasp of intellect, in his foresight and fertility of resource, in his clear and dispassionate judgment, his practical common sense, a helping hand out of their embarrassments. Upon his knowledge and sound principles the philanthropist could rely with confidence for the safe and effectual development of all schemes of improvement and general utility; the man of science for practical assistance in prosecuting his studies, or in making known their result to the world; while the artist—the sculptor and the painter—men of European reputation—were not ashamed to acknowledge their obligation to his fertile genius and cultivated taste.

If to these talents and accomplishments, and to the social qualities that fitted him to shine so eminently in public and private life, we add genuine and unaffected love of virtue and abhorrence of vice*—the latter feeling, however, tempered by the charity that thinketh no evil, springing from innate warmth and kindness of heart—above all, if we look to the childlike purity and innocence of mind, preserved unsullied in deed and in

* "Its presence depressed him, grieved him, horrified him. His tolerance allowed him to make excuses for the vices of individual men, but the evil itself he hated."—*Introduction to Speeches and Addresses of H. R. H. the Prince Consort*, published in 1864, p. 43.

thought, from the cradle to the grave—we have indeed before us a character which may well be held up as a bright and glorious example for the emulation, as well as the love and admiration, of future generations.

How beautiful is the evidence borne to the Prince's goodness and excellence by those who knew him best—by his nearest relatives,* his tutor, and his most intimate friends. What a noble spirit of self-sacrifice and devotion to duty breathes in every line of the beautiful letters to his grandmother, and the friend of his youth, Baron Stockmar, written by him just before his marriage.† Well might it be said of him that "he was one of those few men into whose minds questions of self-interest never enter, or are absolutely ignored when the paramount obligation of duty is presented to them."‡

Then, again, what high aspirations after the power of doing good do we find in the same letters—what evidence of the "presence of a large and loving nature, where the lovingness takes heed of all humanity."§

The Prince's extraordinary "good nature and prompt sympathy forbade him to ignore any question that interested his fellow-men."‖ Indeed, to such an extent was this the case, that it may be too truly said of him that his life fell a sacrifice to his unceasing exertions in their cause.

"To put the cup of this world's gladness to his lips and yet not to be intoxicated—to gaze steadily on all its

* See especially the letter written by his brother, the present reigning Duke of Saxe-Coburg, when the marriage was arranged.—Chap. xi., page 212.

† Chap. x., pages 191, 196, 198, etc.

‡ *Introduction to Speeches*, p. 31.

§ Ibid.

‖ Ibid.

grandeur and yet to be undazzled—plain and simple in personal desires, to feel its brightness and yet defy its thrall—this is the difficult, and rare, and glorious life of God in the soul of man."* And to this the Prince, if any man, most surely attained.

Mixed up as the Prince was of late years with all the most important events of an eventful period, it would be premature to attempt any account of his life which should enter into a detailed history of those events; and without doing this, it would be impossible to do him justice, or to make him known as he ought to be known to a world of which he was so great a benefactor.

We may, however, even now prepare the way for the future biographer, and to do this is the object of the present volume. It will contain a compilation of letters and memoranda, the greater part of those of the Prince himself, and of the Queen, from which materials may, at the proper time, be extracted for such a memoir as may be given to the world. In the mean time, printed privately for the use and study of his children, with such an amount of narrative as appears necessary for their due connection, they will furnish those children, and perhaps children's children to the remotest times, with such an example of unselfish devotion to duty as may well encourage them, in imitation of their great parent, to strive, as he did, to discharge the duties of their high callings without deviating from the path of virtue and true greatness.

These letters and memoranda will speak for themselves. We shall be able to trace in them the whole

* *Robertson's Sermons,* vol. ii., p. 282.

career of the illustrious Prince—his progress from boyhood to manhood—from manhood to the grave. We shall see the boy, scarcely yet emerged from infancy, winning the love as well as the respect of his instructors.* We shall follow him as he advances toward manhood, still keeping the promise of his earliest years, thirsting for knowledge, and laborious and persevering in its acquirement, but seeking after it for the noblest of purposes—that he might be better enabled to promote the happiness and to improve the condition of his fellow-man.†

Grown to man's estate, and raised to the commanding position of the Consort of England's Queen, we shall find his great character developing itself in ever grander proportions: as a husband and a father, fulfilling every domestic duty with the most affectionate care and the tenderest solicitude; as the adviser and assister of the sovereign in her daily communications with her ministers,‡

* See Memorandum by his tutor, Herr Florschütz, at the end of Chap. v., page 89 *et seq.*

† "It was for the 'relief of man's estate' that this amiable Prince delighted most in the extension of the bounds of knowledge."—*Preface to Speeches*, p. 46.

‡ M. Guizot says, in his introduction to his translation of the Prince's Speeches: "A la fois actif et modeste, ne recherchant point, évitant même toute apparence vaniteuse dans le Gouvernement, bien que très sérieusement préoccupé des affaires publiques de l'Angleterre, et des intérêts de la couronne placée sur la tête de sa femme: il a été, pendant vingt et un ans, le premier sujet et le premier conseiller de la Reine Victoria, son intime et seul secrétaire, associé sans bruit à toutes ses délibérations, à toutes ses résolutions, habile à l'éclairer et à la seconder dans ses rapports avec son Ministère, sans gêner ni offusquer le Ministère lui-même, exerçant à côté du trône une judicieuse et salutaire influence, sans jamais

making the interest and prosperity of the kingdom his undivided object; displaying an unusual capacity for public business, and in political and international questions, often of the most complicated nature, giving evidence of a coolness of judgment and fertility of resource which had already given him a weight and an authority in the councils of Europe that bade fair not only to equal, but to surpass those which were conceded by universal consent to the wisdom and long experience of his uncle Leopold, king of the Belgians.*†

In studying such a life, though it may be given to few, if any, to attain the full height of the standard thus set before them, his children will find the strongest incentive to do nothing unworthy of their great sire.

dépasser un rôle, ni porter atteinte aux conditions du régime constitutionnel."

* "If the Prince had lived to attain what we now think a good old age, he would inevitably have become the most accomplished statesman and the most guiding personage in Europe: a man to whose arbitrament fierce national quarrels might have been submitted, and by whose influence calamitous wars might have been averted."—*Preface to Speeches*, p. 55.

† As these sheets pass through the press, the news arrives that the life of this great and enlightened sovereign has been brought to a close; that his long and beneficent reign has ended amid the lamentations of his subjects and with the regret of all Europe. How well he has done his work—how completely he understood and identified himself with the spirit of the age—is proved by the two very remarkable demonstrations in Brussels of Saturday, the 17th, and Sunday, the 18th of December: on the former day by the respectful demeanor and unmistakable expression of sorrow that clouded every brow among the countless thousands that thronged the line of the funeral procession from Brussels to Laeken; on the following day by the no less unmistakable and universal display of popular enthusiasm that marked the entry of his son and successor into

Oh how should England, dreaming of his sons,
Hope more for these than *some* inheritance
Of such a life!—a heart—a mind as thine,
Thou noble father of her kings to be!

Since writing the above I have had the privilege of reading the beautiful address delivered on the last sad anniversary of our loss, by Dr. Macleod, to three of the Prince's children—the Crown Princess of Prussia, Princess Louis of Hesse, and Prince Alfred. How must their hearts have burned within them while they listened to the following glowing summary of their great Father's character:

". . . . . Yet in trying circumstances which constantly demanded from him a positive opinion, advice, decision, and action, on affairs of state and matters of world interest—in addition to those duties, themselves extremely onerous, belonging to his domestic and social life, the Prince not only came out of every ordeal unscathed, but triumphant and nobler than before. Who ever heard one whisper breathed against his moral character? What false step in politics did he ever take? What wrong advice on any subject did he ever tender? What movement, great or small, did he originate which was not beneficial to the state, and worthy of our honor and our greatness? What enemies did he ever make, unless possibly among such persons as have no sympathy with goodness, truth, or justice in any man? So completely did he become identified with all that was worth loving

his capital, and proved the devotion of the Belgians to their constitutional sovereign and to the independence of their country.

in the nation; so intuitively did he discern its wants, and those points on which, while preserving all that was good, true progress toward something better was possible, and therefore desirable—that all classes, all interests, claimed him as their leader. Commerce, agriculture, science, arts, the cottage and the camp, the great men in the nation, as well as the domestic servant and the ragged child, recognized in him their wisest guide and truest friend. For the attainment of whatever could benefit them, 'the Prince of all the land led them on.'

". . . . Few men who have ever lived, no prince certainly of whom we read, could have possessed a mind so many-sided with such corresponding political and social influence. He was, indeed, the type of a new era—an era of power; but not of that kind of power represented by the armor of his noble ancestors, the power of mere physical strength, courage, or endurance, displayed at the head of armies or of fleets, but the moral power of character, the power of intellectual culture, of extensive knowledge, of earnest thought; the power of the sagacious statesman, of the *single-minded good man;* that power which discerns, interprets, and guides the wants and the spirit of the age—the power, in short, of highest wisdom directed by genuine benevolence to higher objects.

". . . . His real strength lay most of all in his character, or in that which resulted from will and deliberate choice, springing out of a nature singularly pure, by God's grace, from childhood.

". . . . It is only now, when he is gone, that all who knew him are made to feel how much they unconsciously depended upon him! like a staff on which the weak have been so long accustomed to lean, that they know not how essential it was to their support until it be removed, and when with a sigh they withdraw the hand from the place, now empty, where it was wont to be!

"It is this feature in the Prince's character," Dr. Macleod adds, "which ought to make every one sympathize to the very utmost with her Majesty, who, of all persons on earth, had the best means of knowing it, and the best means of proving it in a thousand ways in every-day life, and who had the best grounds, therefore, for appreciating its constancy, its tenderness, its unfailing strength." And well may the eloquent preacher appeal to "every true English heart or conscience" to acknowledge the demand which "now arises in mute eloquence from the throne for the sympathy, the prayers, the loyal self-sacrificing aid of every member of her house, and of every citizen of our Christian nation, on her behalf whom God, in His Providence, has been pleased to spare, and in mercy to continue to us, as our beloved Sovereign."

THE EARLY YEARS
OF
HIS ROYAL HIGHNESS
THE PRINCE CONSORT.
1819–1841.

CHAPTER I.
1819–1823.

The Saxe-Coburg Family.—Birth and early Infancy of the Princes.—Birth of Princess Victoria.—Letters from the Duchess of Coburg, and from the Dowager Duchesses of Coburg and of Gotha.

PRINCE ALBERT was descended from the Ernestine, or elder branch of the great Saxon family. That branch had, however, lost its birthright in the course of the 16th century. Frederick the Wise, elector of Saxony, had been the protector of Martin Luther, and was one of the first to embrace the doctrines of the Reformed Church, of which he was the most powerful supporter. His immediate successors adhered to the same religious opinions, and after the defeat of John Frederick the Magnanimous by Charles V., at Mühlberg, in 1547, they paid the penalty of their devotion to the Protestant faith in the forced surrender of their inheritance to the younger, or Albertine branch of the family, by the descendants of which the Saxon throne is still occupied.

It is not easy to trace the arrangement by which, on losing the electorate, now the kingdom of Saxony, the Ernestine branch acquired the several duchies still possessed by its descendants. It would be still more difficult to follow out the laws of succession—the intermarriages, etc., leading to the redistribution or interchange of territory, in consequence of which these different duchies came into the possession now of this, now of that member of the family. The custom of dividing and subdividing their inheritance among their sons seems long to have prevailed with these Saxon dukes. Thus the dukedoms of Saxe-Gotha-Altenburg, of Saxe-Meiningen, of Saxe-Hildburghausen, and of Saxe-Coburg-Saalfeld were, on the death, in 1679, of Ernest the Pious, duke of Saxe-Gotha-Coburg, and great-grandson of the last elector of the Ernestine branch, John Frederick the Magnanimous, divided severally among his sons. Of these, the eldest, Frederick, inherited the duchies of Saxe-Gotha-Altenburg, while that of Saxe-Coburg-Saalfeld fell to the share of the youngest, John Ernest, the immediate ancestor of our Prince.

Francis Joseph, son and successor of John Ernest, had four sons, of whom the eldest, Ernest Frederick, succeeded him as reigning duke in 1764; while the third, Frederick, having greatly distinguished himself in the Austrian service, was made a field-marshal, and commanded the allied armies in the Netherlands for some time in the beginning of the French Revolutionary war.*

* An interesting notice of this generation of the family, and particu-

Ernest Frederick was succeeded, in 1800, by Francis Frederick, his eldest son, who died in 1806, leaving three sons and four daughters.

1. Ernest, the father of our Prince, who succeeded his father as Duke of Saxe-Coburg-Saalfeld, under the title of Ernest I. To this inheritance, by a family arrangement made in 1825, on the death of Frederick IV., the last male descendant of Frederick, duke of Saxe-Gotha-Altenburg, eldest son of Ernest the Pious above mentioned, and confirmed in November, 1826, he added the duchy of Gotha. But, in accordance with the same arrangement, he had to surrender the duchy of Saalfeld to the Duke of Meiningen—Saxe-Altenburg being, at the same time, separated from the duchy of Gotha, and given to the Duke of Hildburghausen, who assumed the former title, Hildburghausen itself being also added to the territory of the Duke of Meiningen.

2. Ferdinand George, who married the heiress of the Prince of Kohary in Hungary, and whose son became King Consort of Portugal by his marriage with Queen Donna Maria II. of that kingdom.

3. Leopold, the late King of the Belgians.

Duke Francis also left four daughters.

1. Sophia, who, after refusing many eligible proposals of marriage of her own rank, married, in 1804, Count Mensdorff-Pouilly, who, emigrating from France at the Revolution, attained high rank and distinction in the Austrian service. The greatest intimacy and friendship existed in youth between her sons, all distinguished in

larly of the field-marshal, will be found in Appendix A., *et seqq.*, containing the Reminiscences of the King of the Belgians.

the Austrian service,* and their cousin Prince Albert,† and an interesting account of his recollections of the Prince, by Count Arthur Mensdorff, will be found in a subsequent chapter.

2. Antoinette, married, in 1798, to Duke Alexander of Würtemberg, brother to the Empress Mother of Russia (mother to the Emperors Alexander and Nicholas), who had a very influential position in Russia, and lived there for many years.

3. Julie, the third, married, at fifteen, to the late Grand-duke Constantine of Russia. But this marriage was not a happy one, and in 1802 she left Russia, fixing her residence finally at Elfenau, near Berne, in Switzerland,‡ where, it will be seen, the Prince, in the course of a pedestrian tour, paid her a visit in September, 1837, as he also did on several occasions afterward.

4. Victoire Marie Louise, the youngest daughter, married, first, the Prince of Leiningen; and, secondly, the Duke of Kent, as whose widow, and as the mother of our Queen, she lived for the remainder of her life in England, beloved by her family and friends, and endeared, by her many virtues and innumerable acts of kindness, to the whole British nation.

Ernest I., eldest son of Duke Francis by Augusta, daughter of Prince Henry XXIV. of Reuss-Ebersdorff, was born in 1784, and, as already mentioned, succeeded

* One of them, Count Alexander Mensdorff, is now [1866] Minister for Foreign Affairs at Vienna.

† See Appendix A.

‡ For more detailed accounts of his sisters and family, see Reminiscences of the King of the Belgians, Appendix A.

his father in 1806 as reigning Duke of Saxe-Coburg-Saalfeld.

The dukedom was at that time in the occupation of the French, and the new duke and other members of the family were objects of great suspicion to the French government. The reminiscences of his brother, the King of the Belgians, which will be found in Appendix A., at the end of the volume, will give a good idea of the difficulties with which Duke Ernest had, in consequence, to contend at his accession and for many years afterward; nor was it till the emancipation of Germany in 1813 from the oppressive domination so long exercised over her by Napoleon that he can be said to have come fairly into possession of his inheritance.

A marriage with a Russian grand-duchess had originally been in contemplation for the young duke; but this was broken off in 1812, and in 1817 he married the Princess Louise, daughter, by his first wife, a Princess of Mecklenburg Schwerin, of Augustus,* last reigning duke but one of Saxe-Gotha-Altenburg. By her he had two sons, Ernest, the present reigning duke, born at the Ehrenburg, the Ducal Palace at Coburg, on the 21st of June, 1818, and Albert, the subject of the following memoir, born at the Rosenau, a charming summer residence belonging to the duke about four miles from Coburg, on the 26th of August, 1819.

In a Memorandum written in 1864, the Queen gives the following account of the duchess:

* He married, secondly, the Princess Caroline of Hesse Cassel, born in 1768, daughter of William, ninth Elector of Hesse, and of Wilhelmina of Denmark. She was the Duchess of Gotha so constantly mentioned in the following pages, and died February 28, 1848.

"The princess is described as having been very handsome, though very small; fair, with blue eyes; and Prince Albert is said to have been extremely like her. An old servant who had known her for many years told the Queen that when she first saw the Prince at Coburg in 1844, she was quite overcome by the resemblance to his mother.

"She was full of cleverness and talent; but the marriage was not a happy one, and a separation took place in 1824, when the young duchess finally left Coburg, and never saw her children again. She died at St. Wendel in 1831, after a long and painful illness, in her 32d year.

"The Duchess Dowager of Gotha, her stepmother, writes to the Duke the following account of her on the 27th of July, 1831:

"'The sad state of my poor Louise bows me to the earth. . . . . The thought that her children had forgotten her distressed her very much. She wished to know if they ever spoke of her. I answered her that they were far too good to forget her; that they did not know of her sufferings, as it would grieve the good children too much.'

"The Prince never forgot her, and spoke with much tenderness and sorrow of his poor mother, and was deeply affected in reading, after his marriage, the accounts of her sad and painful illness. One of the first gifts he made to the Queen was a little pin he had received from her when a little child. Princess Louise (the Prince's fourth daughter, and named after her grandmother) is said to be like her in face.

"On receiving the news of her death, the amiable Duchess of Gotha again writes to the Duke of Coburg:

"'My dear Duke,—This also I have to endure, that that child whom I watched over with such love should go before me. May God soon allow me to be reunited to all my loved ones. . . . It is a most bitter feeling that that dear, dear house [of Gotha] is now quite extinct.' The Duchess Louise was the last descendant of the family. Many years later, her earthly remains were brought to Coburg, and she now reposes next the duke and his second wife in the fine family mausoleum at Coburg, only completed in the year 1860, where the Queen herself placed a wreath of flowers on her tomb in the autumn of that year."

Prince Albert was born, as has been already stated, at the Rosenau, a summer residence of the duke's, about four miles from Coburg. His grandmother, the Dowager Duchess of Coburg-Saalfeld, resided at this time at Ketschendorf, a small villa about a quarter of a mile on the other side of Coburg. A little before seven in the morning of the 26th of August, 1819, a groom from the Rosenau rode into the court-yard of Ketschendorf to summon the duchess to the former place, bringing the news of the safe confinement of her daughter-in-law and of the birth of the young Prince. But let the duchess give her own account of the event. She thus writes to her daughter, the Duchess of Kent, the following day:

"*Rosenau, August* 27, 1819.

"The date will of itself make you suspect that I am sitting by Louischen's bed. She was yesterday morning safely and quickly delivered of a little boy. Siebold, the accoucheuse, had only been called at three, and at six the little one gave his first cry in this world, and looked about like a little squirrel with a pair of large black eyes.* At a quarter to seven I heard the tramp of a horse. It was a groom, who brought the joyful news. I was off directly, as you may imagine, and found the little mother slightly exhausted, but *gaie et dispos.* She sends you and Edward (the Duke of Kent) a thousand kind messages.

"Louise is much more comfortable here than if she had been laid up in town. The quiet of this house, only interrupted by the murmuring of the water, is so agreeable. But I had many battles to fight to assist her in effecting her wish. Dr. Müller found it inconvenient. The Hof-Marshal thought it impossible—particularly if the christening was to be here also. No one considered the noise of the palace at Coburg, the shouts of the children, and the rolling of the carriages in the streets.

"The little boy is to be christened to-morrow,† and to have the name of Albert. The Emperor of Austria, the old Duke Albert of Saxe-Teschen, the Duke of Gotha, Mensdorff, and I, are to be sponsors. Our boys will have the same names as the sons of the Elector Frederick the Mild, who were stolen by Kuntz of Kauffungen—namely, Ernest and Albert. Ernest minor" (he was then just 14 months old) "runs about like a weasel. He is teething, and as cross as a little badger from impatience and

* The eyes, however, were blue.

† This, however, was not the case. He was christened on the 19th of September, in the Marble Hall at the Rosenau.

liveliness. He is not pretty now, except his beautiful black eyes.

"How pretty the *May Flower* will be when I see it in a year's time. Siebold can not sufficiently describe what a dear little love it is. *Une bonne fois*, adieu! Kiss your husband and children. AUGUSTA."

The *May Flower* above spoken of was the Princess (now Queen) Victoria, who had been born on the 24th of May preceding. And it is a curious coincidence, considering the future connection of the children, that Mdme. Siebold, the accoucheuse spoken of above as attending the Duchess of Coburg at the birth of the young Prince, had, only three months before, attended the Duchess of Kent at the birth of the Princess.

The Dowager Duchess, whose letter announcing the young Prince's birth we have just read, had thus written to her daughter on that occasion.

"*June*, 1819.

"I can not express how happy I am to know you, dearest, dearest Vickel, safe in your bed with a little one, and that all went off so happily. May God's best blessings rest on the little stranger and the beloved mother.

"Again a Charlotte* — destined, perhaps, to play a great part one day, if a brother is not born to take it out of her hands.

"The English like queens, and the niece† of the ev-

* The Princess Charlotte of Wales had died the preceding year, and this made the young Princess heiress presumptive to the throne on the death of her father and uncles.

† She was first cousin, but niece as well—the Princess Charlotte having married the little Princess's uncle, Prince Leopold.

er-lamented, beloved Charlotte will be most dear to them.

"I need not tell you how delighted every body is here in hearing of your safe confinement. You know that you are much beloved in this your little home."

The Duke of Kent lived but a short time after the birth of his daughter. On the 23d of January, 1820, only a few days before his father, King George III.,* he died, and left his duchess a widow for the second time.

On the 19th of September the young Prince was christened in the Marble Hall at the Rosenau, when he received the following names in the order in which they are given: Francis Charles Augustus Albert Emmanuel. The name by which he was known, Albert, being the last but one.

When the Queen was at the Rosenau in 1863, the Prince's former tutor, M. Florschütz, gave her a copy of the address pronounced on the occasion of the baptism by the Superintendent Genzler, whose daughter M. Florschütz had married. Nor is it without interest to note in passing that Professor Genzler had before officiated at the marriage of the Duke and Duchess of Kent, which took place in the Palace at Coburg in 1818, and that he received the Queen and Prince at Coburg when they paid their first visit to it after their marriage, in 1844.†

In this address there are two passages so strikingly and completely realized and fulfilled in the beloved Prince's great, pure, and spotless character — so absolutely prophetic of his after life—that it would be an unpardonable omission not to insert them here.

* He died January 29th, 1820.

† Memorandum by the Queen.

"The good wishes," said the preacher, "with which we welcome this infant as a Christian, as one destined to be great on earth, and as a future heir to everlasting life, are the more earnest, when we consider the *high position in life in which he may one day be placed, and the sphere of action to which the will of God may call him, in order to contribute more or less to the promotion of truth and virtue, and to the extension of the kingdom of God.* . . . . The thoughts and supplications of the loving mother are, that her beloved son may one day enter into the kingdom of God as *pure* and as *innocent after the trials of this life as he is at this moment* (the joy and hope of his parents) received into the communion of this Christian Church, whose vocation it is to bring up and form on earth a God-fearing race."

Had these words, pronounced by the officiating clergyman at the Prince's baptism, been used after his premature death, could they, by possibility, have been more descriptive of him? Surely no man ever went beyond him in a constant, persevering devotion of himself "to the promotion of truth and virtue;" and of none could it have been said with more truth over the grave, that the trials and temptations of the world had left him as pure and innocent at that closing scene as when first "received" an infant in his nurse's arms "into the communion of the Christian Church."

On the 22d of May, 1820, when Prince Albert was barely eight months old, his mother thus describes her children: "Ernest est bien grand pour son âge, vif et intelligent. Ses grands yeux noirs pétillent d'esprit et de vivacité. . . . Albert est superbe—d'une beauté extraordinaire; a de grands yeux bleus, une toute petite bouche

—un joli nez—et des fossettes à chaque joue—il est grand et vif, et toujours gai. Il a trois dents, et malgré qu'il n'a que huit mois, il commence déjà à marcher."

"Albert est toujours beau, gai et bon, et a sept dents," writes his mother again in July of the same year—"il marche déjà, quelquefois tout seul, et dit 'papa et maman;' n'est-ce pas," she adds, in all the pride of a young mother's heart, "n'est-ce pas un petit prodige pour dix mois?"

Again, when the young Prince was two years old, she writes: "Albert adore son oncle Léopold, ne le quitte pas un instant, lui fait des yeux doux, l'embrasse à chaque moment, et ne se sent pas d'aise que lorsqu'il peut être auprès de lui. . . . . Il est charmant de taille, blond, et yeux bleus. Ernest est très-fort et robuste, mais pas la moitié si joli. Il est beau, et a des yeux noirs."

And a few months later: "Mes enfans ont faits les délices de leurs aïeuls. Ils grandissent beaucoup et deviennent très amusants. L'aîné surtout parait avoir de l'esprit, et le petit captive tous les cœurs par sa beauté et sa gentillesse."

The Dowager Duchess of Coburg continued to watch with the tenderest affection over the progress of the young princes, her grandchildren; and the letters from her which will be quoted in the course of this Memoir, up to the time of her death in 1831, breathe in every line a spirit of simplicity and love that speaks to the heart. The King of the Belgians, in his reminiscences, describes her as being in every way "a most distinguished person;" and the Queen, speaking of her many years later, thus records her recollections:

"The Queen remembers her dear grandmother perfectly well. She was a most remarkable woman, with a most powerful, energetic, almost masculine mind, accompanied with great tenderness of heart, and extreme love for nature.

"The Prince told the Queen that she had wished earnestly that he should marry the Queen, and as she died when her grandchildren (the Prince and Queen) were only twelve years old, she could have little guessed what a blessing she was preparing not only for this country, but for the world at large. She was adored by her children, particularly by her sons; King Leopold being her great favorite.

"She had fine and most expressive blue eyes, with the marked features and long nose inherited by most of her children and grandchildren.

"Both the Prince and his brother were exceedingly attached to her, and they lived much with her in their younger days. Of an evening the Prince said she was in the habit of telling them the story of Walter Scott's novels, and she used often to employ them in writing letters from her dictation. This was especially the case in 1829 or '30, when there was a question of her son, Prince (afterward King) Leopold, going to Greece."*

The following letters, written by her to her daughter the Duchess of Kent in 1821, show the fond affection with which she regarded her grandchildren.

"10 *February*, 1821.

"Albert is teething like his little cousin,† but he is

* Memorandum by the Queen. † Princess (now Queen) Victoria.

feverish with it and not at all well. He is not a strong child. Ernest gets much more easily over it, because he is more lively."

"11 *July*, 1821.

"Ernest's little boys are very amusing. Little Alberinchen, with his large blue eyes and dimpled cheeks, is bewitching, forward, and quick as a weasel. He can already say every thing. Ernest is not nearly as pretty, only his intelligent brown eyes are very fine; but he is tall, active, and very clever for his age."

"11 *August*, 1821.

"Leopold is very kind to the little boys. Bold Alberinchen drags him constantly about by the hand. The little fellow is the pendant to the pretty cousin; very handsome, but too slight for a boy; lively, very funny, all good nature, and full of mischief. The other day he did not know how to make enough of me because I took him with me in the carriage. He kept on saying, 'Albert is going with grandmamma,' and gave me his little hand to kiss. 'There, grandmamma, kiss.'"

But the children had another loving relative at Gotha in their step-maternal godmother, the Duchess of Saxe-Gotha-Altenburg, second wife of Duke Augustus, father by his first wife of the Prince's mother.* She was a very sensible woman, with the kindest heart, and of the most genuine and unaffected goodness. Charming evidence of these qualities will be found in her letters quoted in this volume; whether she gives expression to her maternal solicitude for the welfare of the people over

* See note, page 29.

whom her husband had so long reigned, or to the devoted love she felt for her grandchildren, in whom, from their earliest infancy, she took an affectionate interest, not surpassed by that of their own grandmother at Coburg. Indeed, their two grandmothers seemed to vie with each other as to which should show them the most love and kindness; and it is from the letters, now of one, now of the other, that we get the best account of the childhood and youth of the young princes.

In the spring of 1822 the Duke and Duchess of Coburg were absent from Coburg, and the dowager duchess being also away for a short time, the children were alone at Coburg. The Duchess of Gotha therefore invited them to go to her in the following letter to their father, and the invitation was at once accepted.

"*Gotha, May* 2, 1822.

"As your dear mother will not return for some time to Coburg, and the dear children will consequently be left alone, I venture to make a proposal, in which my husband joins, that you should intrust the darlings to our care. I need not tell you, my dearest son, that while they are with me, dear to me as they are, they would be the object of my life; nor can I say how much such a mark of your confidence would touch me. However, I leave it for your consideration, and only beg you will consider the proposal as a proof of my motherly affection."

The visit was paid—and on the 26th of June the young princes returned to Coburg, as mentioned by the Duchess of Coburg in the following letter:

"27 *June*, 1822.

"Yesterday morning my dear little boys came back from Gotha, and I was overjoyed. Ernest is very much grown. He is not as handsome as his father, but he will have his good figure. Albert is much smaller than his brother, and lovely as a little angel with his fair curls."

At the beginning of the following year the Dowager Duchess of Coburg again writes:

"14*th February*, 1823.

"The little boys have interrupted me, for you know how little one can do during such a visit. A couple of boys always find means to be noisy, which, and the loud talking, calls for many a scolding from grandmamma. They are very good boys on the whole, very obedient, and easy to manage. Albert used to rebel sometimes, but a grave face brings the little fellow to submit. Now he obeys me at a look. Some weeks ago he alarmed us by an attack of croup, but leeches and a blister quickly relieved it. If any body complains now, he says, very wisely, 'You must put on a blister.'"

M. Florschütz, the tutor, to whose care it will be seen the boys were removed in the course of this year, says that Prince Albert at this time was very subject to attacks of croup.

Again, on the 10th of March of the same year, the duchess writes:

"Ernest's boys have got a picture-book. One of the pictures represents the carrying off of the Saxon princes. This interests them greatly, and Albert makes wonderful eyes in telling that one was called Albert, like himself."

It has been already mentioned that the young princes bore the same names as Ernest and Albert, the sons of the Elector Frederick the Mild, who gave their names to the two branches into which the Saxon family was thenceforward divided. The story represented in the picture above mentioned was, that these princes were stolen in infancy from the schloss of Altenburg by one Kunz of Kauffungen, chamberlain to the Elector, in revenge for having been compelled to restore property that, during some disturbances, had been trusted to his care.

"The boys are very wild"—the dowager duchess writes on the 9th of May—"and Ernest flies about like a swallow. One need not, therefore, be astonished at his catching cold during these few warm days, with the wind getting up in the evening.

"Florschütz, who has been with Mensdorff's boys, will come now to those of Ernest, of which I am glad. Do not yet tease your little puss with learning. She is so young still."

The Princess Victoria, who is thus alluded to, would not be four years old till the 24th of that month.

CHAPTER II.

1823–1826.

The Princes removed to the Care of a Tutor.—Prince Albert's first Journal and Letters.—Visits to Gotha.—Letters from the Dowager Duchess of Gotha.

PRINCE ERNEST was barely five years old, and Prince Albert not yet four, when the change alluded to at the end of the last chapter took place, and the young princes were removed from the care of the nurse to whom they had been hitherto intrusted to that of Herr Florschütz of Coburg.

It is generally a severe trial to a child to be separated for the first time from the nurse by whom it has been hitherto tended and cared for; but the Prince, even as a child, showed a great dislike to being in the charge of women, and rejoiced instead of sorrowing over the contemplated change.* His gentle and docile temper, too—his natural tenderness of heart and readiness to love those from whom he experienced kindness—soon led him to attach himself with all the warmth of a loving nature to his new instructor; and it was a source of just and honest pride to the tutor, that the attachment and friendship thus begun endured till the last moment of the Prince's life. Not that the Prince ever forgot—it was not in his nature to forget—her to whom his infancy

* Memorandum by the Queen.

owed its earliest care; and Mr. Florschütz relates that many little acts of kindness in after years gave Mme. Müller the grateful assurance of his remembrance of her.

From this time forward Mr. Florschütz had the sole direction of the young princes' education till they left Bonn, fifteen years later, at the close of their academical career; and admirably did he perform his task. Nothing could exceed the patience and unintermitting zeal with which he gave himself up to his new duties; and the progress made by both princes—their varied attainments and extensive information, with the habits which they acquired of application, and of careful and accurate investigation of all subjects submitted to them—gave indisputable proof of the skill and judgment with which he directed their studies. The transfer of the children, however, from the care of their nurse to that of a tutor, alarmed their maternal grandmother at Gotha, and in her tender solicitude, fearing danger to their health from the change thus made, she wrote as follows to the duke on the 23d of November, 1823:

"That the precious children are well makes me very happy, and I long intensely to see them again. I am only sorry that they are now in the hands of the tutor. It is, no doubt, quite right, but I could have wished that, being so subject to attacks of croup, they should still have slept with Müller (their nurse); for a woman, accustomed as Müller has been for so many years to be with the children, naturally sleeps much less soundly than a man who is not used to be with little children.

"Should one of them be suddenly seized with a fit of croup, and he should not be awake, the consequences might be serious. I could, therefore, have wished that their careful nurse should still have slept with the children till Alberinchen was seven years old. Forgive the anxiety of a grandmother."

When the Duchess of Gotha wrote thus, Prince Albert was still only four years and three months old—certainly rather an early age at which to remove a boy from the care of a nurse to that of a man who could have no experience in infantine disorders, and could know nothing of the many little cares and attentions on which the comfort and health of children so much depend.

Nothing was more remarkable, even in infancy, than the unselfish affection which united the two brothers. "Brought up together," says Mr. Florschütz, "they went hand-in-hand in all things, whether at work or at play. Engaging in the same pursuits, sharing the same joys and the same sorrows, they were bound to each other by no common feelings of mutual love." And this mutual love endured without interruption and without diminution through life.

"Even in infancy, however," their tutor continues, "a marked difference was observable in their characters and dispositions. This difference naturally became more apparent as years went on, and their separate paths in life were definitely marked out for them; yet, far from leading at any time to any, even momentary estrangement, it seems rather to have afforded a closer bond of union between them."

A striking proof of the warm affection which united them will be found in a touching letter from Prince Ernest to the Queen, written when his brother's marriage was settled, and inserted in its proper place, in which he speaks of the rare qualities and virtues that already distinguished Prince Albert above all his young associates.

Mr. Florschütz describes the young Prince as being singularly easy to instruct; and this, notwithstanding the difficulties thrown constantly in the way by the injudicious, as he considers it, partiality of their mother; by the irregularity of hours, and the interruptions occasioned by their frequent changes of residence, and general mode of life. His complaints on this subject are fully detailed in a memorandum of his early recollections, which will be found presently, inserted at length.

The intellectual and thoughtful turn of the Prince's character, and his love of order, were even at this early age conspicuous. His studies were a pleasure to him, not a task. His constant love of occupation—for, in the words of his tutor, "to do *something* was with him a necessity"—his perseverance and application were only equaled by his facility of comprehension.

This eager desire for knowledge did not, however, lessen his enjoyment of the active sports and amusements which generally have, and ought to have, so much attraction for boys. Indeed, he seems to have thrown himself into his bodily exercises with the same zeal with which he devoted himself to his studies, and to have entered into the games of boyhood with all the glee and zest of an ardent and energetic spirit. In these games with his brother and his young companions, his was the directing mind. Nor was he at times indisposed to resort to force, if his wishes were not at once complied with.*

* Memorandum by Mr. Florschütz.

At this time, however, his tutor says of him that "he was rather delicate than robust, though already remarkable for his powers of perseverance and endurance."

The King of the Belgians, writing to the Queen in 1864, confirms, for the most part, the account of the young Prince thus given by Mr. Florschütz:

"I have seen him," he says, "in 1822, '23, '24, '26, '27, and '29, chiefly at Coburg, but since 1827 also at Gotha. He looked delicate in his youngest days. Arthur puts me most in mind of his looks in those days. He was always an intelligent child, and held a certain sway over his elder brother, who rather kindly submitted to it."

There does not appear to have been much to record during the boyhood of the princes; and, with the exception of the unfortunate circumstances of the year 1824, which resulted in the separation of their parents, to which reference has already been made, their lives flowed on in a singularly even and unvarying, but, at the same time, very happy course. Indeed, the Prince, in after years, frequently alluded to his happy childhood, and often told the Queen that he considered it the happiest period of his whole life.*

The mode of life adopted at this time for the young princes will be found amply detailed in the memorandum of their tutor, Herr Florschütz. But, before proceeding farther to notice this subject, it may be interesting to read a few extracts from a journal kept by the young Prince himself, as well as some of his letters to his father, written before he was six years old.

It is matter for regret that the habit of keeping a jour-

* Memorandum by the Queen.

nal, thus early commenced, was not continued through life, for in after years such a journal could not have failed to have been of immense interest. In these early days the journal dictated by the Prince contains, perhaps, nothing that any child of that age might not have written, though one can not help being pleased with the artless simplicity of his remarks, as well as with the evident *truth* that marks the expression of the child's feelings; and, though there may not be any thing in his letters to distinguish them from those written by other boys of the same age, the more exalted the position, the more distinguished the career of any man has been in after years, the more we like to know him as a boy, thinking, speaking, and writing as we have ourselves done.

The extracts from the journal which are here given are dated from January to April, 1825, when the Prince was not yet six years old. In that year the duke was much away from home, and during his absence the young princes spent most of the summer quietly at the Rosenau, varied only by a short stay occasionally with their grandmother at Ketschendorf, and by a visit to their other grandmother at Gotha.

The journal is as follows:

"*21st January.*

"When I got up this morning I was very happy: I washed myself, and then was dressed; after which I played for a little while, then the milk was brought, and afterward dear papa came to fetch us to breakfast. After breakfast dear papa showed us the English horses. The little white one can trot very fast, but the chestnut one is rather clumsy." (There was an English breeder there.)

"After we had seen the horses we did our lessons, and then put on our boots and went to the Hof-garden. On our way home we met the little Ledermanns. Then we went home to dinner.

"After dinner we drove to the Rosenau. Here dear papa was shooting, and we went a little way with the shooting-party.

"Waldmann was always wanting to run and chase the partridges, but we would not let him. Sometimes, however, he ran away with the string, and we were forced to run fast after him to catch him again. We drove home, played, and then went down stairs to dinner, but that had long been over. We then visited our cousins, came up stairs again and dined, and then wrote our journals.

"Now I am sleepy, I will pray and go to bed."

"*23d January.*

"When I awoke this morning I was ill. My cough was worse. I was so frightened that I cried. Half the day I remained in bed, and only got up at three o'clock in the afternoon. I did a little drawing, then I built a castle and arranged my arms; after that I did my lessons, and made a little picture and painted it. Then I played with Noah's Ark, then we dined, and I went to bed and prayed."

"*26th January.*

". . . . We recited, and I cried because I could not say my repetition, for I had not paid attention. . . . . I was not allowed to play after dinner because I had cried while repeating. Then Parthénai came, and we talked French with him. The little boy Mensel came and brought us some black chalk, with which we drew beautiful pictures. Then we looked over the Picture Academy."*

"*28th January.*

". . . . Papa took us to breakfast, and there I got a beautiful crown piece. After breakfast we continued our lessons. . . . . Then we went down to dear papa, and I took my needles and rings down with me. . . ."

"*11th February*, 1825.

". . . . I was to recite something, but did not wish to do so: that was not right—naughty! . . ."

"*20th February.*

". . . . During our walk I told the Rath (the tutor) a story. When I came home I played with my companions. But I had left all my lesson-books lying about in the room, and I had to put them away: then I cried, but afterward I played again. . . ."

"*28th February.*

". . . . I cried at my lesson to-day because I could not find a verb; and the Rath pinched me, to show me what a verb was. And I cried about it. . . ."

"*26th March.*

". . . . I wrote a letter at home. But, because I had made so many mistakes in it, the Rath tore it up and threw it into the fire. I cried about it. . . ."

"*27th March.*

". . . I finished writing my letter. Then I played. . ."

"*4th April.*

". . . After dinner we went with dear papa to Ketschendorf. Then I drank beer, and ate bread and butter and cheese. . . ."

* Name of a German book.

"*8th April.*

". . . After dinner we went to Ketschendorf, and from Ketschendorf we went to Seidmannsdorf. On the road I cried. From Seidmannsdorf we went home by the Eckartsberg. . . . Then we had a French lesson."

"*9th April.*

". . . I got up well and happy; afterward I had a fight with my brother. . . . After dinner we went to the play. It was Wallenstein's 'Lager,' and they carried out a monk."

"*10th April.*

". . . I had another fight with my brother: that was not right."

"1825.

"DEAR PAPA," he writes about the same time to his father while staying with his grandmother at Ketschendorf, "we have now been a week at Ketschendorf, and are quite well. I hope you have arrived safe at Berlin, but come back to us soon. I long for your return. It is very fine here. We often stay out till near 10 o'clock, as it is much finer in the evening than in the day. We were at the Rosenau a few days ago, but unluckily the weather was not fine. The wind was very high. We are going there again to-day with dear grandmamma. Pikas" (a dog) "is with us at Ketschendorf, but he often runs away from us. Think of me with love.

"Your ALBERT."

"1825.

"DEAR PAPA,—The day before yesterday we went to see the Hof-marshal, and yesterday the colonel. Our finches have such a fine house to live in! Think of me very often, and bring me a doll that nods its head.

"Your little ALBERT."

A visit to their maternal grandmother at Gotha seems now to have become an annual custom, and was the source of much happiness to her, fondly attached as she was to her grandchildren. She also came herself occasionally to Coburg, and in June, 1824, writes during one of these visits:

"The dear children are, thank God! perfectly well, and as happy and merry as one could wish. They delight so much in driving and walking about, that, if one were to ask them, they would say they never wished to go home."

And in July, 1825, when the young princes were again staying with her:

"I can give you," she says, "the very best account of our dear children. Nothing has ailed them, and I think that dear little Albert is grown decidedly fatter since he came. They lead a very simple and regular life, and are out in the open air as much as possible. They are so good and gentle, and give me great pleasure. I shall hope to restore them to you on your return in perfect health. . . . The dear children wrote to you by the last post. The 'Rath' really does all he can for them, and you have a real treasure in him.

"I took the children to Reinhardsbrunn, where we spent a very happy day, and yesterday I went with them to Schnepfenthal, where they were perfectly happy. The director, Saltzmann, was delighted at my bringing them, and invited them to come again. We should make many more such excursions if the weather was not so unsettled."

In the spring of 1826 we find the children spending two months at Gotha under the charge of the good duchess, and, while staying there, the Prince wrote constantly to his father. It might seem too trivial to give all his letters here, and the two following may be taken as fair samples of the rest:

"1826.

"DEAR GOOD PAPA,—I am very well. I hope you are well. Thank you for your letter. We sometimes make expeditions from here. Last Sunday we went to Schnepfenthal, and dined with the school-boys. Three days afterward we went to Reinhardsbrunn, and walked in the Ungeheurer Grund, where we saw many big rocks, and on the biggest rock there was a falcon's nest. I long for the minerals you are going to bring us. There was a fair yesterday, and grandmamma gave me some money, and I bought myself some pretty things—a Turkish crescent, a whip, an eagle, and a cross-bow. Think with love of your little ALBERT."

"1826.

"DEAR PAPA,—I thank you for your letter. We were very merry yesterday. A great many children played with us. I wish you could have seen us. Think with love of your little ALBERT."

The last of the letters quoted above refers to a practice which was commenced in the winter of 1825, and was continued without interruption for the next eight years, of having, every Sunday during the winter months, twelve or thirteen boys of their own age to play with them. In subsequent letters from the Prince, frequent allusion will be found to their young associates, and to the games in which they joined with them. From two till six they were allowed to play as they liked. From six till seven each boy had to recite something; in later years, discussions upon a given subject in some foreign language being substituted for these recitations.*

* Memorandum by the reigning Duke of Coburg.

CHAPTER III.

1826–1828.

Gotha added to the Possessions of the Duke of Coburg. — Difficulties of the Settlement.—Letters from the Dowager Duchess of Coburg.— School Fête at the Rosenau.—Visits to Gotha.—Letters from the Dowager Duchess of Gotha.—Recollections of Count Arthur Mensdorff.

In 1826, after considerable difficulty and discussion, the arrangement was completed by which the duchy of Gotha was given to the Duke of Coburg.

We need not enter here into the difficulties which attended the negotiations farther than they will be found noticed in some of the letters that follow from the Dowager Duchess of Coburg. Suffice it to say that, by the death, in 1825, without issue male, of Frederick, duke of Saxe-Gotha-Altenburg, the direct succession of the Gotha-Altenburg branch of the Ernestine line came to an end, and the inheritance passed to other branches of the same line. After much delay, owing chiefly to the exorbitant pretensions of the Duke of Meiningen, it was finally settled that, in consideration of the acquisition of the duchy of Gotha, the Duke of Coburg should cede that of Saalfeld to the Duke of Meiningen, Hildburghausen being also added to the inheritance of the latter duke; the Duke of Hildburghausen receiving in exchange the duchy of Saxe-Altenburg, and assuming that title.

"Ernest is very busy just now," writes the Dowager

Duchess of Coburg from Ketschendorf, on the 30th of May, 1826, "as the Saxon Commissioners are here to settle about the inheritance. It will be a difficult task, as the Duke of Meiningen and old K—— are very obstinate. General M—— is a good and sensible man, who would like to make all straight, and fears he will have to return to Dresden without any thing having been settled. . . . . He went first to Hildburghausen, taking with him the ultimatum of the old Duke of Meiningen, who is the senior of the Ernestine line. . . . . The ultimatum was to the effect that the duke would enter into no arrangement except:

"1. That he should retain all his possessions, besides acquiring Hildburghausen, Coburg, and Saalfeld; that he should be the only Duke of Coburg, founding a new duchy of Coburg.

"2. Ernest to have Gotha (Hildburghausen, Altenburg), and to give up the name which your great-uncle and your brothers made so celebrated! S—— is gone to Meiningen with the answer that Ernest will neither give up Coburg nor the name of his family."

To the Dowager Duchess of Gotha the termination of the Saxe-Gotha-Altenburg line, and the separation of those duchies, was an event inexpressibly painful; and she gives vent to her feelings in the following touching letter to the duke, which, as it relates exclusively to this subject, we insert here, though somewhat anticipating the date at which it was written. Second wife and widow of Duke Augustus, the predecessor of the duke just deceased, it will be remembered that she was step-mother to Louise, duchess of Coburg, the mother of our princes; and the devoted love she bore to her step-grandchildren, to which all her letters quoted in this memoir bear witness, was of a piece with the affectionate and maternal interest this excellent and most amiable woman now expresses in the welfare and happiness of those who had been her husband's subjects.

"I need not tell you," she writes to the Duke of Coburg from Rumpenheim,* on the 5th of September, 1826, "I need not tell you that I thanked God when I heard that the duchy of Gotha had become yours. It was a great comfort to me, for there is no one in whom I have more confidence than in yourself, my dear duke.† But you must also feel and know that this event opens afresh many wounds. The division of the beloved land, to which it was my happiness to be a mother, naturally grieves me. Yet, my dear duke, I love you, your precious children, and the dear country too well not to keep my heart open to my beloved people of Gotha; and whenever it may be in my power to help these faithful

* Note by the Queen.—Rumpenheim belonged to the Landgraf of Hesse, father to the Duchess of Cambridge, and uncle to the Duke and Duchess of Gotha, who was daughter of the Elector of Hesse-Cassel. It now belongs to the Duchess of Cambridge, her three brothers and two sisters.

† Mr. Perthès, on this occasion, wrote as follows to a friend: "My monarchical principles have gained many new adherents, for all suddenly fall down before the new prince. Certainly he is, like Saul, head and shoulders taller than the rest of the people, full of princely dignity, very judicious, and consequently very popular. He knows and is interested about every subject; in short, the whole world is bewitched with him, and men of all parties have suddenly become *ducalized.*"—*Memoirs of Frederick Perthès, by his son, Professor Perthès, of Bonn.*

subjects by word or deed, or by intercession for them with their kind sovereign, I will do so as long as God shall spare me.

"I am convinced that you, my dear friend, will do all in your power to make your new subjects happy. Their prosperity is now intrusted to you. I shall hope for the pleasure of seeing you and the dear children often at Gotha. Surely, when you come for the first time, you intend to bring these darlings with you, to gratify us all."

In fact, the hope of now seeing more of her beloved grandchildren was almost her only consolation under the pain caused by this change.

It was not, however, till the month of November that the change was completed by the ratification of the family convention giving Gotha to the Duke of Coburg; and it was toward the end of the year that the duke, accompanied by the young princes, made his formal entry into Gotha on taking possession of his new inheritance.

In the mean time the princes continued to reside as usual, under the care of their tutor, at Coburg and the Rosenau, and in the summer of this year we find them attending a fête of school children at the latter place, and taking a principal part in the proceedings of the day. The Dowager Duchess of Coburg, writing from Ketschendorf to the Duchess of Kent on the 4th of July, thus describes what took place:

"I think I told you that the annual school feast had been held on Ernest's birthday, and, to return this compliment, your brother gave a treat to all the school children last Sunday. (He had waited for Leopold.) We dined on the meadow, and watched from a stand overlooking the whole place the arrival of the little ones in their gay attire. They were to be treated, at four long tables, to cake and wine, and later in the evening to sausages. 1300 children were thus assembled, and they must have had lectures on good manners in their schools, for they behaved exceedingly well, not indulging in screaming or excessive merriment. It was a most pleasant sight, that of these happy young people playing on the large meadow, and jumping about like grasshoppers. Ernest and Albert went in full armor to meet a procession of knights and hunters, the whole Freischutz, Samiel included, and led them on to the platform to Leopold. Ernest stammered forth a short address (for his comrades confused him), in which he thanked his kind uncle for having come across the sea to spend the feast with them, and begged his favor for Albert, his comrades, and himself."

Shortly after this the Dowager Duchess of Gotha paid a visit to Baden. Passing Meiningen on her way there, the children were sent to that place to see her, and she thus notices their visit in a letter written from Baden on the 16th of July, 1826:

"How can I thank you sufficiently for having sent the dear children to me to Meiningen? It was the most welcome present for my birthday, the day after. I found them both much improved and grown, looking so healthy; and Albert more handsome than ever. Dear Ernest so good and kind.

"I hope the dear children arrived safely at home the

next day, and have given you many kind messages from me. I kiss them a thousand times. They have been so charming and good.

"Please have the kindness and goodness to write to me as often as possible, and if business prevents your doing so, pray let Florschütz do it, for it would be too painful to me to be left, while so far away, without constant news from yourself and the dear children."

The next letter is from the Dowager Duchess of Coburg to the Duchess of Kent:

"17*th August*, 1826.

"I see by the English newspapers that 'his Majesty* and H. R. H. the Duchess of Kent went on Virginia Water.' The little monkey† must have pleased and amused him. She is such a pretty, clever child. The bigger monkey‡ was always much in favor.

"Alberinchen looks rather pale this summer. He is delicate: the heat tries him, and he grows fast. In jumping and running about he is as little backward as his brother."

We have already read, in a former letter from the Dowager Duchess of Gotha, her strong and touching expression of affectionate solicitude for the continued happiness and prosperity of a people who were very dear to her as the subjects of her late husband; and in the two following letters, expressive of the love she bore to her grandchildren, the feelings naturally excited by the

* George IV. † Princess Victoria.

‡ Princess Feodore, now Princess Hohenlohe.

changes that had occurred at Gotha still show themselves.

"May God spare you and the dearly beloved children," she writes on the 30th of October, 1826, "for many years to come, and grant you every possible happiness. It is natural that I should be much moved; but it will, nevertheless, be a great comfort to see you, and, I hope also, the dear children. I am sure they will never find a more faithful or true friend than myself, and of this I trust you are convinced."

And again, on the 26th of November of the same year:

"How thankful I am that you and the dear children are coming. I will think of this as the only alleviation to my sorrow. . . . . Is it not too long a day's journey from Coburg to Ichtershausen for the dear children; and in this horrible weather? Would it not be perhaps better to make this stage in two days? Excuse this advice, but I am afraid the children might arrive unwell."

Soon after this letter was written the expected visit was paid. The duke, accompanied by his children, made his formal entry into Gotha on taking possession of his new inheritance. He remained there, however, but a short time, and returned to Coburg by the beginning of the new year. The weather was bitterly cold, and the duchess trembled lest the children should suffer on their journey home.

"Thank God!" she writes on the 4th of January, 1827, "that you and the dear children, whom I tenderly embrace, have arrived safely at home, in spite of this terrible weather. I am glad the latter did not stop at Meiningen. The cold rooms might have done them harm."

The accession of their father to the dukedom of Gotha made a necessary change in the usual round of the young princes' lives. Up to this time they had resided constantly at Coburg or in its immediate vicinity, spending the spring and summer months at the Rosenau, those of autumn and winter in the city. After 1826, Gotha, and Reinhardsbrunn in its immediate neighborhood, were added to their regular places of abode at certain seasons of the year.

It will easily be imagined, from the tone of the letters from her, which have been already quoted, how much pleasure this gave to the good duchess their grandmother—how she rejoiced at the arrival of the season which brought them to Gotha, and how fondly she wrote to them, and of them, during their absence at Coburg. Her grandchildren returned her love with equal affection, of which our Prince gives an affecting proof in a beautiful letter, written many years later, to announce his intended marriage.* The duchess writes on the 7th of April, 1827, "Yesterday I received charming letters from the dear children, whom I thank a thousand times. God grant that they may continue well, and may escape the scarlet fever and measles."

It does not appear that, as a child, Prince Albert ever had either of these disorders. He had the measles very many years later in England. But it will be seen in Mr. Florschütz's memorandum that, though he was kept in

* Chap. x., page 197.

bed for eight days when his brother had the scarlet fever in 1829, he showed no symptoms of the disorder, and the only reason for this confinement appears to have been the excessive caution of the doctor, who seems to have assumed that if one brother had the fever the other must of necessity have it also.*

The Prince's birthday was never passed over by his grandmother without a kind letter, and in August, 1827, she writes from Baden: "Kiss your dear children for me, and congratulate dear Albert on his birthday. May God preserve the beloved child to us. I have asked Florschütz to give my present on that day. It is for both boys; may it give them pleasure. I wish with all my heart that you may spend the day happily together, and think sometimes also of me."

In December, 1827, we again find the children on a visit to their grandmother at Gotha, for she writes to the duke on the 22d: "I hasten to give you news of the children, who are enjoying excellent health. Since you left us they breakfast with me, which seems to give them great pleasure. I hope it was not contrary to your wishes that I allowed them to go to the opera last night, as a very good piece was given. The dear children wish to be respectfully remembered to their beloved father, and hope, with me, soon to have the pleasure of seeing him again."

* Notwithstanding what Mr. Florschütz says, who is the authority for the statement in the text, the Queen says Prince Albert certainly had the scarlet fever at this time. "At least," her Majesty adds, "he himself always maintained this, and therefore visited his children regularly when they had it in 1855."

The young princes remained under their grandmother's care at Gotha till the end of January, 1828, and she writes, on their departure on the 30th of that month, "I will not let the dear children go without a line to recall me to your remembrance, my dear duke. God grant that the darlings may arrive safely at home. They leave this perfectly well and happy. Since the 24th they have been my daily guests in the morning and afternoon. I can not say enough in praise of their good behavior, and I shall feel the separation from them very much. To their great delight, I have gratified their ardent wish to have another goat, which has been sent to-day. I entreat that they may be allowed to keep them all three. They have already arranged every thing for two carriages. Albert wishes to drive the little goat. Happy children! how much are they to be envied for the power of being pleased with so little! I allowed them to go to the theatre several times, as they were so delighted with it, and they had borne the confinement to their rooms so patiently. Do not let them take much medicine, nor hear much about their health; it only makes them nervous. A well-regulated diet and mode of life is much better than medicine, and as much air as possible."

"On our dear Ernest's birthday," the duchess again writes, June 26, 1828, "I have also thought much of you, my dear duke. May God grant you much happiness through the good child who, together with his brother, is our comfort and hope."

Count Mensdorff, married, as has been mentioned, to the duke's eldest sister, and holding high rank in the Austrian service, was at this time Governor of Mayence;

and in 1828 the young princes paid a visit there, to his sons their cousins.

Prince Albert, then in his ninth year, gives his father the following account of the visit:

"*Mayence*, 1828.

"DEAR PAPA,—I can not thank you half enough for letting us have the pleasure of coming to Mayence to see our cousins.

"Mayence was hardly in sight when our uncle and cousins met us on horseback. We were very much astonished when we saw the Rhine in the valley, with its bridge of boats; but the water of the Maine and the Rhine is so different that you can not mistake them. The Maine has red and the Rhine green water. . . . . . Yesterday we drove to Wiesbaden, and from Wiesbaden rode on donkeys to the Platte,* which is two hours from Wiesbaden. The day before we were at Biberich. . . . Keep your love for your ALBERT."

The intimacy thus early begun between the cousins seems to have been kept up with undiminished affection throughout life; and Count Arthur Mensdorff, in 1863, gives the Queen the following account of his recollections of those early days. It was written, as will be seen, in answer to a wish expressed by the Queen, through the Duchess of Saxe-Coburg; and in addition to the interest attaching to what he tell us of the Prince's boyhood, and of the traits of character that already distinguished him, it affords pleasing evidence of his own

* A shooting lodge on the hill above Wiesbaden belonging to the Duke of Nassau.

affection for his cousin—of manly sorrow for his loss, and sympathy with the Queen's still greater affliction.

Count Arthur Mensdorff to the Queen.

"*Castle Einöd, March* 16, 1863.

"I was deeply touched by the receipt of your gracious present: the photographs, which are a real treasure to me, and the splendid book on the dear, great Albert.

"The small prints representing you in your widow's dress have moved me deeply, and remind me sadly of the last happy days I spent with you in England in 1848, when Albert, my dear aunt, and the whole group of blooming children were gathered round you. I hardly dare call them children now, for some of them are married princes and princesses, who scarcely remember their old cousin in the mountains of Styria.

"How terribly has all this changed! How many noble and beloved beings has it pleased the Almighty to call into his kingdom, leaving us behind—alone and deserted! But what a dreadful heavy trial God has sent *you*, my broken-hearted cousin! And yet it is through His mercy and loving kindness that you have found strength to support the burden of this joyless life with such beautiful, such exemplary resignation!

"Alexandrine* has written to me that you wish me to write down all I can recollect of the early years of our beloved departed one. I will try and do so.

"Albert, as a child, was of a mild, benevolent disposition. It was only what he thought unjust or dishonest that could make him angry. Thus I recollect one day

* Duchess of Coburg.

when we children, Albert, Ernest, Ferdinand, Augustus, Alexander, myself, and a few other boys (if I am not mistaken, Paul Wangenheim was one) were playing at the Rosenau, and some of us were to storm the old ruined tower on the side of the castle, which the others were to defend. One of us suggested that there was a place at the back by which we could get in without being seen, and thus capture it without difficulty. Albert declared that this 'would be most unbecoming in a Saxon knight, who should always attack the enemy in front,' and so we fought for the tower so honestly and vigorously that Albert, by mistake, for I was on his side, gave me a blow upon the nose, of which I still bear the mark. I need not say how sorry he was for the wound he had given me.

"Albert never was noisy or wild. He was always very fond of Natural History and more serious studies, and many a happy hour we spent in the Ehrenburg,* in a small room under the roof, arranging and dusting the collections our cousins had themselves made and kept there. He urged me to begin making a similar collection myself, so that we might join, and form together a good cabinet.

"This was the commencement of the collections at Coburg in which Albert always took so much interest.

"Albert thoroughly understood the naïveté of the Coburg national character, and he had the art of turning people's peculiarities into a source of fun. He had a natural talent for imitation, and a great sense of the ludicrous, either in persons or things; but he was never severe or ill-natured, the general kindness of his disposition

* The palace at Coburg.

preventing him from pushing a joke, however he might enjoy it, so as to hurt any one's feelings. Every man has, more or less, a ridiculous side, and to *quiz* this, in a friendly and good-humored manner, is, after all, the pleasantest description of humor. Albert possessed this rare gift in an eminent degree.

"From his earliest infancy he was distinguished for perfect moral purity, both in word and in deed, and to this he owed the sweetness of disposition so much admired by every one.

"Even as a child he was very fond of chess, and he, Ernest, Alexander, and myself often played the great four game. This led often to jokes, but sometimes to ridiculous quarrels, which, however, owing to his goodness of heart, always ended good-humoredly.

"While still very young, his heart was feelingly alive to the sufferings of the poor. I saw him one day give a beggar something by stealth, when he told me not to speak of it; 'for when you give to the poor,' he said, 'you must see that nobody knows of it.'

"He was always fond of shooting and fishing, as far as his natural kind feeling would permit, for a wounded animal always excited his warmest compassion.

"One day, out shooting at Coburg, I was hit by a chance shot, and he was the person who showed the greatest concern and evinced the truest anxiety about my accident.

"In order to refresh my memory I have looked over the letters which our mutual grandmother wrote to me when I was a child, and which I still preserve with other relics. In one dated March 1st, 1831, she says: 'Last night your cousins and some playfellows, Paul Wangenheim, the eldest Gilsa, the little Birner, and Emil Piani, acted proverbs in my room, extemporizing the dialogue for the most part. Albert as a quack, with a pigtail and paunch, was too ridiculous. Ernest, as a lady, looked quite like your mother when she was a girl: he distributed the playbills. Piani represented a drunken prompter. In short, there was a good deal of fun and laughter.'

"In later years we saw much less of each other. In 1839, when I was serving in the Austrian Lancers, we met at Töplitz, and from thence drove together to Carlsbad, to see Uncle Ernest. Eôs* was in the carriage. During our journey Albert confided to me, under the seal of the strictest confidence, that he was going to England to make your acquaintance, and that if you liked each other you were to be engaged. He spoke very seriously about the difficulties of the position he would have to occupy in England, but hoped that dear Uncle Leopold would assist him with his advice. We were at that moment approaching the station where we were to change horses. He asked me the name of the place, which I told him was Buchau, a little village known all round as a sort of *Krähwinkel*, famous for all sorts of ludicrous stories about the inhabitants. We drove into the place, the postillion blowing his horn and cracking his whip. Albert, seeing a large crowd assembled round the posthouse, said to me, 'Quick; stoop down in the carriage, and we will make Eôs look out of the window, and all the people will wonder at the funny prince.' We did so,

* A beautiful and favorite black greyhound that the Prince brought with him to England.

and the people had to satisfy their curiosity with Eôs. The horses were soon changed, and we drove off, laughing heartily at our little joke.

"Some time ago I collected all the letters I have of dearest Albert's, and in one of them I found a passage most characteristic of his noble way of thinking, as shown and maintained by him from his earliest childhood.

"'The poor soldiers,' he says, 'always do their duty in the most brilliant manner; but as soon as matters come again into the hands of politicians and diplomats, every thing is again spoiled and confused. Oxenstiern's saying to his son may still be quoted: "My son, when you look at things more closely, you will be surprised to find with how little wisdom the world is governed." I should like to add, 'and with how little morality.'"

"How much these words contain! We again see the Saxon knight, who, as a child, declared that you must attack your enemy in front, who hates every crooked path; and, on the other hand, the noble heart which feels deeply the misfortune of a government not guided by reason and morality.

"I am sorry to say that these are all my recollections of old times. The changes we have had, the wars and revolutions, may have obliterated many dear recollections.

"The noise of the festivities around you will have been most painful to you, causing many a wound to bleed afresh.

"May the Almighty bless this young pair, and may Albert's spirit descend upon his son.

"ARTHUR MENSDORFF."

CHAPTER IV.

1828–1831.

Life at the Rosenau, etc.—Journals and Letters of Prince Albert.—Death of the Dowager Duchess of Coburg.

THE years 1829 and 1830 seem to have been passed by the princes in the quiet routine of their studies and other occupations, their residence at Coburg and the Rosenau being only interrupted by the visits, now grown periodical, to Gotha.

The duke, their father, had been absent for some time in the winter of 1828–29, and on the 16th of January of the latter year we find Prince Albert, now in the tenth year of his age, writing, by direction of his grandmother (probably from Ketschendorf, where she resided), to say how sorry they were at his staying away so long, and to express their joy to hear he was soon coming back. Again, on the 28th of the same month, he gives his father an account of the manner in which he and his brother, with their young companions, the sons of the principal people of Coburg, who came constantly on Sundays and other holidays to play with them, according to the practice established, as already noticed, in 1825, had been amusing themselves.

They dragged some hand-sledges up to the Festung (the old fortress above Coburg), and "there," he writes, "we and some other boys got into our sledges, and went the whole way down to the gate of the schloss."

In March, 1829, we find the young princes, with their tutor, going out to dine with their grandmother at Ketschendorf. The following letter in which this is mentioned is also interesting from the insight which it gives into the sound and liberal views of the duchess. What a salutary influence must she not have exercised over the young and candid mind of our Prince, and how much may she not have contributed, by her precepts and her example, to the development of those truly liberal and constitutional principles by which he was always distinguished?

This letter is written to the Duchess of Kent, evidently in answer to one in which the duchess must have mentioned the introduction, by the government of the Duke of Wellington, of a Bill for the Emancipation of the Roman Catholics.

"In spite of your great prudence, my dear," the duchess writes on the 23d of March, "I must speak of politics —namely, that which now interests me—the Emancipation! I say, 'God save the King;' and again, 'God bless the Duke of Wellington!' It is very right in the hero of the Peninsula to stand up so manfully for what he commenced with so much judgment. How they will laugh at the Prussian general, whom they do not like as it is, at Berlin! Ernest begs to be remembered to you. He is very busy planting. The cold March of this spring is more favorable to it than usual.

"I must leave off now, as my company is just arriving

for dinner, namely, the young gentlemen and Mr. Flor schütz. They are dear boys—so clever and merry. Ernest is beginning to grow handsome. He has very fine brown eyes, white teeth, and a fair and rosy complexion. He will have his father's fine, tall figure. Albert is very good-looking, very clever, but is not so strong as his brother."

In July of this year the brothers were again on a visit to their other grandmother at Gotha: "Let me give you," the duchess writes to the duke, on the 31st of July, "the assurance that our dear children are very well and happy. I see them every day, and often more than once. Yesterday afternoon they dined with me, and rode out afterward. They have just breakfasted with me, and to-morrow they intend making a little excursion to Gleichen."

In a journal kept by the Prince in 1830, when he was not yet eleven years old, he gives an account, which is not without interest, of the manner in which he and his brother were in the habit of amusing themselves with their young companions; he also describes the great Protestant festival, in celebration of the Confession of Augsburg, which was held at Coburg in June of that year.

The princes were very fond of assuming the characters of the most distinguished worthies of old times, and of making the most remarkable incidents in by-gone German history the subject of their games. On the occasion mentioned in the following extracts from Prince Albert's journal, it is not without interest to observe that when the boy selected to play the emperor was missing, he was to be replaced by another boy chosen by lot from among those who were to represent the different dukes. The lot fell worthily on the Prince himself.

But the journal is chiefly interesting from one short entry in it, strongly indicative of that trait in the Prince's character which was, perhaps, the most remarkable, as being, certainly, the most rare in those born to such high rank—his thoughtful consideration, namely, for others. When lamenting the disappointment to himself and his companions of the pleasure which they had promised themselves, and which a wet day had put a stop to, his thoughts seem to turn quite naturally to the still wider disappointment occasioned to the children of the whole town, whose festival was spoiled by the bad weather.

The extracts here given embrace a period extending from January to the end of August, 1830:

"17*th January.*

"*Sunday.* When I woke this morning, the first thing I thought of was the afternoon when we expected our playfellows. The tallest and one of the cleverest, Emil Gilsa, was to be our emperor. Ernest was to be Duke of Saxony, and was to have two Counts Rottenhahn, the elder M. von Schauroth, a Preger and a Borner, and one of our rooms was to be his duchy.

"Paul von Wangenheim was to be Duke of Bavaria, and his followers were to be the younger M. von Schauroth, a Piani and a Müller, and he also had a room; and I was to be Duke of Burgundy, and Herman, Achill, Victor and Edward von Gilsa, were to belong to me, and another of our rooms was to be my duchy. We dined with dear grandmamma. After dinner we returned home, and our playfellows had already arrived; but we heard with great horror that Achill and Emil von Gilsa (our chosen emperor) were ill, and that the two Mess. von Schauroth were gone out sledging and would come later. We therefore decided on choosing an emperor from among the dukes, and lots were to decide who it was to be. Fortune favored me, and I was emperor. We played very happily till half past eight o'clock.

"*8th April.*

"*Thursday.* This morning at eight o'clock we went to the church in the town, where they sang Graun's music. After church we went on foot to the Kalenberg. Here the stork had made us some presents. When we had found all the eggs and cracknels, we dined with dear papa. . . . ."

"*9th April.*

"*Friday.* To-day we went to the town church again at eight o'clock, where they sang the third part of Graun's Passion music. . . . . . After church papa showed us a large leaden bird-cage which he was going to give us on our birthday. In the centre of the cage was an owl, and a fountain of water spirted from his beak up to the top of the cage."

"*17th April.*

"After dinner I played with our companions. We played Wallenstein's Camp. Leopold was Wallenstein. After that we went down stairs, then we came up again, and our companions went away. Then we dined, and afterward went to the play, where Wallenstein was stabbed. . . . ."

"*26th April.*

". . . . We dined with papa at the Rosenau. Then we went home, where I sang with the Rath."

"*21st June.*

"To-day was my brother Ernest's birthday. We spent this day, in spite of the rain, very happily together.

"We drove into the town after dear papa had given Ernest many beautiful presents, and visited dear grandmamma. The bad weather not only spoiled our happiness, but that of the children of the whole town too, as just on this day a school festival happened to fall.

"We spent the afternoon at Ketschendorf with some of our companions.

"In the evening we went to see a menagerie which consisted chiefly of serpents."

Celebration of the third Secular Festival of the Confession of Augsburg. This Festival was celebrated during three days.

"*25th June.*

"*Friday.* This morning we drove into the town in order to take part personally in the proceedings of this day, which is such an important one for Protestants. The ceremony commenced at nine o'clock. It consisted principally of a very fine and long procession, which I will now describe.

"A band of music led the way; then came the students of the Gymnasium, with all their professors: they were followed by all the boys from the school, with their teachers; then came all the clergy, who moved slowly forward, chanting as they went along; next came the two chamberlains with their long wands; they were followed by dear papa and the whole court; and all the officials of the town brought the procession to a close.

"It was a most imposing sight. The procession wound round the market-place to the Church of St. Moritz, at the doors of which the clergy were stationed.

"The* General Superintendent Genzler addressed a few words to dear papa, in which he mentioned the Electors who used to celebrate this festival in these sacred walls. He concluded with a blessing.

"All who stood round were moved to tears by this address. In the church the general superintendent also preached. No procession left the church.

"We spent the afternoon at Ketschendorf, while dear papa paid a visit to the King of Bavaria at Banz."

"*26th June.*

"*Saturday.* This day was devoted particularly to the young people.

"At nine o'clock we went to the school-house, and heard a discourse on the present festival by the Co-rector Gremier. Then we went to General Superintendent Genzler's garden, and afterward to the Gymnasium, where we heard another discourse on the festival by Director Wendel.

"In the afternoon all the school children, joined by several schools from the country and the students of the Gymnasium, accompanied by an immense concourse of people, went up to the fortress."

"*27th June.*

"*Sunday.* We breakfasted to-day in the Hof-garden, and experienced great heat. At ten o'clock we went to church. This day was the third day of the festival. We dined with the company also in the Hof-garden. In the evening Ernest drove with papa to Ketschendorf. I could not go with them, as my nose bled. We did not remain much longer at Coburg, but returned immediately to the Rosenau."

"10*th July.*

"*Friday.* It rained so incessantly the whole morning that we thought there was going to be another Deluge. . . ."

"11*th July.*

"*Sunday.* This was a very pleasant and happy day for us. . . . The Rosenau was visited by town and country people, as if there had been a fête here. . . . In the morning Paul (Wangenheim) paid us a visit, and helped us to draw some of the scenes in our stories. In the afternoon we had the pleasure of having seven of our playfellows to dinner, with whom we then played very happily till the evening."

"28*th and* 29*th July.*

"*Wednesday* passed in the usual manner. On Thursday the bird-shooting began. We had our lessons in the morning as usual, and after dinner drove to Ketschendorf, from whence we were to go with dear grandmamma to the Green, where a party was to be given in honor of Aunt Julia. The heat was oppressive, and many people were there. . . ."

"25*th August.*

"*Wednesday.* Papa is going to Gotha to-morrow; therefore my birthday, which is *really* to-morrow, is to be kept to-day. I was awoke by some beautiful music. At

9 o'clock papa gave me a quantity of beautiful presents. . . . We dined in the afternoon with some of our companions at the Rosenau. After dinner we played very happily with our playfellows. In the evening we were at a ball in the Castle at Coburg, and only got to bed at half past 10 o'clock."

On the 24th of May of this year the young Princess Victoria had completed her eleventh year, and her grandmother, the Dowager Duchess of Coburg, sends the following beautiful letter of congratulation to her daughter on that occasion:

"*May*, 1830.

"My blessings and good wishes for the day which gave you the sweet blossom of May! May God preserve and protect the valuable life of that lovely flower from all the dangers that will beset her mind and heart! The rays of the sun are scorching at the height to which she may one day attain. It is only by the blessing of God that all the fine qualities He has put into that young soul can be kept pure and untarnished. How well I can sympathize with the feelings of anxiety that must possess you when that time comes. God, who has helped you through so many bitter hours of grief, will be your help still. Put your trust in Him!"

Again, after the death of George IV., in June following: "God bless Old England, where my beloved children live, and where the sweet blossom of May may one day reign! May God yet for many years keep the weight of a crown from her young head, and let the intelligent clever child grow up to girlhood before this dangerous grandeur devolves upon her!"

One of the first acts of the Parliament that met after the accession of William IV. was to pass a Regency Bill, by which it was settled that, in the event of the king's death, the regency, during the young princess's minority, should be given to the Duchess of Kent. The following letter refers to this arrangement:

"*Dec.* 7, 1830.

"I should have been very sorry if the regency had been given into other hands than yours. It would not have been a just return for your constant devotion and care to your child if this had not been done. May God give you wisdom and strength to do your duty, if called upon to undertake it. May God bless and protect our little darling! If I could but once see her again! The print you sent me of her is not like the dear picture I have. The quantity of curls hide the well-shaped head, and make it look too large for the lovely little figure."

But we must return to the young princes, who had, as usual, been spending the greatest part of the year at Coburg.

On the 19th of July, the Prince writes to his father to say they are quite well; and, after telling him what they have been doing, adds: "We have plenty of time to work both in the house and in the garden, and employ it well in working hard to become good and useful men, and to give you pleasure.

The Prince was now in his twelfth year, and all his letters give unmistakable proof of his natural warmth of heart. They are full of the most simple and unaffected expressions of his affection for his father, of love for their home, and of his anxious desire to improve himself, and make the most of his time; and this last desire not expressed, as is too often the case, without much thought, or with only a passing wish to please a father, but as the ruling impulse of his heart, which never ceased to influence him till the day of his death.

In January, 1831, the duke seems to have left the princes at the Rosenau while he himself went to Gotha, and on the 30th Prince Albert writes:

"DEAR PAPA,—We were really anxious about your journey, for we feared that you would have been stopped in your sledge, as, with us, it rained nearly the whole day; and we were the more rejoiced to hear yesterday, from dear grandmamma, that you had arrived safely. But the weather has quite changed. It snowed without stopping for three or four days, and the snow is very deep. The drifts are six feet high at the Festung, as we found out ourselves yesterday. We walked to Ketschendorf, and thence through the snow, by an unbeaten track through Herr von Schauroth's garden, to the Festung, and sank several times up to our middle in the snow. To-day it is beautiful, but cold, for it is twelve degrees below the freezing-point.

"You will forgive me, dear papa, for not writing to you before, but we had so much to do all the week that I could not do so till to-day—Sunday. We are quite well, and hope that you are as well at Gotha. Prince Reuss will be present at the Academy to-day, and as soon as I have finished my letter I will work at my poem, that I may get the prize this afternoon."

"'Fünfter'* visits us still very often. We hope soon to see you again, and with this hope I remain your attached son, ALBERT.

"*Coburg, 30th January*, 1831."

This was the year when Europe was so severely visited by the cholera, and (whether owing to this circumstance or not—the Rosenau being probably exempt from the visitation—is not mentioned) Prince and Princess Ferdinand, brother and sister-in-law to the duke, with their children and the Princess Kohary, spent part of the year at the Rosenau. In July of that year, however, the brothers were again here by themselves; and here, with the exception of a short visit to their grandmother at Gotha, they seem to have remained during the absence of the duke, who paid a visit to England in the course of that month. The letters which follow allude to that visit, and give a pleasing account of the life of the young princes meanwhile at the Rosenau:

"*Rosenau, July* 6, 1831.

"DEAR PAPA,—The weather lately, although not cold, has been very dull, and it has rained a great deal. The water was very high. At one time a dreadful storm of hail swept over the valley of our Rosenau, and we were afraid it would have destroyed every thing. However, it did no harm, and at this moment the Rosenau is looking more beautiful than ever in the sunshine.

"Please to give our best remembrances to dear uncle, dear aunt,† and to our dear cousin.‡

* A young Prince Reuss V., who (as is generally the case in that family) was called by his number.

† The Duchess of Kent.

‡ Princess Victoria.

"Hoping soon to see you again, I remain your most loving son, ALBERT."

"*Rosenau, July*, 1831.

"DEAR PAPA,—You will long before this have reached your journey's end, and will already have gone all over London. I wish I was with you, to see all the sights that you will have seen. We heard of you yesterday from Thiel, the last place at which you passed the night; and we were very glad to hear that you were quite well. We are also quite well, dear papa, and though I should like to be with you, yet we like being here also, and are very happy at the Rosenau. The quiet of the place, too, is very agreeable, for our time is well regulated and divided. The day before yesterday was the fête of the Gymnasium at Coburg, to which we were invited; so we drove into the town in the morning, and heard a beautiful speech from Professor Troupheller. I am sure it would have pleased you.

"We staid the whole day at Coburg, as our grand-aunt arrived in the afternoon from Lobenstein, and we visited her immediately. She is staying at Ketschendorf with dear grandmamma.

"We are going next Saturday to Gotha, to which we look forward with much pleasure. We will write to you from thence, and tell you how we made the journey. If the weather is only 'good!'"

The visit to Gotha was paid accordingly, but the letter giving an account of it was not written till after their return to the Rosenau, and was as follows:

"*The Rosenau, July* 19, 1831.

"DEAR PAPA,—Although I hear that this letter will not reach you in England, it shall not prevent my writing to you, both to tell you how well we are, and to give you an account of our journey.

"We found dear grandmamma very well at Gotha, and much pleased to see us again. She was particularly cheerful on her birthday, and said that no birthday-present had ever given her so much pleasure as that we gave her in your name on that day. She was also equally pleased with two little poems that we made for her.

"We staid five days at Gotha, and drove on the fifth day, after dinner, to Wolsdorf, from whence we returned here the next day, coming by the Frauenwalde and Eisfeld. From Schalkau to the Rosenau we walked, and got here by half past five. We took the road by Schalkau because we had never been in that part of the country before.

"We are now quite settled here, at the quiet Rosenau, and have resumed our usual hours. We only want you to be here to be completely happy. We are just returned from Ketschendorf, where we dined with dear grandmamma, and she assured us you would now soon return. You do not know, dear papa, how I long for your arrival. We have been long wishing for you. I am sure you will be glad to see the dear Rosenau again. It is now in great beauty; and I will therefore end now, as I wish to enjoy this beautiful evening a little while longer, and it is already eight o'clock.

"Your ALBERT."

In August, 1831, the mother of the princes died, as has been already mentioned, at Sante Wendel. And in the November following they had to mourn the loss of their kind and beloved grandmother, the Duchess Dowager of Coburg. We have seen her, in a former chapter, watching with the fondest maternal solicitude by the bedside of her daughter-in-law, at the birth of the Prince. We have read her letters, breathing the purest spirit of anxious and devoted love for her grandchildren, and full of high-minded aspirations for their future career, and we can well imagine the blank her death must have left in the family circle. "She had already, at a very early period, formed the ardent wish that a marriage should one day take place between her beloved grandchild Albert and the 'Flower of May,' as she loved to call the little Princess Victoria. How would her kind, loving, and benevolent heart have rejoiced, could she have lived to see the perfect consummation of her wishes in the happiness, too soon, alas! to be cut short, that followed this auspicious union!"*

The duchess died at Coburg on the 16th of November, 1831, in the arms of her two eldest sons, Duke Ernest and Duke Ferdinand. Leopold, her youngest and favorite son, was unavoidably absent from her death-bed. In the summer of that year, however, she had been able to pay him a last visit at Brussels, and had enjoyed the pride and happiness of congratulating him on his recent election as King of the Belgians.

* Memorandum by the Queen.

CHAPTER V.

1832–1833.

Visit of the Princes to Brussels.—Remarriage of the Duke.—Mr. Florschütz's Recollections of Mode of Life, System of Study, etc.

In the summer of 1832 the young princes accompanied their father to Brussels on a visit to their uncle Leopold, who, in the course of the preceding year, had been chosen to be the sovereign of the newly-created kingdom of Belgium.

The King of the Belgians, speaking in 1862, in a letter to the Queen, of this visit, says that it was then that she and Prince Albert met for the first time. This, however, is a mistake. The Queen saw the Prince for the first time at Kensington Palace, during a visit paid by the brothers to England in 1836, and which will be noticed in its place.

The stay of the princes at Brussels at this time was short. But, short though it was, their tutor ascribes to the effect produced by what they saw there—by the spectacle which the Belgian capital then afforded, of liberty and independence bravely acquired, and used with good sense and moderation—that appreciation of the blessings of liberty, that attachment to liberal principles which ever afterward distinguished both the princes. In Prince Albert these liberal principles were tempered by a moderation and love of order, and by a detestation of every thing approaching to license, which were very remarkable at his early age; and this without weakening the devotion to the purest and best principles of constitutional freedom, of which his whole after life in England gave such repeated proof.

The love of art, too, which was natural to the Prince, received, his tutor adds, a great stimulus from the beauty of Brussels, and the study of the art treasures which that city contains.

On their way home the princes passed a few weeks with their aunt and cousins at Mayence, and during that time attended the swimming-school which forms part of the military establishment there. They made so much progress that, before they left, they swam down the stream from the bridge of Mayence to Biberich, a distance of three miles. Soon after their return, Prince Albert writes as follows to his father:

"*Rosenau*, 21*st September*, 1832.

"DEAR PAPA,—Let me assure you that we are perfectly well. I am sorry that, since the day of your departure till yesterday, the weather has not always been fine. It must have spoiled some of your nice shooting-parties.

"We have also had very bad weather here, rain and cold winds; but this has disturbed us very little, for we were all the better able to devote our time to our studies. We are working with the greatest diligence, in order to make up for what we may have lost on our journey. The weather, however, has not prevented us from amusing ourselves out of doors; we are working very industriously at our fortifications, and have already made great progress, so that I am sure that you will give us full credit for our industry in this respect when you return.

"Yesterday we had a windy, but, at the same time, a warm, bright day.

"Besides what I have told you, nothing has taken place worthy of notice. Pray give my respectful love to dear grandmamma, and hoping soon to see you again, I recommend myself to your loving remembrance.

"Your dutiful son, ALBERT."

In the autumn of this year the duke remarried. The new duchess was his own niece, being the daughter of his sister Princess Antoinette, married to Duke Alexander of Würtemberg.* In November the brothers accompanied their father to the Castle of Thalwitz, in Saxony, there to await the arrival of the princess from Petersburg. Thence they escorted her to her new home.

The Prince was now in his fourteenth year, and was fast developing that power of thinking and judging for himself which distinguished him so greatly in after life.

The ardent desire for the acquisition of knowledge, always so characteristic of the Prince, as well as his love of order and method, show themselves, even at this early age, very remarkably, in a programme drawn up by himself at this time for his guidance in the prosecution of his studies. We here see in the boy the same feeling which led him to rebel later against the interruption of his

* NOTE BY THE QUEEN.—Princess Mary of Würtemberg, born September 17th, 1799. She was consequently one year older than the duke's first wife, mother of the princes.

work at the Rosenau,* and to complain of the want of method which marked, he thought, the course laid down for him in the study of English law.†

This programme is given, as written out in the Prince's own handwriting, at the end of an interesting Memorandum by his old tutor, Counselor Florschütz, in which he (the counselor) records his recollections of the Prince as a boy, and gives an account of the nature of his studies and the manner in which they were regulated. It will be seen that, though not neglected, classics and mathematics did not hold the prominent, not to say the exclusive place in their system of education which these branches of study occupy in England. The study of modern languages, of history, of the natural sciences, of music, and generally of those accomplishments which serve to embellish and adorn life, had many hours in each week devoted to them.

The amount of work which the Prince thus traces for himself would probably not only seem excessive to the most studious English school-boy (and we must remember that the Prince at this time was only of the age of a school-boy), but was such as a hard-reading man at one of our universities might almost have shrunk from. Be it also remembered that the principal parts of these studies are what his tutor describes as "self-imposed." From six o'clock in the morning to one in the afternoon, and on two days of the week till two o'clock, there was continuous work, excepting, of course, the time required for breakfast. From one to six was given up to outdoor exercises and recreation, dinner, etc.; and the day

* See pages 175, and 176. † See Chap. XIV.

concluded with two hours' more work, from six to eight.

It must not be supposed, however, that this programme was strictly carried into effect. It will be seen from the Memorandum how much their tutor complained of the interruptions caused by the frequent changes of residence, and by the system of breakfasting in the open air at different places, and sometimes at a considerable distance from home; but as a scheme of study laid down by the young Prince himself, and, as far as was possible, adhered to, it may well command our admiration. It may also be remarked that, though their tutor in this paper seems only to lament the interruption occasioned to their studies, he elsewhere mentions the frequent changes of residence as "advantageous rather than otherwise, and as tending to encourage the habit of observation and to enlarge their minds."

The Memorandum is as follows:

"In May, 1823, when I first undertook the care and education of Prince Albert, he was still so young and little that he willingly allowed me to carry him up and down stairs.

"Every grace had been showered by nature on this charming boy. Every eye rested on him with delight, and his look won the hearts of all. I thus entered enthusiastically upon the discharge of my important task, the more so that I met with the entire confidence of his parents—a confidence never impaired or withdrawn from the beginning to the end of the Prince's education. To the confidence thus reposed in me the success of my labors was mainly due, for without it no uniform plan could have been followed, no certain system observed, but differences of opinion, and an uncertain and fluctuating course of education would inevitably have followed.

"Difficulties indeed there were which showed themselves at the very outset, and, but for the love and confidence with which the young princes attached themselves from the first to their tutor, the peculiar circumstances of the time would doubtless have exercised a pernicious influence.

"Among these difficulties was the partiality shown in the treatment of the children by their mother. Endowed with brilliant qualities, handsome, clever, and witty, possessed of eloquence and of a lively and fervid imagination, Duchess Louise was wanting in the essential qualifications of a mother. She made no attempt to conceal that Prince Albert was her favorite child. He was handsome, and bore a strong resemblance to herself. He was, in fact, her pride and glory. The influence of this partiality upon the minds of the children might have been most injurious; and to this was added the unfortunate differences which soon followed, and by which the peace of the family was disturbed; differences that, gradually increasing, led to a separation between the duke and duchess in 1824, and a divorce in 1826.

"It is a satisfaction to me to reflect that these sad events did not interfere permanently with the happiness of my beloved pupils, and that with the cheerfulness and entire innocence of childhood, they retained their respectful and obedient love for their parents.

"Thus deprived of a mother's love and care, the children necessarily depended more entirely on that shown by their tutor; and he is conscious of having thrown himself with all his heart and strength into his task; of having given himself up with unceasing solicitude and the most entire devotion to the good of his pupils. And he was rewarded by their showing their sense of this by their love and confidence, their liking to be with him, and the entire unreserve with which they showed their inmost thoughts and feelings in his presence. Time only strengthened the cordial relations thus established between the tutor and his pupils, which lasted unimpaired during the whole period of the education of the princes till the close of their residence at Bonn in the year 1838.

"Nor did the regard of Prince Albert for me cease with the termination of his studies. I was ever honored with the proofs of his continued good-will. The last mark of his affection was given to me but a short time before his death; and I stand daily before the valued picture which he then sent me, to weep for my beloved pupil and friend.

"Throughout the course of his education much care was bestowed on the due regulation of hours, though circumstances made it more difficult to adhere to them than could have been wished.

"Up to his tenth year Prince Albert usually rose between six and seven in summer, and between seven and eight in winter. The lively spirits with which he at once entered into the games of childhood, or the more serious occupations of youth, spoke the healthy tone of mind and body. The children breakfasted with their parents between nine and ten. The duke himself summoned them to the meal, unless the breakfast was in the open air, in which case the task of conducting them to the place, seldom the same two days following, devolved on me. As this custom prevailed from early spring to late in the autumn, the breakfast, from Coburg, being constantly held in the Hof-gardens, at the Festung, the Kallenberg, at Ketschendorf, or in the Rosenau; and from Gotha in like manner at various places, the greater part of the forenoon was inevitably wasted, to the interruption of useful studies and occupations.* The duke, however, was indifferent to this, and we can only wonder that the princes, notwithstanding, retained their love for study.

"Dinner, which till his eleventh year Prince Albert had regularly alone with his brother and tutor, was at one o'clock. Between four and five, when the duke's dinner was over, he had to appear before the company, after which he paid a visit to his grandmother, the Dowager Duchess Augusta; and no morning passed, when at Gotha, without a visit to his maternal grandmother, the Duchess Caroline of Saxe-Gotha-Altenburg.

"At seven o'clock the Prince supped, and was glad to retire to bed as soon after as possible. An irresistible feeling of sleepiness would come over him in the evening, which he found it difficult to resist even in after life; and even his most cherished occupations, or the liveliest games, were at such times ineffectual to keep him awake.†

"If prevented from going to bed he would suddenly disappear, and was generally found sleeping quietly in

* Note by the Queen.—The Prince often spoke of this.

† Note by the Queen.—The Prince told me this frequently.

the recess of the window, for repose of some kind, though but for a quarter of an hour, was then indispensable; on one occasion—the first time I was present at his supper—the young Prince suddenly fell asleep and tumbled off his chair, but he was not hurt, and continued to sleep quietly on the ground.

"The hours above mentioned were constantly observed till the Prince was eleven years of age, after which he always dined with his father at three (the place of dinner being as uncertain as that of the breakfast), and attended the evening parties at court.

"Some change necessarily took place in the nature and regulation of the Prince's studies and occupations with the progress of time and changes of place; but the end kept in view was still the improvement of body and mind—his advance in health, usefulness, and goodness.

"Before I came to the Prince he had already had a daily master of the name of Tonnelen, but even after I took him in charge I need hardly say that my chief occupation was at first to promote play and exercise in the open air—to tell stories, or explain pictures to my young charge.

"At six his regular lessons commenced. At first only one hour a day; from his seventh to his ninth year, three hours—one before, and another after breakfast, and one in the afternoon. From his ninth to his eleventh year the time was extended to four hours; but as two hours of this time were given after breakfast, they were too often interrupted by the distance of the place of breakfast. Bodily exercises, also regulated at fixed hours, and amusement, filled up the rest of the day.

"After his twelfth year the course of instruction was considerably extended, but the time given for regular lessons seldom exceeded five hours. Subsequently, when studying at Brussels and Bonn, even that number of hours was seldom reached, for much time was there given to his own particular studies and occupations.

"It will be interesting to read the programme of studies which I inclose, drawn up by the Prince himself, in his fourteenth year, for the regulation of his time at the Rosenau. I need not add that it includes all his own or self-imposed tasks.

"It is difficult for me to specify particularly the instruction given by myself. During his early years I taught him every thing except music and drawing, and up to his going to Brussels he received from me his instruction in religion, in history, geography, philosophy, and Latin. He had masters from his tenth year in German and mathematics. At Brussels I continued to give lectures on two subjects, but when he went to Bonn I ceased to give personal instruction, and merely exercised a general superintendence over his whole course of study. It was not till after he left the University that I parted from the beloved Prince.

"The Prince's establishment, when I entered on my duties, consisted of a man and a maid servant. The former, named Wäschenfelder, was an excellent, trustworthy man, and died a few years ago. The latter still lives at Coburg, a widow, and blind; she depends for her subsistence upon the pension bestowed upon her by the Prince.

"The valet, 'Cart,' was engaged in April, 1829, and at first attended on both princes, but after 1839 on Prince

Albert only. He was a faithful, attentive, and obedient servant, and deserved the confidence reposed in him.*

"Though the Prince's health was generally good, he had more than one illness, and was subject to serious, and sometimes even alarming attacks of croup,† which the most trifling cause, the slightest attack of cold, was sufficient to bring on. At such times the characteristic qualities of H. R. H.'s mind displayed themselves very remarkably. I shall never forget the gentle goodness, the affectionate patience he showed when suffering under slight feverish attacks. His heart seemed then to open to the whole world. He would form the most noble projects for execution after his recovery, and, though apparently not satisfied with himself, he displayed a temper and disposition which I may characterize as being, in thought and in deed, perfectly angelic. I can not recall these recollections, even now, without the deepest emotion!

"These attacks of croup were of frequent recurrence up to the Prince's tenth year, and often occasioned a hoarseness which lasted several days, and gave him much annoyance. It is possible that the remedies adopted may have been insufficient, but it is well that some of the measures proposed were not adopted, such, for instance, as passing a hair through the Prince's throat!

"I have no recollection of Prince Albert's ever having had the *whooping*-cough.‡ Could the Prince have mis-

* NOTE BY THE QUEEN.—He remained with the Prince till August, 1858, when he died.

† NOTE BY THE QUEEN.—Leeches had constantly to be applied for these attacks, the marks of which remained till he was quite grown up.

‡ NOTE BY THE QUEEN.—This is a mistake. He certainly had it.

taken the more severe and lasting cough which, on one occasion, followed the croup for that disorder? or is it possible that this malady of my beloved pupil's should have so entirely escaped my memory, although it usually lasts so long, and worries children so much?

"Nor am I more certain about the scarlet fever.* In the year 1829 this disease was prevalent in Gotha. Dr. Dorl, at that time the resident court physician, though able and learned, was of the old theoretic school, and, unfortunately, both pedantic and nervous. One afternoon a slight redness showed itself on the palm of the left hand, and on the neck of the hereditary prince, which the doctor at once rightly pronounced to be scarlet fever. He was at once ordered to bed; but as the brothers lived entirely together, it was assumed that if one had the disorder the other must have it also, so Prince Albert was also put to bed, and kept there for eight days, though no symptoms of the fever showed themselves upon him, nor even upon the hereditary prince, beyond the redness I have mentioned. In bed, however, the two princes had to remain for eight days, when the doctor was convinced the fever had passed. My own belief is that they never had it at all.

"In his early youth Prince Albert was very shy, and he had long to struggle against this feeling. He disliked visits from strangers, and at their approach would run to the farthest corner of the room, and cover his face with his hands; nor was it possible to make him look up, or speak a word. If his doing so was insisted upon, he resented to the utmost, screaming violently. On one occa-

* Note by the Queen.—This the Prince also mentioned.

sion, at a child's fancy ball given by the duchess, Prince Albert, then in his fifth year, was brought down, and a little girl selected as his partner; but when it came to his turn to move on after the other dancers, nothing could induce him to stir,* and his loud screams were heard echoing through the rooms. The duchess, thus *agreeably* surprised, exclaimed, 'This comes of his *good* education.'

"The duke once undertook to punish the Prince for his supposed obstinacy. When the screams were next heard, therefore, the duke, sending me out with the hereditary prince, resolved to try whether a small cane would not succeed in pacifying the 'little obstinate.' On our return, however, Prince Albert was still crying, and the duke, who had not had the heart to administer the punishment he intended, was glad to be relieved of his self-imposed task.

"Even with his brother the Prince showed, at this time, rather too strong a will of his own, and this disposition came out at times even in later years. Surpassing his brother in thoughtful earnestness, in calm reflection and self-command, and evincing, at the same time, more prudence in action, it was only natural that his will should prevail, and when compliance with it was not voluntarily yielded, he was sometimes disposed to have recourse to compulsion. The distinguishing characteristics of the Prince's disposition were his winning cheerfulness and his endearing amiability. His disposition was always to take a cheerful view of life, and to see its

* Note by the Queen.—An anecdote the Prince remembered quite well. He was dressed as a little Cupid.

best side. He was fond of fun and practical jokes, and on one occasion drew down a scolding from his father by getting his instructor in chemistry to fill a number of small glass vessels, about the size of a pea, with sulphureted hydrogen, which he threw about the floor of the pit and boxes of the theatre, to the great annoyance and discomfiture of the audience, at whose confusion he was highly delighted.

"But the joke was not always on his side. The Princess Caroline of Reuss Ebersdorff,* a clever, witty person, at that time resident at Coburg, and very fond of the young Prince, whom she took under her special protection, resolved to revenge herself for some trick he had played her. For this purpose she took advantage of an aversion he had formed, under the following circumstances, for frogs.

"He was always fond of natural history, and lost no opportunity of collecting specimens, showing no timidity, even as a boy, in his pursuit and seizure of animals of all sorts. One evening, while tea was going on in the garden at Oeslau, Prince Albert occupied himself as usual in searching the hedges and pathsides for objects of interest to him, and hit upon a large and very pretty green frog. Seizing it in both hands, he ran with his treasure to the tea-table. To his astonishment, he was received by the ladies with a general cry of horror; and their fright extending to himself, he threw down the frog in a panic, and from that time forward conceived the most un-

* Note by the Queen.—First cousin to his father and the Duchess of Kent, always called "Linette."

conquerable aversion for every animal of the kind.* Princess Caroline, knowing this, took advantage of it to retaliate on the Prince for the many little tricks with which he loved to torment her. Among other tricks he played her, he had one evening, during a party at the palace, filled the pockets of the cloak left by the princess in the cloak-room with soft cheese; and helping assiduously to cloak her at the conclusion of the evening, he was delighted at the horror with which she threw the cloak away, and turned upon himself as the perpetrator of the joke. For this the princess took ample revenge by collecting a basketful of frogs at the Rosenau, and having them placed unobserved in his bed, to the destruction of his night's rest.

"Of the many virtues that distinguished the Prince, two deserve especial mention, for they were conspicuous even in his boyhood, winning for him the love and respect of all. Growing with his growth, these virtues gained strength with years, till they formed, as it were, part of his very religion. One was, his eager desire to do good and to assist others; the other, the grateful feeling which never allowed him to forget an act of kindness, however trifling, to himself.

"He gave an early instance of the former quality, when only six years of age, in the eagerness with which he made a collection for a poor man in Wolfsbach (a small village close to the Rosenau), whose cottage he had seen burnt to the ground. He never rested till a sufficient sum had been collected to rebuild the poor man's cottage. How many more substantial proofs has

* NOTE BY THE QUEEN.—Particularly toads.

he given of the same virtue since he grew up, particularly in the numerous benevolent institutions founded by him in his native home!

"These two qualities of heart won for him the affection of all, and to them more particularly may be ascribed that peculiar charm which fascinated all who knew our beloved master, awakening those feelings of love, admiration, and respect which attended him from the cradle to his premature grave."

PROGRAMME OF STUDIES DRAWN UP FOR HIMSELF BY THE PRINCE CONSORT WHEN IN HIS FOURTEENTH YEAR.—ROSENAU.

HOURS.	MONDAY.	TUESDAY.	WEDNESDAY.	THURSDAY.	FRIDAY.	SATURDAY.
6–7	Translations from the French.	Exercises in Music.	Reading.	Exercises in Memory.	Exercises in Music.	Correspondence.
7–8	Repetition and Preparation in History.	Preparation in Religion.	Riding.	Repetition and Preparation in History.	Exercises in Memory.	Riding.
8–9	Modern History.	Religious Instruction.	Exercises in German Composition.	Religious Instruction.	Ancient History.	Exercises in German Composition.
10–11	Ovid.	Ovid.	Music.	Modern History.	Exercises in Latin Composition.	Music.
11–12	English.	Logic.	English.	English.	Natural History.	English.
12–1	Mathematics.	Geography.	French.	Cicero.	Logic.	French.
1–2			Drawing.			Drawing.
6–7	French.	English Exercises.	French.	English Exercises.	French.	Geography.
7–8	Exercises in Latin Composition.	Written Translation of Sallust.	Mathematics.	Mathematics.	Latin Exercises. Sallust.	Correspondence.

CHAPTER VI.

1832–1835.

The Rosenau and Reinhardsbrunn.—Excursions in the Thüringerwald. —Confirmation of the Princes.

WHILE the winter months, including perhaps those of early spring and late autumn, were generally spent either at Coburg or Gotha, in the enjoyment of the society and amusements afforded by those cities, the more genial months of the year were passed, for the most part, either at the Rosenau or at Reinhardsbrunn.

The Prince was always a great admirer of fine scenery, and early showed this taste in the excursions for which the residence at either of these places gave so much facility. "Nothing," M. Florschütz says, "could exceed the intense enjoyment with which a fine or commanding view inspired the young Prince;" and the time passed at the Rosenau or at Reinhardsbrunn, delightfully situated as were these summer residences—the one at the southwest, the other at the northeast extremity of that lovely district of wood and hill known as the "Thüringerwald"—enabled him to gratify this taste to an almost unlimited extent.

As the place of the Prince's birth, and one to which he remained through life passionately attached, though not destined often to revisit it, we must here attempt some description of the Rosenau. Distant about four miles from Coburg, it is charmingly placed on a knoll that rises abruptly from and terminates to the south, a ridge running out, their last offshoot, from a range of wooded hills which divide the lovely valley of the Itz from the broad and undulating plain through which passes the main road from Coburg to Hildburghausen, Meiningen, etc.

This ridge is cut a quarter of a mile above the house, and again half a mile higher up, at the little villages of Unter and Ober Wolfsbach, prettily situated on the right or western bank of the Itz, by openings through which country roads ascend to the open country to the west; while from the latter village it runs back in a steep ascent, first to the picturesque ruins of Lauterbourg, and thence to the summit of the Herrn Berg, the last of the range of wooded hills above mentioned.

The eastern side of the ridge falls steeply, covered with wood, to the narrow valley through which serpentines the pretty little stream of the Itz, sometimes, as at the villages above mentioned, drawing close in below the ridge, at others diverging in wide sweeps to the farther side of the valley. To the west the ridge slopes gently, just above the house, to a meadow shut in by thriving plantations, and with a large piece of artificial water in the centre.

The knoll on which the house stands rises, as has been said, abruptly at the southern extremity of this ridge. It falls precipitously on the east side to the Itz, which again draws close in here beneath the house, and by a very steep descent on the other three sides to the plain to the west and south.

The top forms a small plateau, on the southern edge of which stands the house—a solid oblong building of no architectural pretensions, with high gable-ends to the north and south. The entrance is in a round tower on the west side of the house, to which the approach ascends through a thick grove of young spruce firs round the western side of the knoll. A broad winding staircase in the tower leads upward to the principal rooms on the first floor, and downward to the marble hall, or dining-room, to the south, which, from the sudden fall of the ground, stands at a lower level than the rest of the house.

A small terrace-garden at the north end of the house commands a lovely view of the valley of the Itz, beyond which, to the east and north, the country is broken up into a succession of wooded hills and picturesque valleys, with occasional clearings, and smiling, tidy villages, standing in the middle of rich meadows and orchards; the hills gradually rising in height up to the highest points of the Thüringerwald, visible in the far distance.

Below the house the stream winds, fringed with trees, through a bright and cheerful meadow, to the village of Oeslau, half a mile lower down. Here it makes a turn, almost at right angles, to the west, and runs at the foot of a range of hills, thickly wooded, which bound the prospect to the south, and terminate in the commanding eminence on which stands the old Festung overhanging the city of Coburg some three miles lower down.

The marble hall, in which, as has been mentioned, the Prince was christened, opens on a small graveled space to the south of the house, bounded by a neatly-trimmed hedge of roses, and communicating at its eastern corner, by a long and irregular flight of stone steps, with the walk along the banks of the Itz below. Standing on this space in the early morning, before the sun has got upon it, or in the afternoon when he has left it, it is difficult to imagine any thing more bright or enjoyable than the view before you, looking over the meadow below the house, bordered to the left by the trees which mark the course of the stream throughout, and to the right by those which clothe a gentle slope on the top of which runs the road to Coburg, the prospect being closed by the wooded hills to the south of the Itz.*

Pleasant and well laid-out walks lead in all directions through the woods, round the water and meadows, and along the stream from the village of Unter Wolfsbach above to that of Oeslau below the house, and thence round by the Schweitzerei, or dairy-farm.

Prominent among the trees which grow and thrive at the Rosenau is the Abele poplar, of which there are many very good specimens here, some of them, on the road leading to Coburg, really magnificent. This accounts at once for this tree having always been a favorite one with the Prince, for surely no man was ever endowed with a stronger feeling of love for all the recollections and associations of his youth and of his native place. This is a feeling which perhaps no man can be without who is possessed of the amiable and loving disposition that characterized the Prince. It showed itself repeatedly in after life in much that he did in those places of his creation,

* Note by the Queen.—The peaceful beauty of the scene is perhaps still more striking by moonlight.

Osborne and Balmoral. At the former place especially, the cottage architecture bears unmistakable witness to the influence which early associations exercised over him.

Some 200 yards from the house to the west, in the angle made by two roads which lead by different lines to Coburg, stands a small Wirthshaus, the favorite resort on Sundays and holidays of the Coburg citizens, who here sit at tables under the trees, without distinction of rank or class, drinking their beer or coffee, or stroll about the walks above mentioned, for the system of exclusion is unknown here which prevails with regard to our English parks, and the walks and grounds are at all times freely thrown open to those who wish to enjoy them.

Dearly was the Rosenau loved by the Prince, the principal scene, as it was, of what he always fondly looked back to as a most happy childhood. His brother shared his love for the place, and several traces of their joint labors as boys still exist there, particularly at the keeper's house near the little inn, behind which there is a small garden still kept as they made it, and a little summer-house which, if they did not actually build, they decorated within entirely themselves. Here, too, is the small skittle-ground, after which the Prince formed one in after years in the garden at Buckingham Palace. It is a game for which he never quite lost his liking, and he would join in it, with all the eagerness and energy of youth, when the Queen's illness made him unwilling to go to any distance from the Palace.

* NOTE BY THE QUEEN.—The little garden and summer-house were much injured by lawless bands in 1848, and, with the small skittle-ground, had been entirely neglected, till the Queen had them restored in 1863.

Reinhardsbrunn, about eight miles from Gotha, with its magnificent lime-trees, and fine pine-woods, situated close under the highest of the wooded hills that give a character of its own to all this district, though not so dear to the young princes as the Rosenau, the scene of their earliest and happiest associations, is perhaps even more charmingly situated, and affords even more temptation to the excursions the princes delighted in; for here the hills and valleys assume their wildest form, and a succession of beautiful and romantic glens, with their strange mixture of wood and rock, gave a wide scope to their spirit of enterprise and discovery. The brothers were never tired of exploring the inmost recesses of these interesting valleys, and in June, 1829, undertook a lengthened excursion, making a ten days' pedestrian tour through the whole district.

Natural History had always a great attraction for both princes, and it was during such excursions that they collected the specimens of various sorts which they afterward brought together, and from which the museum at Coburg, known as the "Ernest-Albert Museum,"* grew up to its present dimensions. To the end of his life the Prince continued to manifest the warmest interest in this museum by many valuable additions which he neglected no opportunity of making to it.†

When he grew old enough to join in the sports of the field, the Prince often carried his gun on such expe-

* Note by the Queen.—It is now (1864) removed to the Festung, where rooms have been built on purpose for it.

† Note by the Queen.—The Queen continues these contributions to it, and watches over it with the greatest interest.

ditions.* But, though by no means indifferent to such sports, and an excellent shot, he scarcely inherited his father's love for them. In later years, indeed, he seemed to engage in them rather as a means of taking a certain amount of exercise than from any great liking for them in themselves. The only sport which he may be said to have engaged in for itself was that of deer-stalking, and in this, the wildness of the scenery, and the interest attaching to the study, which it promoted, of the habits of the animal, added largely to the pleasure of the chase.

"The active life which the Prince thus led in the open air," says his tutor, "strengthened alike the mind and the body. His thirst for knowledge was kept alive and indulged, while under the influence of his bodily exercises he grew up into an active and healthy boy."

There seems no particular notice of the years 1833 and '34, which were doubtless spent in the usual round between Coburg and Gotha. And the only letter we have to quote is the following short note of usual congratulation on the Prince's birthday from his grandmother, the Dowager Duchess of Gotha.

"*Gotha, Aug.* 24, 1834.

"Accept for the birthday of our beloved Albert my most heartfelt wishes. May God preserve this angel to us, and ever keep him in the right path."

The princes were now in their seventeenth and sixteenth years respectively, and the elder at least had arrived at the age at which it is customary in Germany to go through the ceremony of confirmation. But the

* Memorandum by M. Florschütz.

younger was, his tutor relates, "of a singularly earnest and thoughtful nature," and as up to this time they had gone hand in hand in all their studies, it was not wished that any separation should take place between them in this, the first important step in their young lives, and it was therefore determined that "they should make their public profession of faith together."*

It will be seen in a future chapter that a similar course was pursued when the hereditary prince came of age, and that Prince Albert was, by a special act of the Legislature, declared to be of age at the same time as his brother.

On Palm Sunday, 1835, the young princes were accordingly confirmed, and Mr. Florschütz speaks warmly of the earnestness with which Prince Albert prepared himself for the solemn ceremony, and of the deep feeling of religion with which he engaged in it.

The profession now made by the Prince he held fast through life. His was no lip-service. His faith was essentially one of the heart, a real and living faith, giving a color to his whole life. Deeply imbued with a conviction of the great truths of Christianity, his religion went far beyond mere forms, to which, indeed, he attached no especial importance. It was not with him a thing to be taken up and ostentatiously displayed with almost Pharisaical observance on certain days, or at certain seasons, or on certain formal occasions. It was part of *himself*. It was ingrafted in his very nature, and directed his every-day life. In his every action, the spirit—as dis-

* Memorandum by M. Florschütz.

tinguished from the letter—the spirit and essence of Christianity was his constant and unerring guide.

In the Appendix will be found a somewhat abridged translation of the account, printed at the time, of this event, which took place on the 11th and 12th of April, 1835, in the schloss at Coburg.*

* Appendix B.

CHAPTER VII.

1835–1837.

Visit to Mecklenburg, and Tour through Berlin, Dresden, Prague, Vienna, etc.—First Visit to England.—Residence at Brussels.—Letters of the Prince.

IMMEDIATELY after their confirmation the young princes went to Mecklenburg to congratulate their great-grandfather the Grand-duke of Mecklenburg-Schwerin* on the 50th anniversary of his accession to the grand dukedom, and after a few days spent there they joined their father at Berlin. Their stay at that capital at this time was short, as they merely remained till they had been presented at court, after which the princes set out on a tour by themselves, visiting Dresden, Prague, Vienna, Pesth, and Ofen, and returning to Coburg toward the end of May. On the 11th of that month, while they were still at Berlin with their father, the Duchess of Gotha writes to congratulate the duke on the success which the young princes had every where met with. "I was sure beforehand," she says, "that you would be received with the accustomed friendship at Berlin. It is really most satisfactory that our dear children bore every thing so well, and have every where made themselves so beloved by their nice manners. May God con-

* The mother of the princes was the daughter of Duke Augustus of Saxe-Gotha, by his first marriage to a daughter of this Grand-duke of Mecklenburg.

tinue to protect them. I would, however, entreat you not to tire them too much, particularly by too much traveling at night."*

Again, on the 23d of the month, the duchess speaks of the arrival of the young princes in Vienna; of their having visited their uncle, Count Mensdorff, and their aunt at Prague,† and with true grandmotherly solicitude repeats the expression of her anxiety that they should not be over-fatigued.

At every court which they visited they seem to have been received with the greatest kindness, and to have created the most favorable impression.

On the 27th of June, after the return of the duke to Coburg, where the princes had already been settled some time, the duchess writes: "Accept my best thanks for your dear letter of the 24th, announcing your safe arrival at the lovely Rosenau. Thank God that you and the dear children arrived quite well after your great fatigues; but I must scold you a little for having made your journey back such a fatiguing one."

It would be interesting to read the Prince's own account of their tour, and of the impression made upon him by all he saw; and he doubtless wrote fully to his parents and his grandmother during his travels; but the following short letter to his step-mother, the new Duchess of Coburg, is the only letter of his written at this time that is at present forthcoming:

* A caution, the Queen remarks in a note, very necessary, but which was unheeded.

† Count Mensdorff had been transferred, at this time, from the command of the fortress of Mayence to that of the troops at Prague.

"*Berlin, May* 9, 1835.

"DEAR MAMMA,—I hope you will excuse my long silence, for I can assure you that I have never been able to find a moment's leisure; even the time for this letter is, as it were, snatched from other things, for we are already expected at a review.

"I can assure you, dear mamma, that we are quite well, and that we have enjoyed ourselves in Mecklenburg as well as in Berlin. It requires, however, a giant's strength to bear all the fatigue we have had to undergo. Visits, parades, rides, déjeûners, dinners, suppers, balls, and concerts follow each other in rapid succession, and we have not been allowed to miss any of the festivities."

At the beginning of July the young princes went to Gotha for their grandmother's birthday, and she writes on the 12th, when they had again left her, to express the pleasure it had given her to have "the dear children with her on her birthday." After describing the manner in which it had been kept, she adds: "I would willingly have kept them longer with me, but good Florschütz said it was not good that their studies should be longer interrupted, particularly as they were to have a new master to-morrow. I submitted, and must again assure you how very much I was pleased with the dear young people. May God protect them!"

Early in 1836 we find the Prince corresponding from Gotha, where the brothers were again residing, with Dr. Seebode, director of the Gymnasium (High School) at Coburg; and his letters give us a pleasing insight into the literary nature of his pursuits, and the philosophical and inquiring turn of his mind, even at this early period of his life, for he was not yet seventeen years old. On the 5th of February he writes:*

"VEREHRTESTER HERR CONSISTORIALRATH,—In spite of all the distractions (*Zerstreuungen*) of our life here at Gotha, in spite of innumerable visits, in spite of the howling of the wind and storm, in spite of the noise of the guard under our windows, I have at length completed the frame-work (*Disposition*) of my Essay on the Mode of Thought of the Germans (*die Anschauungsweise der Deutschen*); and I send it with this for your perusal, begging you not to judge too severely the many faults which your critical eye will doubtless discover in it.

"You have my work without head or tail (*ohne Kopf und Schwanz*). I have sketched no form (*kein Skelett entworfen*) of introduction or conclusion, thinking it unnecessary, for my desire is to trace through the course of History the progress of German civilization (*Culturgang der Deutschen*) down to our own times, making use, in its general outlines (*in allgemeinen Umrissen*), of the division which the treatment of the subject itself commands.

"The conclusion will contain a retrospect of the shortcomings of our time, with an appeal to every one to correct those shortcomings in his own case (*jene Mängel zuerst aus seinem eignen Benehmen zu verbannen*), and thus to set a good example to others.

"If this idea should not please you, pray write and tell me so, and I will then endeavor to find another conclusion.

"*Gotha, 5th February,* 1836."

* See original of this and following letters in Appendix C.

Again, on the 12th of March, he writes:

"We have heard with great regret of the accident you have met with. I would not believe it at first, but your letter confirms it. I hope you may very soon be well again.

"The work on the History of German Literature gets on but slowly, owing to our Gotha engagements (*Gothaischen Verhältnissen*). Accept again my heartfelt thanks for the correction of my last essay. As I go on with it, I will change and modify the points on which you raise some doubts.

"The time for our departure to Brussels draws certainly nearer, yet still so far off that we shall, under any circumstances, first go once more to Coburg, probably toward Easter. We shall then certainly call at your house, and hope to find you perfectly recovered.

"*Gotha, March* 12, 1836."

Another letter to the same gentleman, written from Brussels toward the end of the year, relates to the same subject. It is therefore inserted here, though somewhat out of its proper place. On the 18th of December the Prince writes:

"Accept my most heartfelt thanks, as well for your kind letter as for the beautiful present that accompanied it. You could not have given me any thing that would have pleased me more than this great work. I intend immediately to study and to follow the thoughts of the great Klopstock into their depths (*dem grossen Klopstock in seinen Tiefen nachzudenken*), though in this, for the most part, I do not succeed.

"I often think back with the greatest pleasure of the interesting hours spent with you at Coburg; with what pleasure my ear took in your praises of our German masters.

"Here, where one is only surrounded by foreign literature, lives only in foreign literature, one learns to appreciate our own at its real value. But it is painful to see the mean idea which the French and Belgians, and even the English, have of our German literature. It consoles one, however, to find that this undervaluing proceeds from an utter incapacity (*völligen Unfähigkeit*) to understand our German works. To give you a slight idea of this incapacity, I add to this letter a French translation of Goethe's *Faust*, which, in the most literal sense of the word, makes one's hair stand on end (*die Haare zu Berge steigen*). Certainly from such productions foreigners can not understand the profound genius of our literature, and they explain why so much in it appears to them weak and ridiculous.

"You will not think me ungrateful for having been so long in answering your kind letter. In excuse I may tell you that but little time is given us to ourselves, and that an extensive correspondence consumes the few moments that we are at liberty. And though we really make the best use of the time we have, there are also many interruptions inseparably connected with a court.

"Our residence at Brussels will last till Easter. Where we shall then go in search of more wisdom we do not yet know. First to Coburg, to which affection draws us, then probably to some German University. To which? This is still undecided.

"In the hope of soon seeing you again well and happy at home, I remain your grateful ALBERT.

"*Brussels, December* 18, 1836."

The princes not only paid the visit to Coburg to which the Prince looked forward, but, before settling at Brussels, they also visited England with their father, traveling by steam-boat down the Rhine to Rotterdam, and crossing thence direct to London. The following letter describes this first part of their journey:

"*Rotterdam, May* 17, 1836.

"DEAR MAMMA,—Let me give you some account of our journey here. I am still writing from Rotterdam, as we arrived after the departure of the steamer, and must wait for the next, which is to start this afternoon.

"Our journey to Mayence, traveling day and night, was very cold and dusty, but we did it in twenty-two hours. We slept at Mayence, and started the following morning by the boat for Coblentz, papa going the same evening by himself to Rüdesheim. On board the steamer we made the very agreeable acquaintance of the two Princes of Isenburg, and we dined with them at the hotel. Major Josa, who was very glad to see us again, and Major Hübner, who built Ehrenbreitstein, were also at dinner. Major Hübner had been ordered by the general commanding here to show us the fortifications. We went over Ehrenbreitstein the same afternoon, and the next morning visited Forts Alexander and Franz, which we admired very much.

"In the afternoon we went on board the steamer, where we met dear papa, and proceeded with him to Cologne. Here we heard that it was impossible for us to be in London on Saturday, or even to leave Rotterdam before Tuesday next, for which we have to thank some Dutch speculators, whose object it is to detain travelers as long as they can.

"We arrived here after two days more on board the steamer, during which time I tried to practice my English in conversation with some Englishmen whom we met. The day before yesterday we made a little excursion to the Hague and Scheveningen. We traveled incognito, which succeeded perfectly, till the chamberlain of the Princess of Orange, saluting us with a malicious smile, unmasked us.

"Ernest and myself are quite well, and only afraid of sea-sickness. The only thing that spoils our pleasure is the absence of good Mr. Florschütz."

From London he again writes on the 1st of June, and as it may be interesting to those who understand German to read his first impressions of England in his own words, the original of the letter is added in the Appendix.*

"DEAR MAMMA,—Accept mine and Ernest's heartfelt thanks for your dear, kind letter. I would have answered you sooner if I had not been suffering for some days from a bilious fever. The climate of this country, the different way of living, and the late hours, do not agree with me. I am now, however, fairly upon my legs again.

* See Appendix C. In the Appendix will also be found the original of many of the Prince's letters.

"My first appearance was at a levee of the king's, which was long and fatiguing, but very interesting. The same evening we dined at court, and at night there was a beautiful concert, at which we had to stand till two o'clock. The next day the king's birthday was kept. We went in the middle of the day to a Drawing-room at St. James's Palace, at which about 3800 people passed before the king and queen, and the other high dignitaries, to offer their congratulations. There was again a great dinner in the evening, and then a concert which lasted till one o'clock. You can well imagine I had many hard battles to fight against sleepiness during these late entertainments.

"The day before yesterday, Monday, our aunt gave a brilliant ball here at Kensington Palace, at which the gentlemen appeared in uniform, and the ladies in so-called fancy dresses. We remained till four o'clock. Duke William of Brunswick, the Prince of Orange and his two sons, and the Duke of Wellington, were the only guests that you will care to hear about.

"Yesterday we spent with the Duke of Northumberland at Sion, and now we are going to Claremont. From this account you will see how constantly engaged we are, and that we must make the most of our time to see at least some of the sights in London. Dear aunt is very kind to us, and does every thing she can to please us; and our cousin also is very amiable. We have not a great deal of room in our apartment, but are nevertheless very comfortably lodged.

"I hope to give you more full accounts from Brussels, dear mamma. . . . ."

From his earliest years the Prince had to struggle constantly of an evening against the feeling of sleepiness, of which he complains in the above letter. This propensity has been already noticed in a memorandum by M. Florschütz, given in a former chapter. Nor did the Prince, manfully as he strove against it, ever entirely conquer it. But, independently of this feeling, he never took kindly to great dinners, balls, or the common evening amusements of the fashionable world, and went through them rather as a duty which his position imposed upon him than as a source of pleasure or enjoyment to himself.* Indeed, on such occasions he loved to get hold of some man eminent as a statesman or man of science, and to pass the hours he was thus compelled to give to the world in political or instructive conversation.†

In a letter dated Gotha, 31st of May, 1836, the dowager duchess speaks of having received a letter from the Duke of Coburg from Kensington, and of her anxiety on account of the sea voyage, as well as of the fatigues and late hours to which the young princes were exposed.

During their stay in England the duke and his sons were lodged at Kensington, and it was on this occasion that the Queen saw the Prince for the first time. They were both now seventeen years old—the Queen completing her seventeenth year during the visit, the Prince three months later.

* Note by the Queen.—Yet nothing, at the same time, could exceed the kind attention he paid to every one, frequently standing the whole evening that no one might be neglected.

† See in Chapter IX., page 166, the remark of the Grand-duke of Tuscany on seeing the Prince talking to the Marquis Capponi during a ball at Florence—"Voilà un prince dont nous pouvons être fiers. La belle danseuse l'attend—le savant l'occupe."

On leaving England they staid a short time at Paris, leaving it a short time before the attempt of Fieschi against the life of Louis Philippe. From Paris they went to Brussels, where their father left them under the care of Baron Wiechmann, a retired officer of the English German Legion. They resided here for the next ten months, preparing by a course of diligent study, in which modern languages and history held a prominent place, for their removal in the course of the following year to the University of Bonn.

Among those by whose society and instruction the young princes chiefly profited during their residence at Brussels was M. Quetelet, to whom many years later, when presiding over the International Statistical Congress, of which M. Quetelet was a member as deputy from Belgium, the Prince paid a graceful compliment, as one to whom he himself principally owed whatever information he possessed on such subjects.

Both princes profited greatly by the time thus spent in Brussels, but the absence it necessarily entailed from their own country was a source of much lamentation to their grandmother, the Duchess Dowager of Gotha. In writing to the duke on the 7th of July, to congratulate him on his safe return to Coburg, while she "thanks God that you have returned in good health and have left the dear children well"—"it makes me sad," she adds, "to think that you are come back without them, and I can not reconcile myself to this long separation from them. Thank God that you were able to assure me you had left them well."

The following letters from Prince Albert to his father

and step-mother, written during their residence at Brussels, gives some insight into their life there, and will speak for themselves:

TO THE DUCHESS OF COBURG, ETC.*

"*Brussels, June* 30, 1836.

"DEAR MAMMA,—I take advantage of the opportunity of papa's return to Coburg to write to you at last once more. I would have written to you before this from Paris if I had had time. We all thought the Hôtel des Princes,† where we lived, a most horrible place—such a noise in the street that you could not hear your own voice. Ernest Würtemberg had been in the same house a short time before.

"We not only saw all the sights to be seen in Paris itself during our stay there, but also made several very pleasant excursions in the neighborhood. We visited St. Cloud, Meudon, Montmorency, Neuilly, Versailles, Trianon, etc., and were much struck by the beauty of the scenery on all sides. We were received at court with the greatest kindness and civility, and we must all join to the fullest extent in the great praise which every one bestows on the royal family.

"After all our fatigues and amusements we are now settled in our new home, and are really glad to be able to lead a quiet and regular mode of life. We live in a small but very pretty house, with a little garden in front,

* See Appendix C. for original of this letter.

† It was in the Rue Richelieu, the most noisy thoroughfare in Paris, and, happily for those who might have been doomed to pass a night in it, no longer exists as a hotel.

and though in the middle of a large town, we are perfectly shut out from the noise of the streets. The masters selected for us are said to be excellent, so that every thing is favorable to our studies, and I trust there will be no lack of application on our part.

"Uncle Leopold is not expected before the 15th, and by the time he arrives we shall have settled to our daily routine. We have already arranged every thing, and mean to devote the next few days to paying the necessary visits before settling, next week, to our new mode of life.

"When this letter reaches you, you will also be about to commence a new mode of life, for I hear that your journey to the sea-side is fixed for the 10th. I hope this trip will answer to you in every way. The journey to England has given me such a disgust for the sea that I do not like even to think of it."

To the Duke of Coburg.

"*Brussels*, *July*, 1836.

"Dear Papa,—Accept the warmest thanks from us both for your dear letter, which we received yesterday evening. . . . . The eagerness shown at Coburg for the building of the theatre is really delightful, and proves that the spirit of improvement is there, and only requires encouragement to develop itself. We mean to make a strong appeal to Aunt Kent to contribute somewhat to this national work. We have been for some time in active correspondence with her. . . . . Uncle Leopold arrived at Laeken last night. We have not yet seen him. And now good-by, dear papa. Always keep the same love for your devoted son Albert."

To the Duke of Coburg.*

"*Brussels, August* 15, 1830.

"Dear Papa,—We accompanied uncle to the camp of Beverlow, which is on a large plain, on which, on a circumference of ten leagues, not a house is to be seen. The camp itself is about five miles round, and is well built. The barracks and stables are much better arranged than is usually the case. We lived in a very nice little hut, close to the royal one, over which the Belgian and Saxon flags were hoisted.

"There was a different field-day every day, and two of them were particularly interesting. The last of these two was really beautiful, and, in the opinion of experienced officers, gave a perfect idea of real war. The victorious army was commanded by Generals Goetals, Magnan, and Marneff; the losing army under Generals d'Olivier and De Lime; and when the latter were at a loss how to extricate themselves from a difficult position, uncle himself conducted the retreat.

"After the fatigue of the manœuvres the soldiers amused themselves by playing at various games, at which we were present, such as running races, climbing high poles, jumping in sacks, fencing and wrestling, etc., in all of which they showed great dexterity. Upon the whole, the troops showed to so much advantage that every one was astonished. Toward evening there was sometimes excellent music, the bands of all the regiments being assembled, in which 160 musicians played together."

* See Appendix C.

TO THE DUKE OF COBURG.

"*Ostend, Sept.* 1, 1836.

"DEAR PAPA,—Thank you a thousand times for your dear letter, and for the pretty ring which I received in your name from the 'Rath' when I awoke on the 26th. I have not taken it off my finger since I got it, and it shall always remain there, and remind me of you when I am not with you.

"How sorry I was to spend this happy day without you, and to be so far from you!"

In the same letter the Prince speaks of having been out shooting with his brother, and of their having killed some sea-gulls.

TO THE DUKE OF COBURG.

"*Brussels, Oct.* 17, 1836.

"DEAR PAPA,— . . . . Yesterday (Sunday) we made an excursion to Waterloo, and went on foot all over the field of battle. Colonel von Wiechmann, who had been at the battle, was our cicerone. We found, to our great indignation, that the French, who marched over the field on their way to the siege of Antwerp, had knocked off the iron cross of the monument. . . . ."

TO THE DUKE OF COBURG.

"*Brussels, Nov.* 29, 1836.

"DEAR PAPA,—We should be so glad to accept your invitation to go to Coburg for a few days and to spend Christmas there. But if we are to profit by our stay here, I am afraid we must deny ourselves that pleasure.

Such an expedition would require five or six weeks, and our course of study would be quite disturbed by such an interruption. We told dear uncle the purport of your letter, and he said he would write to you on the subject."

We do not often find a young man of eighteen objecting to a holiday because it would interrupt his studies!

CHAPTER VIII.

April, 1837, *to the close of* 1838.

Residence at Bonn.—Death of William IV.—Tour through Switzerland and North of Italy.—Letters from the Prince.

THE young princes were now to enter upon their academical career. In April, 1837, they left Brussels for Bonn, at which University, with the exception of the usual vacations, they remained for the next year and a half. A small detached house had been taken for them, not far from the Cathedral, and overlooking the alley that leads up to the Kreutzberg; and here they resided with their tutor, M. Florschütz, who bears witness to the diligence and steadiness with which they applied themselves to their studies. Of our Prince more particularly, he says that "he maintained the early promise of his youth by the eagerness with which he applied himself to his work, and by the rapid progress which he made, especially in the natural sciences, in political economy, and in philosophy." "Music also," he adds, "of which he was passionately fond, was not neglected, and he had already shown considerable talent as a composer."*

* The Prince also excelled in manly exercises, and at a great fencing-match, in which there were from twenty-five to thirty competitors, carried off the first prize, as recorded by an English student at the University, now holding a government situation in Dublin, and who himself obtained the second prize.

Their principal instructors at the University were Messrs. Bethman-Holweg, Schlegel, Fichte, Löbell, Kaufmann, Perthès,* d'Alten, etc., of most of whom the Prince retained throughout life the most affectionate recollection.

Among the students who were at Bonn at this time were the present reigning Duke of Mecklenburg-Strelitz, Prince William of Löwenstein-Werthheim, and Count Erbach, a relation of Prince Leiningen's. With these, from their connection with them, the princes naturally lived on terms of the greatest intimacy, and, indeed, with their fellow-students generally they seem always to have been on the most cordial and friendly footing. With none, however, did Prince Albert form so close and intimate a friendship as with Prince William of Löwenstein, who has lately sent the Queen an account, which will be found at the end of this chapter, of his recollections of their college life. He has also sent several letters, written to him by the Prince at various times after they left the University, which will be found inserted in their place, and which, particularly those written about the time of the marriage, will be read with much interest.

Since the visit of the princes to England in the preceding year the idea had become very general that a marriage was in contemplation between Prince Albert and the Princess Victoria; and during their late residence in Brussels reports to that effect had become still more prevalent, though most prematurely, as nothing

* See extract of letter from M. Perthès on the occasion of the Prince's marriage, quoted from Memoirs by his son, Chap. XIII.

was then settled.* Prince Albert's letters to his father at this time are chiefly interesting from their allusion to England and the young Queen. The first is dated from Bonn, only a few days before the death, on the 20th of June, 1837, of William IV., when Queen Victoria, who had only just completed her eighteenth year, ascended the throne. In that letter, after mentioning a visit to Cologne which he had made a few days previously with his brother and the hereditary Grand-duke of Weimar, and alluding to two pictures† which they had given a commission to have bought at a sale of old pictures which was to be held there, he goes on:

"A few days ago I received a letter from Aunt Kent, inclosing one from our cousin. She told me I was to communicate its contents to you, so I send it on with a translation of the English. The day before yesterday I received a second and still kinder letter from my cousin, in which she thanks me for my good wishes on her birthday. You may easily imagine that both these letters gave me the greatest pleasure."

On the 4th of July, after dwelling on the beauty of the Ahrthal, to which he and his brother had just made an excursion, and telling his father of their attendance at a swimming-school on the Rhine close to Bonn, he adds: "The death of the King of England has every where caused the greatest sensation. From what Uncle Leopold, as well as aunt, writes to us, the new reign has begun most successfully. Cousin Victoria is said to have

* Memorandum by the Queen.

† One was a sketch by Albert Durer, the other a negro's head by Vandyck.

shown astonishing self-possession. She undertakes a heavy responsibility, especially at the present moment, when parties are so excited, and all rest their hopes on her. Poor aunt has again been violently attacked in the newspapers, but she has also found strenuous supporters."

On first hearing of the king's death, the Prince had already written the following beautiful and characteristic letter to the young Queen. It is the first of his which we have, written in English,* and, allowing for a somewhat foreign turn and formality of expression, it shows what proficiency he had already made in a language which, from the correctness with which he both spoke and wrote it, he soon made his own. "How much," says one who had deeply studied his character, "of the Prince's great nature is visible in it. Though addressed to a young and powerful queen, there is not a word of flattery in it. His first thought is of the great responsibility of the position, the happiness of the millions that was at stake. Then comes the anxious hope that the reign may be glorious." (Did he feel a presentiment at the time how much he would help to make it so?) "And then how gracefully and naturally the tender regard of an affectionate relation comes in at the last." But let us quote it:

"*Bonn, 26th June*, 1837.

"MY DEAREST COUSIN,—I must write you a few lines to present you my sincerest felicitations on that great change which has taken place in your life.

* All the other letters which have been quoted from the Prince to his parents and grandmother, and from them to him, are translated from the German.

"Now you are Queen of the mightiest land of Europe, in your hand lies the happiness of millions. May Heaven assist you and strengthen you with its strength in that high but difficult task.

"I hope that your reign may be long, happy, and glorious, and that your efforts may be rewarded by the thankfulness and love of your subjects.

"May I pray you to think likewise sometimes of your cousins in Bonn, and to continue to them that kindness you favored them with till now. Be assured that our minds are always with you.

"I will not be indiscreet and abuse your time. Believe me always your Majesty's most obedient and faithful servant, ALBERT."

"Uncle Leopold," the Prince writes to his father on the 30th of July, 1837,* "has written to me a great deal about England and all that is going on there. United as all parties are in high praise of the young Queen, the more do they seem to manœuvre and intrigue with and against each other. On every side there is nothing but a network of cabals and intrigues, and parties are arrayed against each other in the most inexplicable manner. . . . . Uncle Leopold advises us to make a journey to the South of Germany and Switzerland, or even to the North of Italy. Sorry as I shall be to lose the opportunity of seeing our dear uncle again soon, I feel that his opinion is right, and I am sure you will also agree in thinking his reasons imperative and conclusive."

The object of the King of the Belgians in advising this

* See Appendix C.

journey seems to have been to draw attention from the young princes, as, during their residence at Brussels, a report had been very generally spread (as already mentioned) of a marriage being in contemplation between Prince Albert and the young Queen.

The brothers accordingly employed the vacation in making a tour through Switzerland and the North of Italy. Leaving Bonn on the 28th of August, and sleeping on their way at Andernach, Coblentz, Mannheim, Baden-Baden, and Kenzingen, they arrived on the 3d of September at Basel. The first days of their tour had been attended by almost constant rain, in spite of which they visited every thing best worth seeing at Baden, Strasburg, and other places through which their route lay. Ascending the Jura by the Münsterthal, they reached Moutiers, where they slept in the evening of the 4th, and after halting the next day at Biel in order to visit the "Peters Insel" celebrated by Rousseau, they arrived on the 6th at Elfenau, half an hour's drive from Berne. Here they remained three days on a visit to their aunt, the Grand-duchess Anne, widow of the Grand-duke Constantine.

The weather had cleared up the day before they arrived at Elfenau, and, though very cold at the early hour at which they generally set out on their day's journey, the young travelers thoroughly enjoyed their tour and the fine scenery through which it led them. This is so well known, and has been so often described, that it is not necessary to do much more than record the names of the places they visited. Leaving Elfenau on the 9th, they slept that night at Brienz, from whence next morning their pedestrian tour began. Passing by the Brünig-

Pass and Sarnen to Alpnach, where they slept on the 10th, on the 11th they crossed the lake of the four cantons to Lucerne. Here they only remained long enough to see what was best worth seeing in the town, and left again at eleven o'clock in a boat for Küssnacht, whence they ascended the Rigi on foot, arriving, in company with the family of Prince Fürstenberg, with whom they had fallen in at Küssnacht, at six in the evening.

The next morning we find them at break of day admiring the glorious sunrise from the top of the Rigi; descending thence to Goldau, they there took a carriage to Brunnen, and thence a boat to Flüelen, where they passed the night.

On the 13th they drove by the Gothardsstrasse, by Altdorf and Amsteg, the Devil's Bridge, etc., to Andermatt, where they slept. On the 14th they ascended the valley of the Reuss to Hospenthal and Realp, and crossed the Furka in a storm of wind and snow, descending to the Glacier of the Rhone, where they rested for the night in a miserable house. Prince Albert alone refused this day to make use of the ponies that accompanied them. His wish had been to make a pedestrian tour, and such he was determined it should be.

The next morning they set out at eight o'clock to cross the dangerous Mayenwand, a steep ascent made more difficult by the snow that lay as far as they could see to a depth of two and a half feet. Thick mist obscured the fearful abyss below them, and the Grimsel Hospice, which they reached at ten o'clock, was a welcome sight. Descending thence by Handeckfall, they slept that night at Gutlau; the next at Meyringen; the 17th, after visiting the fall of the Reichenbach, at the Rosenlaui Glacier; and on the 18th, after a very fatiguing day, they reached the top of the Faulhorn. A glorious sunset rewarded their toil, and the next morning at five o'clock they were enjoying an equally glorious sunrise. Continuing their route, they slept on the 19th at Grindelwald. On the 20th they crossed the Wengern Alp to Lauterbrunn; whence, passing by Interlaken and Thun, where they slept on the 21st, they again arrived at Elfenau, to pay a second visit to their aunt, early on the morning of the 22d. Here they remained for the day; but, though the next day, the 23d, was the grand-duchess's birthday, they left again at nine in the morning for Freyburg.

On the 25th, having slept the preceding night at Lausanne, they took the steam-boat at Ouchy, and reached Geneva in the evening, after a passage of three and a half hours. The 26th was given up to seeing what was to be seen at Geneva and in the neighborhood, ending with the theatre at night. On the 28th they arrived at Chamouni, and on the 29th, accompanied by three guides, of whom Balmat the younger, son of the first man who had ascended Mont Blanc, was one, they set out for "Jardin," taking mules as far as Montanvert; the rest of the way, by the Mer de Glace, etc., was necessarily performed on foot. The Jardin was reached at half past one, and after half an hour to rest and enjoy the view of the peak of Mont Blanc, hanging right over them, they redescended, and got back to Chamouni at seven o'clock. On the 30th they ascended the Col de Balme, sleeping that night at Martigny, and on the 1st they came by St. Maurice, Bex, etc., to Vernex, where they were received for the third time by their aunt, the Grand-duchess Anne. In the forenoon of the 2d they made an excursion to Vevay, etc., returning to Vernex, which, however, they left at ten in the evening, in order to extend their tour into Italy. But we need not follow them farther step by step. Perhaps we have already been too minute in the enumeration of the places visited by them in Switzerland. But, while these lines are being written, Prince Arthur is following* nearly the exact route taken by his father twenty-seven years before, and it is interesting to think of him visiting the same scenes, sleeping at the same resting-places, and eagerly searching the visitors' books for some record of that earlier tour.

But, except the unchangeable features of the scenery, little remains the same as it was in those days. The facilities of modern travel, and the consequent overwhelming flood of annual tourists, have caused hotels and villages to spring up where there was formerly little better than a hut to repose in, and only in one place did Prince Arthur find an inn the same as it had been in his father's time. Only at one place, too, did he find the inn books preserved so far back as 1837, and his father's name recorded among the visitors.

Having crossed by the Simplon into Italy, the young travelers visited the Italian lakes, Milan, etc., and arrived at Venice on the 12th of October, whence Prince Albert thus writes to his father:

"What thanks I owe you, dear papa, for having allowed us to make such a beautiful tour! I am still quite

* September, 1865.

intoxicated by all I have seen in so short a time. The reports of Herr Rath (Florschütz) will have told you how we have been able to explore every part of Switzerland, and, favored as we were by the weather, we could enjoy the beauties of the country to the fullest degree. . . . . Milan, and, still more, heavenly Venice, contain treasures of art that astonish me."

The Queen, alluding to this tour in 1864, relates that the Prince sent her a small book containing views of all the places above enumerated except two. From one of these, the top of the Rigi, he sent her a dried "Rose des Alpes;" and from the other, Voltaire's house at Ferney, which he visited from Geneva, a scrap of Voltaire's handwriting, which he obtained from his old servant.

"The whole of these," the Queen adds, "were placed in a small album, with the dates at which each place was visited, in the Prince's handwriting; and this album the Queen now considers one of her greatest treasures, and never goes any where without it. Nothing had at this time passed between the Queen and the Prince; but this gift shows that the latter, in the midst of his travels, often thought of his young cousin."*

Only two days were at this time given to Venice. The vacation was drawing to a close, and it was necessary to think of their return journey, so as to allow of a stay of some days, on their way back, at their native Rosenau. Accordingly, at ten o'clock on the night of the 14th, the princes left Venice, and, traveling night and day through the Tyrol, arrived at Innsprück at four

* Memorandum by the Queen.

o'clock on the afternoon of the 16th. Here they only remained long enough to see what was best worth seeing, and went on without stopping at Munich, where they arrived at two o'clock on the 17th.

After one day's rest and sight-seeing at Munich, they left again in the afternoon of the 18th, and arrived at the Rosenau on the 20th.

The above enumeration of the places visited by the princes during this autumn tour is taken from a diary kept at the time by Herr Florschütz, by whom they were accompanied. M. Florschütz has not, unfortunately (at least not in his diary), recorded any particular anecdotes of the tour, with the exception of their having been made prisoners at the top of Strasburg Cathedral by the slamming, in the wind, of the tower door, and being only released by the opportune arrival of other visitors.

The princes remained for some days at the Rosenau, leaving it again on the 3d of November, on their return to the University. On the way they paid a visit to their grandmother at Gotha, and the duchess thus mentions their visit in a letter to the duke:

"*Gotha, Nov.* 4, 1837.

"The visit of the dear children has given me the greatest pleasure, though it was so short; for they only arrived yesterday at half past ten o'clock, and at a quarter to eight this morning they again left me. The whole visit seems like a dream, though a very happy one, for they were both so nice and good. How tall and handsome Albert is grown, and dear Ernest also looks well and amiable. They were very grateful to you for the permission to make this beautiful tour, though a little uneasy at having been forced to leave you unwell. To-morrow they hope to be at Bonn. It is, no doubt, good for *them* to devote so much time to their studies, but it is very bad for *us* to see so little of them."

Returned to Bonn, they resumed their studies with a diligence by no means impaired by their late pleasant excursion. The following letters from the Prince will give some insight into their life, and also refer to an event that created much sensation at the time; the arrest, namely, of the Archbishop of Cologne in consequence of his opposition to the government:*

"*Bonn, Nov.* 12, 1837.

"DEAR PAPA,—The last term really ended before we had time to collect our thoughts about it.

"We have already plunged into the midst of the new one.

"This winter will be one of very hard work for us, for we are overwhelmed with lectures, papers, exercises, etc., etc.

"The chief subjects of our studies at present are Roman law, state right and political economy (*Staatswirthschaftslehre*), and the principles of finance. We also attend two courses of historical lectures by Löbell and A. W. von Schlegel, and a philosophical lecture (Anthropology and Philosophy) by Fichte. At the same time we shall not fail to give attention to the study of modern languages."

* See Appendix C. for original of this and the next letters from Bonn.

TO THE DOWAGER DUCHESS OF SAXE-GOTHA.

"*Bonn, Nov.* 19, 1837.

"The day before yesterday I received a letter from Uncle Leopold, expressing a wish that we should visit him at Brussels during Christmas week, when there will be no lectures. You may easily imagine, dear grandmamma, how we look forward to this short visit. I am the more glad of it, because we shall then have an opportunity of learning more distinctly what uncle thinks of the coming separation, next spring, of our hitherto united lives, and also of giving him, at the same time, our own views of it.

"That moment is, in its saddest form (*in seiner trüben Gestalt*), ever before me. We would, therefore, as long as time allows us, do all we can to soften its pain and to gild the pill."

TO THE DUKE OF COBURG.

"*Bonn, Nov.* 24, 1837.

"DEAR PAPA,—. . . . . . The subject which engrosses every one here and in this neighborhood, at this moment, is the arrest of the Archbishop of Cologne. The Catholic party is furious, and vows death and destruction to all Prussians and Protestants. Yesterday, being St. Clement's day, an insurrection was apprehended both at Aix-la-Chapelle and Cologne; but the fear of the troops being called out seems to have prevented it, and every thing remained quiet.

"You no doubt know how the archbishop has behaved toward the University with reference to the doctrines of

Hermes; that he has forbidden the professors to read—that he has broken up the seminary here—and that he has declared open war against the Prussian government. Upon this the king sent his minister, Rochow, to Cologne, to treat with the archbishop, who, however, refused to receive him, nor would he allow any professor or clergyman to defend his principles before him.

"Latterly the archbishop has prohibited marriages between Protestants and Catholics, unless it were agreed that the children should all be Catholics.

"When the king summoned him to resign his office, he replied that the king had no authority in the affairs of the Church.

"The result was, that the archbishop was secretly arrested and carried off by night.

"A rich Catholic, much respected here, said, 'The government *must* act with us, for no government can go against us. Things must go as far as they have done in Belgium. Let the Prussians have a care, lest they be driven out of the country with flails.'"

On the 22d of December the Prince writes to his father that he had been prevented from writing by the necessity of working hard at their studies on the approach of Christmas, which he and his brother were to have spent with their uncle, King Leopold, at Brussels. Their doing so, however, was prevented by an accident by which the Prince hurt his knee, and was laid up for several days.*

* Note by the Queen.—Riding in the riding-school, the Prince got his knee jammed between his horse and the wall, in consequence of the horse refusing a leap. The knee was severely injured, and retained a deep scar ever after.

The dowager duchess, writing from Gotha on the 17th of December, says:

"How distressed I am to hear that our beloved Albert has hurt his knee, and suffers a good deal of pain, and that he can not walk, as dear Ernest writes to me. It is no joke to hurt the knee. How little do young people take care of themselves, and how much anxiety and care do they not occasion! But as the careful Florschütz has not written to me about it, I hope it is not serious."

On the 26th of December the Prince thus writes to his grandmother:*

"*Bonn, Dec.* 26, 1837.

"DEAR GRANDMAMMA,—A thousand thanks for the beautiful Christmas present which M. Florschütz has given me in your name. On such a day, when so far separated from home and the dear ones there, any token of remembrance that recalls them to us is doubly welcome.

"I have reviewed in thought all the past Christmas-eves, most of which we spent with you, always receiving from you such valuable presents! This Christmas-eve also I was near you, at least in spirit. The glass is really quite beautiful, and I hope soon to adorn myself with the pretty waistcoat. As you know, dear grandmamma, we had intended to spend Christmas week in Brussels, but my unlucky knee has prevented us. Though not yet strong enough to bear without injury the fatigue of such a journey, and the exertions which would be unavoidable at Brussels, it is now almost well again. We

* See Appendix C.

are exceedingly sorry to have had to give up this pleasure; but, on the other hand, it gives us more time to repeat our lectures and college work, and to wait patiently for the cure of my foot.

"At the same time, dear grandmamma, allow me to lay my most hearty good wishes at your feet. May every blessing of heaven rest upon you, and may continued health and unclouded cheerfulness be yours in the coming year. Keep also for me in the years to come the love and kindness which I have hitherto rejoiced in from you.

"I still owe you many thanks for two letters which I have not been able to answer sooner, as the work always increases so much before the vacations as to occupy the whole day. How glad I was to hear that you were quite well again.

"Of our dear Bonn I have nothing to tell you. The controversy respecting the Hanoverian affairs, and that with the Archbishop of Cologne, engrosses at present the interest and speculation of all conversation here. Farewell now, dear grandmamma, and keep in affectionate remembrance your faithful grandson, ALBERT."

On the same day the Prince wrote to his father* a letter, which is very characteristic of the habit, early acquired by him, of weighing the *truth* of all he heard or saw. What he says of the people of the Rhine shows how little liable he was to be deceived by eye-service or lip-loyalty, while all his remarks speak for the liberality and tolerance of his own religious views. "We had

* See Appendix C.

thought," he says, "of celebrating your birthday with our dear uncle at Brussels, but the tiresome blow I gave my knee prevented us from having that pleasure. I am, however, quite well again, only I must still spare my leg a little, so that, on the one hand, I could not undertake the fatigues of Brussels, and, on the other, I shrank from being seen limping about. We therefore remained quietly at Bonn, where we are busy with our studies. . . . . You will no doubt have taken much interest in the affairs at Cologne. Here it is the all-engrossing subject, and it is very evident that the much-extolled loyalty of the Rhine people is wonderfully loose. 'Prussian' and 'Lutheran heretic' are common terms of contumely. The party of the priests seems to be very strong. They find their chief support in the aristocracy and the common people; the aristocracy, in particular, being very bigoted."

On the 21st of January, 1838, the Prince informs his father that he is again "quite well and strong, and once more able, after the hard work he had gone through, to amuse himself by making long expeditions on foot."

Having paid the visit to Brussels, which had been prevented by the accident to his knee, he writes to his father, on his return to Bonn, dated March 6th, to say he had returned quite satisfied with the result of his visit, and that the king had spoken fully to him respecting his future prospects. "The Queen," he continues, "had in no way altered her mind, but did not wish to marry for some time yet." "She thought herself," the Queen says in a memorandum on this subject written in '64, "still too young, and also wished the Prince to be older when he made his appearance in England. In after years she often regretted this decision on her part, and constantly deplored the consequent delay of her marriage. Had she been engaged to the Prince a year sooner than she was, and had she married him at least six months earlier, she would have escaped many trials and troubles of different kinds."*

"The chief question," the Prince continues in the same letter, "is now as to the arrangement of my mode of life in the mean time. For the first half year it is settled that I should remain at Bonn. We have now got through the most difficult of our studies, and intend to turn the summer to account in learning modern languages, and reading political works. After that I am to travel in accordance with your wishes and those of my uncle, in order to learn to depend more upon myself. This plan is also most agreeable to myself, and uncle is trying to get for me as traveling companion a well-informed young Englishman—a Mr. Seymour."†

The details of the proposed journey were to be afterward settled with his father when he returned to Coburg, and with the King of the Belgians, to whom he was shortly to pay another visit.

* From a Memorandum by the Queen.

† NOTE BY THE QUEEN.—Now Major General Seymour, C. B., lately of the Scots Fusilier Guards. General Seymour was appointed Groom in Waiting to the Prince, and is now in the same capacity with the Queen. The Prince told the Queen, in after years, how good a young man he was, and how anxious he had been to keep every thing that was bad or impure from approaching him, though, God knows, vice itself would ever have recoiled from the look alone of one who wore "the lily of a blameless life;" but still it is pleasing to record such conduct.

In June, 1838, the coronation of the Queen took place, to which the Duke and Duchess of Coburg were invited, the invitation being accepted by the duke, but declined by the duchess.

"So you go to England to the coronation," the Prince writes to his father from Bonn on the 23d of May, 1838, "and afterward we shall have the happiness of seeing you with us. Inconvenient and tiring as the doings will be in London, they will still be very interesting. It is really a pity that mamma should not be going also; it would have been more natural, and I am sure the Queen will be very sorry not to see her. At the same time, I must say that I never thought dear mamma would make up her mind to accept such an invitation."

On this occasion the Queen conferred the Order of the Garter on the duke, and the Dowager Duchess of Gotha, writing to him on the 7th of August, takes blame to herself for not having sooner congratulated him upon it. "I know," she says, "this fine Order so well. My revered father,* and my father-in-law,† both had it."

On the 4th of August the Prince wrote again from Bonn:

"Dear Papa,—You will, by this time, have arrived in your dear home; and I am sure, after so many fatigues, and being so constantly on the move, that you will not be sorry to spend some time quietly at the Rosenau. . . . . The end of the term is fast approaching, and we are hard at work at our studies. The removal of our

* Elector of Hesse-Cassel, and son of a daughter of George II.

† Duke of Gotha, nephew to the Princess of Wales, who was mother to George III.

whole establishment will resemble the migration of the Jews from Egypt."

This is the last letter we have from the Prince from Bonn. Their residence there was to end with the end of the term, and the time was to come to which in some of the foregoing letters he has already alluded with such sadness. At the close of their University career, the brothers, hitherto inseparable, were to go their different ways into the great world.

We can not do better than end this chapter with the following account, by Prince William of Löwenstein, of his recollections of the time spent by him with the young princes at Bonn, which he wrote at the request of the Queen in 1864.

"In 1837 I had the good fortune to make the acquaintance of Prince Albert of Saxe-Coburg at the University of Bonn. Among all the young men at the University he was distinguished by his knowledge, his diligence, and his amiable bearing in society. He liked, above all things, to discuss questions of public law and metaphysics, and constantly, during our many walks, juridical principles or philosophical doctrines were thoroughly discussed. On such occasions the Councilor Florschütz, who had accompanied the two princes from Coburg, used to turn the conversation to subjects of general interest.

"Such professors as Fichte, Perthès, and Hollweg could not fail to exercise a stimulating influence over the youthful minds of their hearers; and even August Wilhelm von Schlegel, in spite of his extraordinary vanity, will not easily be forgotten by those who attended his lectures.

"Among his other social qualities, Prince Albert possessed a lively sense of the ridiculous, as well as great talent for mimicking; and it could scarcely fail but that the immediate subjects for the exercise of this talent should be his own attendants, and the professors, who, while absorbed in their lectures, exhibited some striking peculiarities and odd manners. Prince Albert could take these off inimitably, and was enabled by his good memory to reproduce whole sentences out of their lectures to the general amusement of his company. At the same time, the Prince's perfect good taste prevented his ever giving offense, even when he allowed the most uncontrolled play to his fun.

"The somewhat stiff military nature of the princes' governor, Colonel von Wiechmann, gave occasion to many disputes with the young princes, and frequently led to the most comical scenes. It is impossible to give an idea in writing of the many trifling occurrences of this kind, for the ludicrous effect depended more on the mimicry and accentuation than upon the subject itself.

"Among those who, without knowing it, contributed largely to our amusement, was Oberberg Hauptmann von Beust. He had a very pleasant house, to which he often invited us, and spoke with the most genuine Saxon accent. He was a little, thick-set, very good-humored, but somewhat awkward man. One day he showed us a picture of Venice, and it is impossible to forget the gesture and accent with which, pointing to a row of houses, he said, 'This is the Ponte Rialte.'

"Another person who afforded us much amusement was Rath Wolff, in attendance on the Count of Erbach; as, for instance, when one day tasting some red wine, he exclaimed, 'This is not real Walportzheimer'—a very simple remark, but which was for years brought up against him; or when, at another time, he fell in a race, and had to look for his spectacles.

"Prince Albert had a great turn for drawing caricatures, and among the scenes of his University life of which he has thus perpetuated the memory, Professors Fichte and Löbell, and the spectacles of Rath Wolff, are favorite subjects.

"The Prince's humor and sense of the ludicrous, however, found a natural counterpoise in his other great and sterling qualities; and the great business of his later life, the many important duties he had to fulfill, soon drove into the background the humorous part of his character, which had been so prominent at the University.

"As the Prince excelled most of his contemporaries in the use of intellectual weapons, in the art of convincing, in strictly logical argument, so he was distinguished also in all kinds of bodily exercise. In fencing and the practice of the broadsword he was very skillful. In fencing especially he excelled so much, that once in a fencing-match he carried off the prize from all his competitors.

"I recall with much pleasure our excursion on foot to the neighboring Siebengebirge, so rich in legend; to the valley of the Aar, where the celebrated Walportzheimer wine is produced; and up and down the Rhine.

"Two fine greyhounds usually followed the princes,

one of which, called Eôs" (already mentioned as having been brought by the Prince to England), "was remarkable for sagacity and beauty, and was so fast that she could in the shortest time catch a hare and bring it back. On this account she was Prince Albert's favorite.

"Music was also a favorite pursuit of the students. To the despair of Colonel von Wiechmann, we learned several students' songs, and even practiced the 'Glocke' of Romberg for four voices. In spite of many false notes, we went resolutely on, and passed many an evening in song. Prince Albert was looked upon among us as a master of the art.

"Attempts were even made at dramatic performances, some scene or intrigue being invented and spoken, and then at once represented. These improvisings had doubtless little artistic merit, but they were not the less amusing. Prince Albert was always the life and soul of them, and acted the principal parts.

"He entered with the greatest eagerness into every study in which he engaged, whether belonging to science or art. He spared no exertion either of mind or body; on the contrary, he rather sought difficulties in order to overcome them. The result was such an harmonious development of his powers and faculties as is very seldom arrived at. WILHELM, *Prince Löwenstein.*

"*Kreuzwertheim on Main, May* 12, 1864."

CHAPTER IX.

1838–1839.

Separation of the Brothers.—The Prince's Tour in Italy.—Baron Stockmar.—Majority of Prince Ernest.—Prince Albert declared of Age at the same Time.—Letters.

THE brothers were now to be separated for the first time in their lives, and deeply was the separation felt by both. At the close of their University career, the elder, Prince Ernest, was to go to Dresden to enter the Saxon service, while Prince Albert was to set out shortly afterward for Italy, where he was to spend the winter, according to the plan which, as we have seen, had been already determined upon for him.

They had, however, still two months to spend together at Coburg before the final separation took place, and, attached to each other as they were, we may easily imagine how dear to them must have been the last days spent together at a home which they both loved so much. These last days had, however, been nearly marked by a sad catastrophe, of which the Prince gives the following account in a letter to his grandmother; and it will be seen that it was only averted by a combination of coolness and good sense very rare at such moments. Had they opened the doors to call for assistance in the first alarm, as would have been only natural, instead of "shutting themselves in with the fire," the consequences might have been most serious.*

"*Coburg*, 18*th Oct.*, 1838.

"DEAR GRANDMAMMA,—I have again delayed writing to you, but when a man is once sunk in idleness, it is difficult to get out of it.

"I learned from your dear letter to Ernest that you are better, and that you have moved into your pretty winter residence in all its new splendor.

"How perishable such splendor is we felt seriously yesterday, when, if God had not held his protecting hand over us, the whole palace of Coburg might have become a prey to the flames, nor we ourselves able in any way to escape.

"A fire is lit in our rooms every morning lest we should find them cold when we come to town occasionally in the afternoon. It happened the day before yesterday that we staid in town after the play, in order not to catch cold driving back to the Rosenau. The next morning I was awoke by an unpleasant smell; I sprang out of bed to see whether the register had not been forgotten to be opened in one of the stoves. The smoke met me thicker and thicker, but I could not discover any thing. In the fourth room I was met by the flames darting toward me; it was all on fire. I called out 'Fire! fire!' when Ernest and Cart came from their rooms to my assistance. No living soul was in this wing of the palace except us three; it was also so early that nobody was astir in the neighborhood. You can fancy our alarm. We did not take long to consider, but closed all

* See original letter in Appendix C.

the doors and shut ourselves up with the fire. There were only two jugs with water, and a jug of chamomile tea at our command, of which we made the most. Ernest took my cloak and his own and threw them upon the flames, while I dragged all my bedding there, and pressed the mattresses and large counterpanes against the burning wall. Cart lifted a marble table with incredible strength and threw it against the bookcase enveloped in flames, causing it to fall down. Having thus subdued the fire, we could think of calling for more help.

"Ernest ran just as he got out of bed down stairs to the sentry, who gave the alarm, while I and Cart* were still working up stairs. The heat and smoke were so powerful that all the windows had fallen out; even the glasses of the framed pictures were cracked, and the pictures shriveled in, and the paint of the doors is quite charred.

"Help now came in haste from all sides: a number

* Note by the Queen. — Cart came over to this country with the Prince on his marriage, and remained in his service as valet till he died in August, 1858, having been with him twenty-eight years. The Prince received the news of his death at Dusseldorf just as he was starting with the Queen for Hanover and Babelsberg, and they were both deeply affected by the news. Cart's devotion to the beloved Prince was really quite like that of a nurse for a child, and the Prince never ceased to lament the loss of that faithful servant and true friend, whose discretion and independence of character were most striking. When he died the Prince said to the Queen that many recollections of his childhood were gone with Cart to the grave. He was a link, he added, with his happy childhood and dear native country which was peculiarly precious to him, living as he did in a foreign land; for that even the Queen could only talk of those times as of history, and as of things of which she personally knew nothing. Cart was a native of Nion, near Geneva.

of workmen brought water up and extinguished the smouldering fire. A bookstand with many books and all our prints, two chairs, a table, a looking-glass, etc., have been burnt.

"There is no other harm done, but that Cart and I have burnt the soles of our feet as we got barefooted into the cinders.

"The accident was caused by the ignorance of a stoker who had heated a stove that was not meant to be used, and on which books and prints were lying, and against which a quantity of maps were standing.

"The only picture that was not injured is the one of the fire at the Palace of Gotha.

"Farewell now, dear grandmamma, and always love your faithful grandson, ALBERT.

"*Rosenau*, 18*th Oct.*, 1838.

"P.S.—I shall soon be able to send you the promised picture."

On the same day that the above narrative of their escape from fire was written, the dowager duchess was herself writing to the duke, to express her pleasure at having seen Prince Albert again, and to bewail the approaching separation of the brothers.

"It was most kind," she writes, October 18, 1838, "to allow the dear children to spend a day with me, and our dear Albert gave me a most delightful surprise. I regretted very much that dear Ernest could not come also. I sympathize deeply with the poor children on their approaching separation. With that moment I am sure the merriest and happiest periods of their lives will have passed. Who could be otherwise than sad on such an occasion? Every day that now passes adds to my sorrow for them."

Among those who have been mentioned as fellow-students at Bonn with the Prince and his brother, there was no one, as has been already mentioned, with whom the former was more intimate, or to whom he was more attached, than Prince William of Löwenstein, whose recollections of their University life conclude the preceding chapter. For some years after leaving the University, the Prince kept up an occasional correspondence with him, and he has lately given the Queen some of the letters he received, which are very characteristic of the Prince's warm heart and affectionate disposition. While the brothers were now awaiting at Coburg the dreaded moment which was to bring with it their first separation from each other, the Prince thus writes to his college friend:*

"*Coburg, October* 26, 1838.

"DEAR LÖWENSTEIN,—A thousand thousand thanks for your dear friendly letter, which is a proof to us that you still sometimes think of your true friends. I believe that the pleasant days which we spent together, partly in useful occupations, partly in cheerful intercourse (*in froher Unterhaltung*), will ever appear to me as the happiest of my life. In spite of our unrestrained intimacy (*Ungenirtheit*) and our many practical jokes (*den vielen Neckereien*), the utmost harmony always existed between us. How pleasant were our winter concerts—our theatrical attempts—our walks to the Venusberg—the swim-

* See Appendix C. for the original.

ming-school—the fencing-ground! I dare not think back upon all these things.

"Ernest is now going to Dresden in order to sacrifice himself to Mars (*um sich dort dem Mars zu opfern*). He will there throw himself entirely into a military existence.

"I shall shortly begin my Italian travels. I will occasionally give you news of myself from different places; but you must also write to me; I will always let you know where to. In ten or twelve days I shall already have left my home behind. I shall not set out till Ernest also launches his vessel, so that he may not be left behind alone. The separation will be frightfully painful to us. Up to this moment we have never, so long as we can recollect, been a single day away from each other. I can not bear to think of that moment."

Referring to Prince Ernest's intended residence at Dresden, and the approaching separation, the dowager duchess again writes on the 1st of November, 1838:

"I was sure that the good King of Saxony would be delighted at our dear Ernest's spending some time at Dresden. I should think happily of this well-selected residence for him if dear Albert were only there with his brother! The thought of the separation of such fondly-attached brothers quite breaks my heart, and I can not reconcile myself to the great distance which separates him (Prince Albert) from us."

And again, when the coming separation was yet more imminent: "I can well imagine, my dear duke," the duchess writes, "how painful for you will be the separation from your dear sons. May they soon return to their country, and not easily be induced again to leave it; for where else could they be so useful and so safe?"

Toward the end of November the separation was consummated by the departure of Prince Ernest for Dresden. Prince Albert accompanied him a certain distance on his road, and on his return to Coburg sat down to give his grandmother the following most touching account of his brother's departure and of his own loneliness. It was, indeed, a wrench to those young and loving hearts; and it had been well arranged that the Prince should not be left to brood over the change at home, but should proceed upon a tour, which would necessarily occupy and interest his active and inquiring mind:*

"Now I am quite alone. Ernest is far off (*über alle Berge*), and I am left behind, still surrounded by so many things which keep up the constant illusion that he is in the next room. To whom could I turn, to whom could I pour out my heart (*meinem Herzen Luft machen*) better than to you, dear grandmamma, who always take such interest in every thing that happens to us; who also know and understand us both so well?

"We accompanied Ernest as far as Lobenstein, where we spent an evening and the following morning together with our dear old great-aunt.† She was delighted to have us with her once more, maybe for the last time, for she is eighty years old, and very poorly. The two cousins were also very kind to us.

* See Appendix C.

† Louise, princess of Reuss-Lobenstein, eldest sister of the Prince and Queen's maternal grandmother.

"During the evening we were very happy together. The next morning brought the pain of parting. We only staid till twelve o'clock, and then drove home, this time without Ernest, arriving at ten o'clock at night, almost frozen to death.

"We went, as usual, in an open carriage, and had to endure the cold of 16 degrees (Reaumur's) while crossing the lovely Frankenwald.

"Now Ernest has slept through his first night at Dresden. This day will also bring to him the feeling that something is wanting. (*Es wird ihm der heutige Tag doch auch etwas leer vorkommen.*) I wrote to him to-day, and expect a few lines from him to-morrow or the day after, which I will send to you at once if you like it.

"If I have not written to you for some time, it was because during the last days we really had so much to talk and to care about. I am sure you will not be angry with me. I must now give up the custom of saying *we* and use the *I*, which sounds so egotistical and cold (*des so egoistisch und kalt lautenden Ich's*).

"*In *we* every thing sounded much softer, for the *we* expresses the harmony between different souls, the *I* rather the resistance of the individual against outward forces, though also confidence in its own strength (*den Widerstand des Einzelnen gegen die äusseren Kräfte, jedoch auch das Vertrauen auf eigene Stärke*).

"I am afraid of tiring you with my talk, and yet in this present silence it is a comfort to be able to talk.

"*Coburg*, *Nov.* 29, 1838."

* Note by the Queen, *June*, 1865.—No one felt the truth and the anguish of this more than the Queen after Dec. 14, 1861, and never can she speak of "my children," but always says "our."

"A thousand thanks for your last gracious and very affectionate letter. How pleasant it is to know that somebody shares the feelings which animate us. I have had a letter from Ernest, but as it is of older date than yours, I do not send it. I was very glad thus to hear of him more frequently.

"*Coburg, Dec.* 5, 1838."

Prince Albert did not remain long at Coburg after the departure of his brother for Dresden. In the second week of December he set out for Italy, his father accompanying him—as we gather from the following letter from the Dowager Duchess of Gotha—as far as Munich.

"*Gotha,* 9 *Dec.*, 1838.

"DEAR DUKE,—In a letter I have just received from our dear Albert, he tells me that your journey is fixed for next Monday, and that you will go with him as far as Munich. I hasten to assure you of my best wishes for a happy journey, and that I can well imagine how painful the separation from dear Albert will be to you. My most affectionate wishes, my prayers, and my blessings follow him. May God grant that he may return to us as unspoiled in soul and body as he leaves us! The thought of his departure makes me melancholy. Dear good Ernest wrote me a very sad letter from Dresden on the day of his arrival there. He feels himself so alone, which is only natural."

Herr Florschütz, who had had the constant direction of the young princes' education from the time they were five and four years old respectively, had ended his duties as tutor with the close of their University career. Prince Albert was now accompanied to Italy by Baron Stockmar—Stockmar, whose name must be associated in the remembrance of all who had the happiness of knowing him during the many years of his residence at the English court, with all that they have known of most good and true! Long indeed will the name of "the Baron" live as a household word in the English palace. What member was there of the Queen's household who could not point, with grateful remembrance, to some act on his part of kind and considerate friendship? But, above all, what was he to the chief objects of his care and love! Rarely has it fallen to the lot of Queen or Prince to be blessed with so real a friend, in the best sense of that word—with so wise, so judicious, so honest a counselor. A native of Coburg, and attached to the King of the Belgians from the time when, as Prince Leopold of Saxe-Gotha, he first came to England to marry our Princess Charlotte, his whole life may be said to have been devoted to the Coburg family.

Watching the youth of the young princes, he was not slow to discover and appreciate the remarkable qualities of head and heart that distinguished even the boyhood of Prince Albert; and he had early looked forward to his marriage with the young princess, his cousin, as being better qualified than any other prince he knew to fill the difficult position of consort to the sovereign of this great empire.

For many years after that hope had been realized—indeed, till within three or four years of the Prince's untimely death—the English court was his chief residence, and he had the satisfaction of seeing for himself how all the expectations he had formed of the happy results of such a marriage were more than fulfilled.*

Revered and beloved by all who were brought into contact with him—deserving and enjoying the unbounded confidence, not only of the Queen and Prince, but of the leading statesmen† of all parties—employing his great influence for no selfish end, but seeking only to do good and to be of use, there was but one feeling of sorrow when advancing years and failing health led him to think the time was come when he should withdraw from a palace where he had so long lived, the beloved and trusted friend of all beneath its roof, from the Queen on the throne to the humblest member of her household.

From the time that he thus withdrew from the English court he lived almost entirely at Coburg, and it is perhaps not too much to say that a main inducement to the visit which the Queen and Prince made to that place in 1860 was the wish to see their old friend once again. Little could it then have been foreseen that it was the

* NOTE BY THE QUEEN.—The Queen, looking back with gratitude and affection to the friend of their early married life, can never forget the assistance given by the Baron to the young couple in regulating their movements and general mode of life, and in directing the education of their children.

† NOTE BY THE QUEEN.—Lord Melbourne had the greatest regard and affection for, and the most unbounded confidence in him. At the commencement of the Queen's reign the Baron was of invaluable assistance to Lord Melbourne. Lord Aberdeen also, speaking of him to the Queen, said: "I have known men as clever, as discreet, as good, and with as much judgment; but I never knew any one who united all these qualities as he did. He is a most remarkable man!" The Baron had the greatest regard, in return, for "my good Aberdeen," as he called him.

last time "the Prince" and "the Baron" (with what fond affection one still lingers over those beloved and familiar names!) were to meet again in this world. Still less could the Baron have anticipated, when rejoicing with the Queen over the Prince's providential escape, during this visit to Coburg, from an accident that might well have proved fatal*—that he himself, full of years and shattered as he was in health, would live to see the object of so much love, of such anxious and affectionate care, such fond expectation, borne before himself to the tomb; that the life which had been thus providentially preserved would, within a few months, by the inscrutable decree of Heaven, be suddenly cut short, apparently in the full vigor of its strength, and in the full career of its usefulness.

Once again, in 1862, did the Queen see the good old man, to weep together over the sore affliction that had fallen upon them since they met only two short years before. But, ere another year had come round, and while the Queen, in 1863, was looking forward to another visit to Coburg, in the hope of once more seeing the dear Baron, the intelligence arrived that his health had suddenly given way, to be followed, in a post or two, by the news that this kindest, best, and most devoted, as well as

* As the Prince was returning from a morning visit to the Katenberg in a carriage belonging to the Duke of Coburg, the horses took fright and ran away. After running for some distance at a frightful pace, the Prince, seeing that they were fast approaching the crossing over the railroad, where the gates were shut, and that a fearful crash was inevitable, watched his time and jumped out, escaping with a few rather severe bruises and scratches about the face. The coachman, who kept his seat till the collision occurred, was much hurt.

most disinterested of friends, was no more. On the 9th of July, 1863, the Baron followed his beloved Prince to the grave.

And thus was fulfilled the anticipation in which he had himself indulged, when, during that last visit to Coburg, "the crushed and broken-hearted widow, speaking to him of their beloved Prince, and showing him the pictures and photographs of him which covered the table, the Baron exclaimed, 'My dear, good Prince—how happy I shall be to see him again! And it will not be long.'"*

After some stay at Munich, where he parted from his father, the Prince proceeded on his journey to Italy, and arrived at Florence on the 24th of December, 1838, where he remained till the beginning of March, 1839. He thus describes his journey:

"*Florence, Dec.* 30, 1838.

"Last night we at last arrived at the place of our destination—the far-famed Florence. I make it my first duty, dearest papa, to give you an account of our journey. In general we made very short days' journeys, on account of Baron Stockmar's health, and slept at the following places: Kufstein, Innsprück, Sterzing, Trent, Verona, Mantua, Modena, Bologna, Conigliano, Florence. The road over the Brenner offered no difficulties. There was very little, and sometimes no snow on the road, but for five days we had cold of 12 degrees.†

"Since we have left the Alps behind the cold is indeed less severe, but the whole of North Italy is covered with snow three feet deep. We found so much snow in the Apennines that we took five hours to accomplish what

* Memorandum by the Queen.

† Reaumur.

should have been done in less than three, though we had six horses and two oxen to the carriage. I often fancied myself at Oberhof."*

On the 9th of January, 1839, he again writes: "We are now established in the Casa Cerini, a house belonging to the Marquis Cerini, which is very well situated. We have very airy and pretty rooms, still furnished in the style of Louis XIV." (After mentioning that he had been the week before to Pisa, to attend the funeral of Princess Marie of Würtemberg,† he proceeds): "I left immediately after the funeral and returned to Florence, having heard that the Duc de Nemours wished to leave Pisa the same day, in order to get away as soon as possible from a place connected with so many painful recollections."

In his letters toward the end of his stay at Florence, the Prince describes his life as having been very gay; dining out a great deal, and attending balls; one of which, given at the Pergola Theatre, he mentions as having been particularly brilliant, and of his having danced at it till he was quite tired. But we may be sure that his time was also more usefully spent in studying all that was best and most remarkable in art, for, though he never visited Florence again, the intimate acquaintance he displayed in after years with all the best art treasures of that city afforded indisputable proof of the impression

* A shooting lodge in the Thüringerwald, belonging to the duke, between Gotha and Coburg.

† Daughter of King Louis Philippe. Her husband, Duke Alexander, was first-cousin of the Prince, being the son of the Duke of Coburg's sister, Antoinette, married to the Duke of Würtemberg. *See* Appendix A.

made upon him by what he now saw. He was always a great admirer of the buildings at Florence, and among these there was none he admired more than the Palazzo Pitti, which he especially mentions for the beauty of the external architecture and the magnificence of the apartments.*

On the 9th of February, 1839, the Prince was joined at Florence by Lieutenant (now Major General) Seymour, of the 19th Regiment, who, at the request of the King of the Belgians, had obtained leave of absence from his regiment in order to travel with his nephew. Mr. Seymour, in a memorandum of his recollections of his journey, written in 1863 by the Queen's command, describes the Prince, whom he then saw for the first time, as being "slight in figure and rather tall, his face singularly handsome and intelligent, his features regular and delicate; his complexion, which later, from exposure to an Italian sun, became brown, was then fair and clear. He had, in addition to these advantages, a great look of goodness and distinction, which, young as he was in years, impressed all who were fortunate enough to be thrown into his society."

Of the Prince's life at Florence he gives the following account:

"The Prince was staying at the Casa Cerini, Via del Coromen. . . . . He rose at six o'clock. After a light breakfast he studied Italian under a Signor Martini, read English with me for an hour, played on the organ or piano, composed, sung till twelve o'clock, when he generally walked, visiting some gallery, or seeing some artist.

* Memorandum by the Queen.

He returned home at two to a simple dinner, which he hurried over as much as possible, giving as a reason that 'eating was a waste of time.'* His drink was water. After dinner he again played and sang for an hour, when the carriage was announced, and he usually paid some visits. The visits over, the carriage was dismissed, and the great delight of the Prince was to take long walks in the beautiful country round Florence. This he appeared heartily to enjoy. He became at once gay and animated. 'Now I can breathe—now I am happy !† Such were his constant exclamations. He seldom returned home till seven o'clock, his hour for tea; and, if not going to the Opera or an evening party, he joined in some interesting and often amusing conversation with Baron Stockmar, when the latter felt well enough to come to tea. At nine, or soon after, he was in bed and asleep, for he had been accustomed to such early hours in his own country that he had great difficulty in keeping himself awake when obliged to sit up late."

The Grand-duke Leopold, Mr. Seymour says, was ex-

* Note by the Queen.—The Queen has constantly heard the Prince say this.

† Note by the Queen.—This the Prince constantly expressed on arriving at Osborne and Balmoral, and on leaving London. "How sweet it smells." How "delicious the air is! One begins to breathe again!" And how he delighted in the song of birds, and especially of nightingales—listening for them in the happy, peaceful walks he used to take with the Queen in the woods at Osborne, and whistling to them in their own peculiar long note, which they invariably answered! The Queen can not hear this note now without fancying she hears him, and without the deepest, saddest emotion. At night he would stand on the balcony at Osborne, in May, listening to the nightingales.

tremely attentive to the young Prince, expressing not only a sincere personal regard for him, but an unfeigned admiration of his character and disposition. "On one occasion," Mr. Seymour relates, "the grand-duke was much struck by observing the Prince engaged in a warm discussion with the blind Marquis Capponi, a very eminent and respected member of the Tuscan aristocracy, and said to Lady Augusta Fox" (wife of the Hon. Henry Fox, afterward Lord Holland, who was then English minister at Florence) "here is a prince of whom we may be proud. Lovely partners wait for him, while he is occupied with the learned."

To his old college friend, Prince Löwenstein, the Prince himself describes his life, and his impressions of Florence as follows :*

"*February* 25, 1839.

"DEAR LÖWENSTEIN,—I have long wished to write you a few lines, to thank you for your dear letter of the 3d of January, which I received here, sent after me from Gotha. But you know that the best intentions are ever the most rarely carried out, and thus it is that I am so late in writing.

"Oh! Florence, where I have been for two months, has gathered to herself noble treasures of art. I am often quite intoxicated with delight when I come out of one of the galleries. The country round Florence, too, possesses extraordinary attractions. I have lately thrown myself entirely into the whirl of society (*in den Strudel der Gesellschaften*). I have danced, dined, supped, paid

* See original letter in Appendix C.

compliments, have been introduced to people, and had people introduced to me; have spoken French and English—exhausted all remarks about the weather—have played the amiable—and, in short, have made 'bonne mine à mauvais jeu.' You know my *passion* for such things, and must therefore admire my strength of character that I have never excused myself—never returned home till five in the morning—that I have emptied the carnival cup to the dregs (*Carnevalsbecher bis auf den Boden geleert habe*).

"My stay at Florence will not last much longer. On the 10th of March I go to Rome, where I shall remain three weeks. Thence I shall hasten to Naples, and before the overpowering heat begins, hope to have the white peaks of the Alps once more in sight.

"I must now again say good-by, dear Löwenstein. Think sometimes with affection of your sincere friend,

"ALBERT."

The Prince left Florence with much regret on the 12th of March, being anxious to arrive in Rome before the Holy Week. He slept at Arezzo, Perugia, Terni, and Cività Castellana, and arrived at Rome in a storm of rain on the fifth day. He immediately wrote to his father, and thus describes his journey, and his impressions ("any thing but favorable," according to Mr. Seymour) of the Eternal City:*

"*Rome*, 17 *March*, 1839.

"DEAR PAPA,—We arrived yesterday evening in the world-renowned (*weltberühmten*) city of Rome, and I at

* See Appendix C. for original of this and following letters.

once sit down to announce it. We took four days to perform the journey, visiting several places of note on our way, such as the celebrated waterfall at Terni, which is really more grand than any of those we saw in Switzerland; the Lake of Trasimene; the bridge of Augustus at Narni, etc.

"Yesterday I took a walk with Mr. Seymour through the streets of Rome, but I find it hard to persuade myself that I am really in Rome. But for some beautiful palaces, it might just as well be any town in Germany. By the 1st of April I expect to have seen all the sights here, and on the first days of next month to be able to continue our journey to Naples."

During the time the Prince remained in Rome he devoted himself assiduously to seeing all that was best worth his attention. "He rose," Mr. Seymour says, "at daybreak, wrote his letters, and at nine o'clock began his visits to the different galleries and studios, returning only to partake of a hurried dinner; after which he again set out, and spent the time till sunset in visiting some of the interesting remains of ancient Rome."

On the 31st of March he describes all he had seen during Easter week. He says he had been interested, but that the only ceremony which had not disappointed him, as being less grand and imposing than he had expected, was that of the "Pope's blessing the people, assembled before the Vatican, from the balcony, amid the ringing of bells, firing of cannon, and military music." "It was," he says, "really a most imposing scene," though what followed was tedious, "and savored strongly of idolatry."

"Last Tuesday," he adds in the same letter, "I had the honor of an interview with his holiness.* The old gentleman was very kind and civil. I remained with him nearly half an hour, shut up in a small room. We conversed in Italian on the influence the Egyptians had had on Greek art, and that again on Roman art. The Pope asserted that the Greeks had taken their models from the Etruscans. In spite of his infallibility, I ventured to assert that they had derived their lessons in art from the Egyptians."

In the same letter the Prince mentions his having unexpectedly met the Crown Prince of Bavaria, also Prince and Princess Peter of Oldenburg, and of having also seen Don Miguel, the ex-King of Portugal. In this and other letters H. R. H. speaks enthusiastically of the beautiful things with which Rome is filled.

At the beginning of April the Prince left Rome for Naples, from whence he thus writes to his father on the 11th:

"I have now been here about five days, and occupied with seeing the lions, of which, however, Naples has not many to show. The natural beauties of the place, which are really wonderful, are what strike one. But I have not been able to enjoy them as I could wish, as the southern coloring is quite wanting. The surrounding mountains, and even Vesuvius, are covered with snow; and the sky and the sea are so dull and gray, that one might fancy one's self transported to the North Sea. They say when the moon changes, which it will do in a few days, that we may expect a change for the better.

* Pope Gregory XVI.

"The day before yesterday I paid a visit to the King and Queen. . . . ."

And again on the 25th of the same month:

"A thousand thanks for your last letter, which puts me in possession of the plans for your journey. To-morrow early I leave Naples, and shall now step by step, but without making a long halt at any place, ascend the west coast of Italy, and expect to be at Turin toward the end of next month. How rejoiced I shall be to see you again either on Italian soil or in the Swiss mountains! You will, at all events, find a letter from me at Milan, 'poste restante,' in which I will give you the latest news of my travels. My stay at Naples has been most interesting, and I have profited by it to see all the sights. Nothing struck me so much as Pompeii, a most singular and interesting place.

"I have visited the most interesting places in the neighborhood: Vesuvius, Pæstum, Sorrento, and the island of Capri. In spite of all this, I should much like to be with you at Vienna."

On the 5th of May we find him again at Pisa, on his way home. "We left Naples," he writes on that day, "on the 26th ult., going direct to Rome, where I remained two days; one in order to take a general glance at the objects which, during my long stay, I had seen in detail, the other in order to visit Tivoli. We are now come here direct by Viterbo and Sienna, without going near Florence. I shall remain here to-day, go to-morrow to Leghorn, and return here. I shall then take my way by Lucca to Genoa, which I hope to reach by the 9th. My stay there will only be for two or three days, so that

I hope certainly to leave by the 13th, and to pursue my journey to the north by the route of Novi. If I there hear positive news of you from Milan, I will hasten to that place; if not, I shall go to Turin and stay for a few days there. Thence I should cross by the St. Bernard to Lausanne, and so on to Berne, where I shall, at all events, await your coming."

The Prince spent some days at Milan, where, as he had hoped, he was joined by his father and his cousin, Count Hugo Mensdorff. On their arrival Baron Stockmar left the Prince, and returned to his family at Coburg.

The Prince spent several days at Milan, and on the 19th of May proceeded with his father and cousin to the Lake of Como, and thence, crossing into Switzerland by the Simplon, they traveled by the Lake of Geneva to Vevay, where they remained for a day. From Vevay they descended the lake to Geneva, where the Prince met his aunt, the Grand-duchess Anne of Russia.* Here Mr. Seymour, whose leave of absence had expired, left the Prince and returned to England.

Having remained some days at Geneva, the Prince set out with his father on his return to Coburg, where the coming of age of his brother, the hereditary prince, on the 21st of June, was to be celebrated with all the customary formality and rejoicings.

By a special act of the Legislature, Prince Albert was at the same time declared to be of age; and in a letter the next day to his grandmother, after mentioning that his brother had been delighted with her letter and pres-

* Married to the Grand-duke Constantine (brother to the Emperor Nicholas), from whom, however, she had been long separated.

ent, which "he had given him as soon as he awoke," he goes on to express the gratification it had been to him, that in this important step of their lives he and his brother had "still been allowed to go hand in hand."

"I appreciate," he adds, "this proof of papa's affection and confidence as I ought. And this assurance is what makes this step so agreeable to me; for without it, the thought that I had ceased to be a child of the house would have been rather a source of sorrow than of pleasure. I shall do my best to show myself in all things deserving of his confidence. How I should like now to be with you for a few moments!"

We will conclude this chapter with another letter to his old college friend,* interesting from the unreserved and familiar tone in which it is written, as well as from the insight it gives into the Prince's character, in his lamentations over what he considers the idle life he was leading, the retrospect of his Italian tour, the expressed determination, under all circumstances, to maintain his independence, and, above all, in the warmth of affection with which he speaks of his home, of his brother, and of the friend to whom the letter is addressed.

"*Coburg*, 30*th June*, 1839.

"DEAR LÖWENSTEIN,—Your dear letter from Berlin has given me great pleasure, for I had heard nothing of you for very long. So you are well and happy, and bear your fate, in being an inhabitant of the Berlin Sand Regions (*Sandsteppe*), with fortitude and patience. I can, however, imagine that the University, and the many distinguished and celebrated men who labor there, afford a

* See Appendix C.

rich compensation. When I say the word 'University,' and remember all the good resolutions which I there made, I am quite ashamed of my present life, which consists chiefly in dawdling (*herumschlendern*) about and exchanging compliments. I must, however, acknowledge that my late Italian tour was of great advantage to me. It has made an impression upon me, not so much by its particular incidents as by its general character. My sphere of observation (*Gesichtskreis*) has been doubled, and my power of forming a right judgment will be much increased by having seen for myself.

"Italy is truly a most interesting country, and an inexhaustible source of knowledge. One contrives, however, to taste extraordinary little of the enjoyment which one there promises one's self. In many, many respects the country is far behind what one had expected. In the climate, in the scenery, in the study of the arts, one feels most disagreeably disappointed.

"On the whole, my life was very pleasant. The society of a man so highly distinguished as Baron Stockmar was most precious and valuable to me. I was also accompanied by a young and very amiable Englishman, a Mr. Seymour, with whom I have become very intimate. Above all, that complete harmony which is so necessary for any enjoyment of life always existed among us.

"On the 21st of June we celebrated Ernest's birthday here, his twenty-first, when he became of age (*mündig wurde*). I had also the great happiness of being declared on the same day, by a government patent, of full age, and I am now my own master, as I hope always to be, and under all circumstances.* In consequence of this event we have had great fêtes here, in which the whole country has most heartily taken part.

"On the 13th (July) I shall accompany Ernest to Dresden, and stay with him for about fourteen days. Then must I go to a place that I hate mortally, that charming Carlsbad, where papa is taking the waters, and much wishes me to be with him. I hope this campaign will be over by the middle of August.

"You will easily believe the great pleasure it has been to me to see Ernest and dear Coburg again. I have found the Rath† married! Wiechmann‡ I saw at Geneva, with my aunt the grand-duchess. Oh that I could come across your path somewhere or other! It would please me so much to be able to spend only a few hours with you!

"Engrossed by this thought, I go on talking to you for hours, and forget that you have something else to do than to read my scrawls.

"At once, therefore, good-by! Let me soon hear from you, and do not forget your true friend, ALBERT."

In explanation of what the Prince says in the above letter of his proposed visit to Carlsbad, it should be added that, in writing to Baron Stockmar from Geneva on the 28th of the preceding May, after expressing his regret at having there parted from Mr. Seymour, "the last of our pleasant traveling party," the Prince proceeds: "The happy prospect of approaching nearer and nearer to dear

* NOTE BY THE QUEEN.—How truly this was ever carried out.

† M. Florschütz.

‡ He died in October, 1861.

Coburg would sustain me, were it not for a proposition of papa's which makes me shudder, namely, to accompany him to Carlsbad." Alluding then playfully to the advice given him, that he should "accustom himself more to society," and "pay more attention to the ladies," which, "as an occupation," he particularly disliked,* he adds: "I had, on the contrary, formed the finest plans for the study of the English language and history, for which the quiet of the Rosenau would have been particularly well suited. (*Ich hatte dagegen die schönsten Pläne zu Englischen Sprach- und Geschichts-studien gemacht, zu welchen mir die Stille der Rosenau sehr zu Statten kommen konnte.*)"

The Prince's love of music has been already noticed, and the singing-parties at Bonn described by Prince Löwenstein† will scarcely be forgotten.

During his last visit to Gotha he had formed a singing society, in which he himself bore part, and the following letter, written during the stay with his brother at Dresden, which he had announced his intention of making, shows the interest he continued to take in it:

To CONCERT-MASTER SPAETH.‡

"MY DEAR CONCERT-MASTER,—You will have received through Privy Councilor Florschütz the last parcel of my contributions to the singing society got together by me at Gotha.

"I send you to-day Beethoven's much-wished-for and

* Memorandum by the Queen. † See Chapter VIII., p. 149.

‡ For original of letter, see Appendix C.

highly admired *Praise of Music.* As parts of it only could be got here, I had to write to Leipzig for it, which accounts for your only now receiving it. You will find the instrumental music written out in parts, as well as that for the vocal performers, which, by a lucky mistake of the shopkeeper, is in duplicate. The whole comes more expensive than I at first expected. It will amount to a sum of about sixty florins, showing that we shall not be able to make any important acquisitions out of our funds.

"You may now hand over this cantata to the library of the singing society. I would only ask you to send me back the music for the piano-forte (*den Klavierauszug*) after the concert has taken place.

"I offer myself for the bass solo in the cantata, which, though not important, seems to be very interesting. It will, perhaps, give you some trouble to find *two* good sopranos. For the part of the violin obligato, which is extremely beautiful, Eichhorn will suit very well.

"Now good-by, my dear concert-master. Send me some account to Carlsbad of the rehearsals of Handel and Nencini. Ever yours sincerely, ALBERT.

"*Dresden, July 23d*, 1839."

After leaving Dresden, the much-dreaded visit to Carlsbad was paid, and he writes thence to Baron Stockmar on the 9th of August, complaining of having been asked to go to Reinhardsbrunn immediately after returning to Coburg, which, as an interruption to his proposed course of study, he disliked as much as the visit to Carlsbad. His going to Reinhardsbrunn, however, was not insisted upon, for on the 6th of September he writes to the Baron from the Rosenau to announce his arrival there, "having at last carried my point, in order to enjoy some days of quiet and regular occupation."

The stay at the Rosenau was, however, short, for early in October he had again to leave it, to pay that eventful visit to England, which will be the subject of the next chapter.

CHAPTER X.

1839.

Visit to England.—The Marriage of the Queen and Prince settled.

THE time was now approaching when the marriage, to the possibility of which the grandmother of the Queen and Prince, the Dowager Duchess of Coburg, had so fondly looked forward when they were both children, and which, for the last year, had been the object of such anxious wishes and such sanguine expectations, was to be finally settled.

From a very early period the hope expressed by the Dowager Duchess of Coburg had assumed the form of a definite idea, that might some day be realized; and the Prince used to relate that "when he was a child of three years old, his nurse always told him that he should marry the Queen, and that when he first thought of marrying at all, he always thought of her."*

As the children grew up this idea was warmly encouraged by the King of the Belgians, from whom, indeed, the Queen first heard of it. He had always taken the most affectionate and parental interest in her welfare and happiness, and she herself ever looked up to him with the love and respect of a daughter. Baron Stockmar also had early formed the highest opinion of the young Prince, and his letters to the King of the Bel-

* The Queen's Journal, June 23d, 1840.

gians, written in the spring of 1836, express his strong conviction that no prince whom he knew was so well qualified to make the Queen happy, or fitly to sustain the arduous and difficult position of Prince Consort in England.*

"How this early promise of distinction was fulfilled," the Queen says in the memorandum from which this account is taken, "how immeasurably all the most sanguine expectations were surpassed—how the king's fondest hopes were realized ten thousand-fold—and how the fearful blow which took him from us put an end to all this happiness, and cut short his brilliant and useful career, we all know!"

But the idea of such a marriage met also with much opposition, and the late King William IV. did every thing in his power to discourage it.† No less than five other marriages had been contemplated for the young Princess; and the king, though he never mentioned the subject to the Princess herself, was especially anxious to bring about an alliance between her and the late Prince Alexander of the Netherlands, brother to the present King of Holland. In his anxiety to effect this object, he did every thing he could (though, as has been seen, ineffectually) to prevent the Duke of Coburg's visit to England in 1836, when he came over with his sons and spent nearly

* Memorandum by the Queen, March, 1864.

† Note by the Queen.—Queen Adelaide, in later years, said to the Queen, that if she had told the king that it was her own earnest wish to marry her cousin, and that her happiness depended on it, he would at once have given up his opposition to it, as he was very fond of, and always very kind to, his niece.

four weeks at Kensington Palace with the Duchess of Kent.*

It was then that the Queen and the Prince met for the first time, and her Majesty thus records her impressions of the visit:

"The Prince was at that time much shorter than his brother, already very handsome, but very stout, which he entirely grew out of afterward. He was most amiable, natural, unaffected, and merry—full of interest in every thing—playing on the piano with the princess, his cousin—drawing; in short, constantly occupied. He always paid the greatest attention to all he saw, and the Queen remembers well how intently he listened to the sermon preached in St. Paul's when he and his father and brother accompanied the Duchess of Kent and the princess there on the occasion of the service attended by the children of the different charity schools. It is indeed rare to see a prince, not yet seventeen years of age, bestowing such earnest attention on a sermon."†

Though nothing at this time had passed between the Queen and Prince themselves (nor, indeed, till after the arrival of the princes in England in 1839), yet, after the visit of 1836, the belief in a marriage being intended had become very general, and it was in order to divert public attention from the subject that the King of the Belgians had counseled the tour in Switzerland, which was undertaken in May, 1838.

It was probably in the early part of that year that the king, in writing to the Queen, first mentioned the idea

* Memorandum by the Queen.

† Memorandum by the Queen, March, 1864.

of such a marriage; and the proposal must have been favorably entertained, for in March, 1838, the king writes to Baron Stockmar, and gives an account of the manner in which Prince Albert had received the communication which, of course with the Queen's sanction, he had made to him. In this and other letters the king strongly expresses the high opinion he had formed of the young Prince.

"I have had a long conversation with Albert," the king writes to Baron Stockmar in March, 1838, "and have put the whole case honestly and kindly before him. He looks at the question from its most elevated and honorable point of view. He considers that troubles are inseparable from all human positions, and that therefore, if one must be subject to plagues and annoyances, it is better to be so for some great or worthy object than for trifles and miseries. I have told him that his great youth would make it necessary to postpone the marriage for a few years. . . . . I found him very sensible on all these points. But one thing he observed with truth. 'I am ready,' he said, 'to submit to this delay, if I have only some certain assurance to go upon. But if, after waiting, perhaps, for three years, I should find that the Queen no longer desired the marriage, it would place me in a very ridiculous position, and would, to a certain extent, ruin all the prospects of my future life.'" . . . . "Now again," the king proceeds farther on, "about Albert. If I am not very much mistaken, he possesses all the qualities required to fit him completely for the position he will occupy in England. His understanding is sound—his apprehension clear and rapid—and his feelings in all matters appertaining to personal appearance quite right. He has great powers of observation, and possesses much prudence, without any thing about him that can be called cold or morose."

In the same letter the king mentions the opinions of the instructor of the princes, Colonel Wiechmann, who, while praising both the princes, describes Albert as possessing great power of self-control for so young a man; adding that "he will find this quality most useful to himself in after life."

But both the Prince and his father seem to have objected from the first to the proposal that a few years should elapse before the marriage should take place; and the king, in another letter to Baron Stockmar of the 12th of September, 1838, again says:.

"The young gentlemen arrived here yesterday. Albert is much improved. He looks so much more manly, and from his 'tournure' one might easily take him to be twenty-two or twenty-three." (At this time he was not nineteen.)

"I have spoken to Albert," he adds. . . . . "What his father says upon the subject of the marriage is true.

"Albert is now past eighteen. If he waits till he is in his twenty-first, twenty-second, or twenty-third year, it will be impossible for him to begin any new career, and his whole life would be *marred* if the Queen should change her mind."

The Queen says she never entertained any idea of this, and she afterward repeatedly informed the Prince that she would never have married any one else. She expresses, however, great regret that she had not, after her accession, kept up her correspondence with her cousin, as she had done before it.

"Nor can the Queen now," she adds, "think without indignation against herself of her wish to keep the Prince waiting for probably three or four years, at the risk of ruining all his prospects for life, until she might feel inclined to marry! And the Prince has since told her that he came over in 1839 with the intention of telling her that, if she could not then make up her mind, she must understand that he could not now wait for a decision, as he had done at a former period, when this marriage was first talked about.

"The only excuse the Queen can make for herself is in the fact that the sudden change from the secluded life at Kensington to the independence of her position as Queen Regnant, at the age of eighteen, put all ideas of marriage out of her mind, which she now most bitterly repents.

"A worse school for a young girl, or one more detrimental to all natural feelings and affections, can not well be imagined than the position of a queen at eighteen, without experience and without a husband to guide and support her. This the Queen can state from painful experience, and she thanks God that none of her dear daughters are exposed to such danger."*

In the month of July, 1839, after the majority of the princes had been celebrated at Coburg, as related in the last chapter, Prince Albert had accompanied his brother, who was then in the Saxon service, on his return to Dresden. The King of Saxony had often expressed a

* Memorandum by the Queen.

wish to see him, and his regret at not seeing them both oftener at Dresden. From thence Prince Albert went to Töplitz, where he met his cousin, Count Arthur Mensdorff, with whom he joined his father at Carlsbad.

How reluctantly he gave this time to Carlsbad, which he thought might have been so much better employed in the study of the English language and history at the Rosenau, has been already mentioned.

But the visit to England was now to be paid, which was to decide the fate of the young Prince's life. At the beginning of October we find him with his brother at Brussels, from whence they set out on the 8th of that month, charged with the following letter from the King of the Belgians to the Queen:

"*Laeken, Oct.* 8, 1839.

"MY DEAREST VICTORIA,—Your cousins will be themselves the bearers of these lines. I recommend them to your 'bienveillance.' They are good and honest creatures deserving your kindness, and not pedantic, but really sensible and trustworthy. I have told them that your great wish is that they should be quite 'unbefangen' (quite at their ease) with you.

"I am sure that if you have any thing to recommend to them they will be most happy to learn it from you. . .

"My dear Victoria, your most devoted uncle,

"LEOPOLD R."

Leaving Brussels on Tuesday, the 8th of October, the princes arrived at Windsor Castle on Thursday the 10th, at half past seven in the evening. They here met with the most cordial and affectionate reception from the

Queen, who received them herself at the top of the staircase, and conducted them at once to the Duchess of Kent.

The three years that had passed since they were last in England had greatly improved their personal appearance. Tall and manly as both the princes were in figure and deportment, Prince Albert was indeed eminently handsome. But there was also in his countenance a gentleness of expression, and a peculiar sweetness in his smile, with a look of deep thought and high intelligence in his clear blue eye and expansive forehead, that added a charm to the impression he produced in those who saw him far beyond that derived from mere regularity or beauty of features. "Their clothes not having arrived," the Queen says, "they could not appear at dinner, but came in after it, in spite of their morning dresses." Lord Melbourne, who, as well as Lord Clanricarde, Lord and Lady Granville, Baron Brunnow, Lord Normanby, was staying in the Castle at the time, said at once to the Queen "that he was struck with Prince Albert's likeness to her."*

The way of life at Windsor during the stay of the princes was much as follows: The Queen breakfasting at this time in her own room, they afterward paid her a visit there; and at two o'clock had luncheon with her and the Duchess of Kent. In the afternoon they all rode—the Queen and duchess and the two princes, with Lord Melbourne and most of the ladies and gentlemen in attendance, forming a large cavalcade. There was a great dinner every evening, with a dance after it three times a week.

* The Queen's Journal, October 10, 1839.

But on the 15th there was an important interruption to the ordinary routine of the day. The Queen had told Lord Melbourne the day before that she had made up her mind to the marriage, at which he expressed great satisfaction, and said to her, as her Majesty states in her Journal, "'I think it will be very well received; for I hear that there is an anxiety now that it should be, and I am very glad of it;' adding, in quite a paternal tone, 'You will be much more comfortable; for a woman can not stand alone for any time, in whatever position she may be.'"* Can we wonder that the Queen, recalling these circumstances, should exclaim, "Alas! alas! the poor Queen now stands in that painful position!"

An intimation was accordingly given to the Prince, through Baron Alvensleben, master of the horse to the Duke of Coburg, and long attached to his family, who had accompanied the Prince to England, that the Queen wished to speak to him the next day.

On that day, the 15th, the Prince had been out hunting early with his brother, but returned at twelve, and half an hour afterward obeyed the Queen's summons to her room, where he found her alone. After a few minutes' conversation on other subjects, the Queen told him why she had sent for him; and we can well understand any little hesitation and delicacy she may have felt in doing so, for the Queen's position, making it imperative that any proposal of marriage should come first from her, must necessarily appear a painful one to those who, deriving their ideas on this subject from the practice of private life, are wont to look upon it as the privilege and

* The Queen's Journal, October 14, 1839.

happiness of a woman to have her hand sought in marriage, instead of having to offer it herself.

How the Prince received the offer will appear best from the following few lines which he wrote the next day to the old friend of his family, Baron Stockmar, who was naturally one of the first to be informed of his engagement: "I write to you," he says, "on one of the happiest days of my life, to give you the most welcome news possible," and having then described what took place, he proceeds, "Victoria is so good and kind to me that I am often at a loss to believe that such affection (herzlichkeit) should be shown to me. I know the great interest you take in my happiness, and therefore pour out my heart to you;" and he ends by saying, "More, or more seriously, I can not write to you, for that, at this moment, I am too bewildered.

"'Das Auge sicht den Himmel offen,
Es schwimmt das Herz in Seligkeit.'"*

The Queen herself says that the Prince received her offer without any hesitation, and with the warmest demonstration of kindness and affection; and, after a natural expression of her feeling of happiness, her Majesty adds, in the fervor and sincerity of her heart, with the straightforward simplicity that marks all the entries in her Journal, "How I will strive to make him feel as little as possible the great sacrifice he has made! I told him it *was* a great sacrifice on his part, but he would not allow it. . . . . . I then told him to fetch Ernest, who congratu-

* SCHILLER's *Lied von der Glocke*, a poem of which the Prince was very fond, and knew mostly by heart.

lated us both, and seemed very happy. . . . . He told me how perfect his brother was."*

The Queen thus announces what had occurred, the next morning, to the King of the Belgians.

"*Windsor Castle, Oct.* 15, 1839.

"MY DEAREST UNCLE,—This letter will, I am sure, give you pleasure, for you have always shown and taken so warm an interest in all that concerns me. My mind is quite made up, and I told Albert this morning of it. The warm affection he showed me on learning this gave me great pleasure. He seems perfection, and I think that I have the prospect of very great happiness before me. I love him MORE than I can say, and shall do every thing in my power to render this sacrifice (for such in my opinion it is) as small as I can. He seems to have great tact, a very necessary thing in his position. These last few days have passed like a dream to me, and I am so much bewildered by it all that I know hardly how to write; but I do feel very happy. It is absolutely necessary that this determination of mine should be known to no one but yourself and to Uncle Ernest until after the meeting of Parliament, as it would be considered, otherwise, neglectful on my part not to have assembled Parliament at once to inform them of it.

"Lord Melbourne, whom I have of course consulted about the whole affair, quite approves my choice, and expresses great satisfaction at this event, which he thinks in every way highly desirable.

"Lord Melbourne has acted in this business, as he has

* See the Queen's Journal, October 15, 1839; also Letter from Prince Consort toward the end of next chapter.

always done toward me, with the greatest kindness and affection. We also think it better, and Albert quite approves of it, that we should be married very soon after Parliament meets, about the beginning of February.

"Pray, dearest uncle, forward these two letters to Uncle Ernest, to whom I beg you will enjoin strict secrecy, and explain these details, which I have not time to do, and to faithful Stockmar. I think you might tell Louise of it, but none of her family.

"I wish to keep the dear young gentleman here till the end of next month. Ernest's sincere pleasure gives me great delight. He does so adore dearest Albert.

"Ever, dearest uncle, your devoted niece, V. R."

While this was passing at Windsor, the King of the Belgians was writing on the same day from Laeken:

"*Oct.* 15, 1839.

"MY DEAREST VICTORIA,—I was greatly pleased and interested by your dear letter of the 12th, which reached me yesterday evening. . . . . The poor cousins had all sorts of difficulties to encounter" (during the journey to England). "It was, however, a good omen that once, when they were in danger on the Scheldt, the 'Princess Victoria' came from Antwerp to their assistance. To appear in their traveling dress was a hard case, and I am sure they were greatly embarrassed.

"I am sure you will like them the more the longer you see them. They are young men of merit, and without that puppy-like affectation which is so often found with young gentlemen of rank; and, though remarkably well informed, they are very free from pedantry.

"Albert is a very agreeable companion. His manners are so gentle and harmonious that one likes to have him near one's self. I always found him so when I had him with me, and I think his travels have still improved him. He is full of talent and fun, and draws cleverly. I am glad to hear that they please the people who see them. They deserve it, and were rather nervous about it. I trust they will enliven your séjour in the old castle, and may Albert be able to strew roses without thorns on the pathway of life of our good Victoria. He is well qualified to do so. . . . .

"My dearest Victoria, your devoted uncle,

"LEOPOLD R."

Ten days later the king writes from Wiesbaden, in answer to the Queen's letter of the 15th:

"*October* 24, 1839.

"MY DEAREST VICTORIA,—Nothing could have given me greater pleasure than your dear letter. I had, when I learnt your decision, almost the feeling of old Simeon: 'Now lettest thou thy servant depart in peace.' Your choice has been for these last years my conviction of what might and would be best for your happiness; and just because I was convinced of it, and knew how strangely fate often changes what one tries to bring about as being the best plan one could fix upon—the maximum of a good arrangement—I feared that it would not happen.

"In your position, which may and will perhaps become in future even more difficult in a political point of view, you could not EXIST without having a happy and agreeable 'intérieur.' And I am much deceived (which I think I am not), or you will find in Albert just the qualities and disposition which are indispensable for your happiness, and which will suit your own character, temper, and mode of life.

"You say most amiably that you consider it a sacrifice on the part of Albert. This is true in many points, because his position will be a difficult one; but much, I may say *all*, will depend on your affection for him. If YOU *love* him, and are *kind* to him, he will easily bear the bothers of his position, and there is a steadiness, and, at the same time, a cheerfulness in his character which will facilitate this.

"I think your plans excellent. If Parliament had been called at an unusual time, it would make them uncomfortable; and if, therefore, they receive the communication at the opening of the session, it will be best. The marriage, as you say, might then follow as closely as possible. LEOPOLD R."

On the 29th of October the Queen again writes to the king, to inform him that the intention of communicating the intended marriage in the first instance to Parliament had been abandoned. "Before I proceed farther," she says, "I wish just to mention one or two alterations in the plan of announcing the event. As Parliament has nothing whatever to say respecting the marriage—can neither approve or disapprove it (I mean in a manner which might affect it)—it is now proposed that as soon as my cousins are gone (which they now intend to do on the 14th of November, as time presses), I should assemble all the Privy Council, and announce my intention to them."

Though the intention of waiting till the meeting of Parliament to announce the marriage had been thus abandoned, it was still thought necessary to conceal it for some time, till the declaration could be made to the Council. "In the mean time the Queen and Prince saw a great deal of each other, and often discussed his future position—what his title should be—whether or not he should be a peer (though to this both he and the Queen objected). He was, however, naturally to take precedence of every one else."*

The 2d Battalion of the Rifle Brigade was at this time quartered at Windsor, under the command of Colonel, afterward General Sir George Brown,† and on the 1st of November it was reviewed in the Home Park by the Queen, accompanied by Prince Albert, who appeared in the green uniform of the Coburg troops. The hereditary prince was unable to attend, having been for some days confined to the house by an attack of jaundice.

The following is the account of this review given by the Queen in her Journal:

"At ten minutes to twelve I set off in my Windsor uniform and cap, on my old charger 'Leopold,' with my beloved Albert, looking so handsome in his uniform, on my right, and Sir John Macdonald, the adjutant general,

* Memorandum by the Queen.

† Sir G. Brown died August 27, 1865. He was a fine specimen of a soldier of the last war, when the discipline and efficiency of the British army were at their highest pitch, and was much esteemed and regarded by the Prince.

on my left; Colonel Grey and Colonel Wemyss preceding me; a guard of honor, my other gentlemen, my cousin's gentlemen, Lady Caroline Barrington, etc., for the ground.

"A horrid day! Cold—dreadfully blowing—and, in addition, raining hard when we had been out a few minutes. It, however, ceased when we came to the ground. I rode alone down the ranks, and then took my place, as usual, with dearest Albert on my right, and Sir John Macdonald on my left, and saw the troops march past. They afterward manœuvred. The rifles looked beautiful. It was piercingly cold, and I had my cape on, which dearest Albert settled comfortably for me. He was so cold, being 'en grande tenue,' with high boots. We cantered home again, and went in to show ourselves to poor Ernest, who had seen all from a window."*

On the 1st of November the Prince writes again to Baron Stockmar from Windsor, in acknowledgment of the baron's reply to the announcement of his marriage.

"DEAR BARON STOCKMAR,—A thousand thousand thanks for your dear, kind letter. I thought you would surely take much interest in an event which is so important for me, and which you yourself prepared.

"Your prophecy is fulfilled. The event has come upon us by surprise, sooner than we could have expected; and I now doubly regret that I have lost the last summer, which I might have employed in many useful preparations, in deference to the wishes of relations (*verwandtschaftliche Rücksichten*), and to the opposition of

* The Queen's Journal, November 1, 1839.

those who influenced the disposal of my life (*die auf die Eintheilung meines Lebens wirkten*).

"I have laid to heart (*recht beherzigt*) your friendly and kind-hearted (*wohlwollenden*) advice as to the true foundation on which my future happiness must rest, and it agrees entirely with the principles of action which I had already privately (*im Stillen*) framed for myself. An individuality (*Persönlichkeit*), a character, which shall win the respect, the love, and the confidence of the Queen and of the nation, must be the groundwork of my position. This individuality gives security for the disposition which prompts the actions; and even should mistakes (*Missgriffe*), occur, they will be more easily pardoned on account of that personal character; while even the most noble and beautiful undertakings fail in procuring support to a man who is not capable of inspiring that confidence.

"If, therefore, I prove a 'noble' Prince (*ein edler Fürst*) in the true sense of the word, as you call upon me to be, wise and prudent conduct will become easier to me, and its results more rich in blessings (*segensreicher*).

"I will not let my courage fail. With firm resolution and true zeal on my part, I can not fail to continue 'noble, manly, and princely' (*edel, männlich, fürstlich*) in all things. In what I may do good advice is the first thing necessary, and that you can give better than any one, if you can only make up your mind to sacrifice your time to me for the first year of my existence here.

"I have still much to say to you, but must conclude, as the courier can not wait longer. I hope, however, to discuss the subject more fully with you by word of mouth at Wiesbaden. Hoping that I shall there find you well and hearty, I remain yours truly, ALBERT.

Windsor, 1st November, 1836."

It was a remarkable feature in the Prince's character that, though no man was more capable of forming a sound and dispassionate judgment upon all things, or had a keener sense of what was right and fitting, no man, perhaps, was ever more ready to listen to and even court advice. When he tells the baron that "good advice is the first thing needful," he only expresses the rule on which he invariably acted. To listen patiently to all that could be said, and then to judge calmly for himself what it was right to do, and, having convinced himself what was *right* (not what was merely *pleasant*), to do it without faltering, was his practice through life. It is perhaps characteristic of a weak mind always to fear being supposed to be guided by the advice or dictation of others.

On the 5th of November the Prince alludes to the coming change in his position in a few lines to his stepmother, so characteristic of his great and noble nature that they must by no means be omitted here; for they show, in simple, unaffected language, his yearning for the power to do good, which may be said to have been the one great object of his life. As his first thought in writing to the Queen on the occasion of her accession to the throne had been the influence this would give her over the "happiness of millions,"* so now his mind was at once occupied by the thought of the power he would

* See letter, p. 130.

himself obtain by his marriage of "promoting the good of so many."

"DEAR MAMMA," he writes to his mother—"With the exception of my relations toward her" (the Queen), "my future position will have its dark sides, and the sky will not always be blue and unclouded. But life has its thorns in every position, and the consciousness of having used one's powers and endeavors for an object so great as that of promoting the good of so many will surely be sufficient to support me!"

But another letter had to be written before he left England, from which he shrank, with a natural disinclination to give pain. He had yet to announce his intended marriage to his grandmother, and how would she bear to hear of an event that involved a separation from one whom she loved so dearly, and over whom, from his earliest infancy, she had watched so anxiously and tenderly? It had to be done, however, and on the 11th he nerved himself to write her the following touching letter:

"DEAR GRANDMAMMA,*—I tremble as I take up my pen, for I can not but fear that what I am about to tell you will at the same time raise a thought which can not be otherwise than painful to you, and oh! which is very much so to me also, namely, that of parting. The subject which has occupied us so much of late is at last settled.

"The Queen sent for me alone to her room a few days ago, and declared to me in a genuine outburst of love and affection (*Ergüsse von Herzlichkeit und Liebe*) that I had gained her whole heart, and would make her intensely

* See original letter in AppendixC.

happy (*überglücklich*) if I would make her the sacrifice of sharing her life with her, for she said she looked on it as a sacrifice; the only thing which troubled her was that she did not think she was worthy of me. The joyous openness of manner in which she told me this quite enchanted me, and I was quite carried away by it. She is really most good and amiable, and I am quite sure heaven has not given me into evil hands, and that we shall be happy together.

"Since that moment Victoria does whatever she fancies I should wish or like, and we talk together a great deal about our future life, which she promises me to make as happy as possible. Oh, the future! does it not bring with it the moment when I shall have to take leave of my dear, dear home, and of you!

"I can not think of that without deep melancholy taking possession of me.

"It was on the 15th of October that Victoria made me this declaration, and I have hitherto shrunk from telling you; but how does delay make it better?

"The period of our marriage is already close at hand. The Queen and the ministers wish exceedingly that it should take place in the first days of February, in which I acquiesced after hearing their reasons for it.

"We have therefore fixed our departure for the 14th inst., so as to have still as much time as possible at home. We shall therefore follow close upon this letter.

"My position here will be very pleasant, inasmuch as I have refused all the offered titles. I keep my own name, and remain what I was. This will make me very independent, and makes it easy for me to run over occasionally (*einen Sprung nach der Heimath zu machen*) to see all my dear relations.

"But it is very painful to know that there will be the sea between us.

"I now take leave of you again. Victoria is writing to you herself to tell you all she wishes.

"I ask you to give me your grandmotherly blessing in this important and decisive step in my life; it will be a talisman to me against all the storms the future may have in store for me.

"Good-by, dear grandmamma, and do not take your love from me.

"Heaven will make all things right.

"Always and ever your devoted grandson,

"ALBERT.

"*Windsor, Nov.* 11, 1839.

"May I beg of you to keep the news a secret till the end of the month, as it will only then be made known here?"

The letter written by the duchess to Prince Albert in acknowledgment of this communication is not forthcoming; but she wrote as follows to the Duke of Coburg:

"*Gotha, Nov.* 24, 1839.

"Our dear Albert is to be torn from us! May this separation, so sad for us, be for his own happiness. God bless and preserve him! His letter, which you sent me from Wiesbaden, brought me the news of his future destiny. God be thanked that he feels painfully the separation from us. He seems also very happy. God keep him so! The little Queen has written me a charming letter indeed, in which she does not express herself as Queen, but as a very happy bride, and full of grateful feelings toward Albert that he will share her fate. I am really touched that she remembered me. I look upon it as a proof of her love to Albert that she feels kindly toward me because I am so fond of him. It is only sad that our Albert must leave so soon, and I know not yet how we shall bear it.

"You do not doubt my sympathy with your feelings, dear duke. I find it, however, quite natural that the Queen should have chosen Albert. She could not have found a more handsome, clever, and lovable husband. But that we must lose him is very painful. May God strengthen us for *all* that is before us."

In answer to that to himself, the Prince thus wrote to the duchess on the 28th of November, and the terms in which he alludes to the contents of her letter must make us lament still more that it is not to be found. The evidence we possess, in the letters already quoted, of the high sense of duty that animated the duchess, of her devoted love to her family and her country, and of her unaffected piety, assures us that the letter written on this solemn occasion deserved to be characterized as the Prince characterizes it—as containing exalted and noble ideas. The Prince writes, in answer, as follows:*

"Dear Grandmamma,—How very grateful I am to you for your dear, gracious letter, which I received yesterday. I had to read it over several times in order to take in fully the noble ideas which you therein express.

* See Appendix C.

"Every word is a reflection of your excellent heart! Certainly, dear grandmamma, my cherished home, my beloved country, will always be dear to me, and in my heart will find a friend who will frequently remind me of her.

"To live and to sacrifice myself for the benefit of my new country does not prevent my doing good to that country from which I have received so many benefits. While I shall be untiring in my efforts and labors for the country to which I shall in future belong, and where I am called to so high a position, I shall never cease to be a true *German*, a true *Coburg* and *Gotha* man (*ein treuer Deutscher*, *Coburger*, *Gothaner zu sein*). Still, the separation will be very painful to me.

"I rejoice in the thought of the few days which I shall be able to spend with you before I go. They will be very few. But we will enjoy them. . . .

"Your devoted grandson, ALBERT.

"*Coburg*, 28*th November*, 1839."

On the 14th of November the princes left Windsor on their return to Coburg, and on their way home stopped first at Bonn, and afterward at Wiesbaden, where the King of the Belgians was then staying, who writes to the Queen on the 22d of November to announce their arrival.

"I have on purpose," he says, "kept back a courier, to be able to send you the latest news from here of Albert. The young people arrived here only on the morning of the 20th, having very kindly stopped at Bonn. I find them looking well, particularly Albert. It proves that happiness is an excellent remedy, and keeps people in better health than any other. He is much attached to you, and modest when speaking of you. He is, besides, in great spirits, full of gayety and fun. He is a very amiable companion."

On his return to Coburg from the visit which had thus determined the course of his future life, the Prince again opens his heart to his college friend :*

"*Coburg*, 6 *Dec.*, 1839.

"DEAR LÖWENSTEIN,—Although I am quite overwhelmed with a confusion of business and work of all sorts, I must find a few minutes in order to give you, my true friend, the news of my happiness direct from myself.

"Yes—I am now actually a bridegroom! and about the 4th of February hope to see myself united to her I love!

"You know how matters stood when I last saw you here. After that the sky was darkened more and more. The Queen declared to my uncle of Belgium that she wished the affair to be considered as broken off, and that for four years she could think of no marriage. I went, therefore, with the quiet but firm resolution to declare, on my part, that I also, tired of the delay, withdrew entirely from the affair. It was not, however, thus ordained by Providence; for on the second day after our arrival the most friendly demonstrations were directed toward me, and two days later I was secretly called to a private audience, in which the Queen offered me her hand and heart. The strictest secrecy was required. Ernest alone

* See Appendix C.

knew of it, and it was only at our departure that I could communicate my engagement to my mother.

"I think I shall be *very* happy, for Victoria possesses all the qualities which make a home happy, and seems to be attached to me with her whole heart.

"My future lot is high and brilliant, but also plentifully strewed with thorns. Struggles will not be wanting (*an Kämpfen wird es nicht fehlen*), and the month of March already appears to have storms in store.

"The separation from my native country—from dear Coburg—from so many friends, is very painful to me. When shall I see you again, dear Löwenstein?

"Pray show no one this letter. I write you these details, relying upon your silence, for I know your friendship for me. Now good-by, and think sometimes of your

"ALBERT."

A letter on the approaching marriage of the Queen and Prince, written in 1839 to the editor of one of the journals by a gentleman of English birth, but brought up and educated in Germany, will fitly conclude this chapter. It will be seen that it was written after the public announcement of the intended marriage, and that the writer was well acquainted with the Prince, and with the whole course of his life up to that time. The letter shows a just appreciation of his character, and will be read with interest.

On the Marriage of the Prince to Queen Victoria.

At a moment when all eyes are turned toward the future husband of our Queen, and public attention is drawn to Prince Albert, it may be, perhaps, not uninteresting to the numerous readers of your far-famed journal to peruse a brief sketch of this prince.

It would be superfluous to revert to the period of his childhood when only the germs of future hoped-for goodness and ability could be traced. Suffice it, therefore, to remark, that he, with his brother, the Hereditary Prince Ernest, received the most careful education under the superintendence of their tutor, now Geheimerath Florschütz, a man of high character and excellent principles. He accompanied the princes to the University of Bonn, whither they were also attended by a Hanoverian officer of distinction and merit, to instruct them in military tactics. Here the Prince Albert occupied himself not only in the branches of a superior education, but studied in his leisure hours the ornamental sciences of botany, chemistry, mineralogy, conchology, and ornithology, etc., and, with his brother, laid the foundation of a cabinet of specimens in those various departments. Nor were the arts neglected among these various pursuits. Prince Albert has a talent for painting, and a love for and a proficiency in music, in which he composes, which will always secure to the respective artists a warm patron, capable of appreciating excellence and merit. His college themes on political economy and jurisprudence, etc., as well as on classical subjects, perused by one of the first German statesmen, are declared to be extraordinary for his age, and would not disgrace a man of far maturer years. They will secure him a high place among distinguished men. Although he has a predilection for field-sports, engaging in them never causes him to forget the necessity of a close application to his present attainments and pursuit of farther knowledge, and he therefore more rarely indulges in these amusements than he would otherwise do.

Graceful and handsome, yet he shows no vanity. A pattern for princes, his amiability renders him a model of domestic life. He is an object of the warmest attachment to all surrounding him. In his filial and fraternal duties he is not less admirable. The respectful attention and love toward the charming reigning duchess, his mother-in-law,* is delightful to witness, as well as his devotedness to the excellent Dowager Duchess of Saxe-Gotha, whom he designates and considers as his grandmother. It was for the first time that the princes were separated last year, when the hereditary prince entered the Saxon service, and Prince Albert departed for his tour in Italy. Neither liked to be the one left. They therefore quitted Coburg, and separated without taking leave. Prince Albert is kind, affable, and gay, joining freely in the mirth of those about him; sensible to any committed absurdity, but showing in his laughter that it proceeds from a really good-humored temper. To flattery and intrigue he is a decided enemy, while he possesses an extraordinary insight into character; looks well into all things; weighs and considers them in every point of view, and is able, by the aid of a powerful and strong mind, to form highly correct judgments. Many interesting anecdotes might be related of him which are not given for fear of offending the ear of the amiable prince. It remains, therefore, only to be added, that every Englishman, be he Whig or Tory, must rejoice at the union of his sovereign with a prince so fully capable of filling the exalted station to which he is called.

* Step-mother.

Prince Albert;

at the age of twenty.

From a Miniature by Sir W. Ross. Engraved by William Holl.

CHAPTER XI.

1839.

Declaration of the Marriage to the Privy Council.—List of Privy Councilors present.—The Queen's Journal.—Proceedings at Coburg and Gotha.—Letter from Prince Ernest to the Queen.—Preliminary Arrangements.

THE public declaration of the intended marriage had been necessarily delayed till it should have been officially communicated to the Privy Council; but on the 15th, the day after the departure of the princes, the Queen mentions in the memorandum from which the account of her betrothal has been chiefly taken, that she wrote letters to the queen dowager, and to the other members of the English royal family, announcing her intended marriage, and received kind answers from all.

On the 20th of November the Queen, accompanied by the Duchess of Kent, came up from Windsor to Buckingham Palace, and on the same day Lord Melbourne brought for her approval a copy of the declaration which it was proposed to make to the Privy Council.

The Queen relates that she had much conversation with him at the same time on the various arrangements to be made, and the steps to be taken with regard to the marriage. £50,000 was the amount of annuity which it had been proposed to settle on the Prince; and in this

Lord Melbourne said that the cabinet (most erroneously as it turned out) anticipated no difficulty whatever, except perhaps in case of survivorship.

The Queen records in her Journal that she observed "she thought this would be very unfair," and that Lord Melbourne expressed his entire concurrence with her, hoping, however, that the difficulty might not arise.

On the same occasion, Lord Melbourne told the Queen of a "stupid attempt to make it out that the Prince was a Roman Catholic!" Absurd as such a report was, the Prince, as the Queen remarks in her Journal, "being particularly Protestant in his opinions," Lord Melbourne told the Queen that he was afraid to say any thing about the Prince's religion, and that the subject would not therefore be alluded to in the proposed declaration.* It will be seen that this omission was afterward severely commented upon in the House of Lords.

The Privy Council met on the 23d, when upward of eighty members assembled in the bow room on the ground floor in Buckingham Palace. "Precisely at two" (the Queen records in her Journal) "I went in. The room was full, but I hardly knew who was there. Lord Melbourne I saw looking kindly at me with tears in his eyes, but he was not near me. I then read my short declaration. I felt my hands shook, but I did not make one mistake. I felt most happy and thankful when it was over. Lord Lansdowne then rose, and, in the name of the Privy Council, asked that 'this most gracious and most welcome communication might be printed.' I then left the room, the whole thing not last-

* Memorandum by the Queen.

ing above two or three minutes. The Duke of Cambridge came into the small library where I was standing and wished me joy."*

The Queen always wore a bracelet with the Prince's picture, and "it seemed," she adds in her Journal, "to give me courage at the Council." She returned the same evening, with the Duchess of Kent, to Windsor.

The declaration made by the Queen is thus recorded in the *Gazette*, Nov. 23d, 1839:

"I have caused you to be summoned at the present time in order that I may acquaint you with my resolution in a matter which deeply concerns the welfare of my people, and the happiness of my future life.

"It is my intention to ally myself in marriage with the Prince Albert of Saxe-Coburg and Gotha. Deeply impressed with the solemnity of the engagement which I am about to contract, I have not come to this decision without mature consideration, nor without feeling a strong assurance that, with the blessing of Almighty God, it will at once secure my domestic felicity, and serve the interests of my country.

"I have thought fit to make this resolution known to you at the earliest period, in order that you may be apprised of a matter so highly important to me and to my kingdom, and which, I persuade myself, will be most acceptable to all my loving subjects."

"Whereupon," it is stated in the Minutes of Council, "all the Privy Councilors present made it their humble request to her Majesty that her Majesty's most gracious

* The Queen's Journal, November 23, 1839.

declaration to them might be made public, which her Majesty was pleased to order accordingly.

"C. C. GREVILLE."

Of the eighty-three members of the Privy Council present on the occasion, including the illustrious names of the Duke of Wellington, Lord Lansdowne, Sir Robert Peel, etc., etc., upward of sixty are now dead. But they are gone, for the most part, full of years and honors—their mission on earth fulfilled. Alas! that he, to hear the announcement of whose selection as her husband by their Queen they were now met, should also have gone from us—gone in the full vigor of his age, ere more than half his race was run—the goal scarce yet in sight—his work of good—thus far how nobly performed—still incomplete!*

The settlement of this marriage was not a source of joy to the members of the Queen's family alone, and especially to her mother the Duchess of Kent, who was much attached to her nephews; its announcement was received with great rejoicing throughout the country, and congratulations flowed in from all sides. People not only indulged in the most loyal and heartfelt wishes for the happiness of their beloved sovereign, they also hailed with satisfaction the prospect of a final separation between England and Hanover—the union with which, no less than the monarch who now occupied the Hanoverian throne (and who, failing the Queen, would have ascended that of England), was in the highest degree unpopular.

* See Appendix D. for the list of Members of Privy Council present at the declaration. Those marked with an asterisk are since dead.

After the Prince returned to Germany, the Queen corresponded constantly with him, and says, in the memorandum already so largely quoted, "that the letters she then received from the Prince are the greatest treasures now in her possession. During this time," she adds, "precedents were searched for to see what the Prince's household should consist of; and, unfortunately, the one commonly referred to was that of Prince George of Denmark, the very stupid and insignificant husband of Queen Anne. He was a peer, and also for some time Lord High Admiral of England, but seems never to have played any thing but a very subordinate part."*

What a noble contrast to the acceptance of these offices by Prince George of Denmark is afforded by the refusal of our Prince to accept the command of the army when pressed upon him many years afterward by no less a man than the great Duke of Wellington! It has already been mentioned that he had determined, even before his marriage, to accept no English title that should be offered to him. He was known only as Prince Albert till very many years later, when, a more correct estimate being formed of his position, and it becoming more generally understood how completely he was identified with every act of the Queen's, it was thought advisable that he should assume the title of Prince Consort.

But while in England the news of the Queen's intended marriage was received with universal satisfaction, and her choice of a husband met with very general approval, far different was the feeling in the Prince's own country. In Coburg and in Gotha, in both of which duchies he

* Memorandum by the Queen.

was equally beloved, but one voice of lamentation was raised for his loss!

Yet what was the sorrow of the people of the duchies, deep and general as it might be, to that of the grandmother left behind at Gotha?

She could be under no delusion on the subject; she felt that the coming separation from her beloved grandson, if not absolutely final, must be complete and lasting. And what consideration of earthly grandeur or high position could reconcile her to the thought? In a letter to the Duke of Coburg, written on the 12th of December, 1839, the duchess gives the following affecting expression to her feelings:

"*Gotha, December* 12, 1839.

"MY DEAR DUKE,—I received your letter of the 8th the day before yesterday, and thank you much for it. I was also pleased to hear from Wangenheim, who brought me, in your name, the programme of last Sunday's festivities, and also from Von Stein, that you are very well and happy.

"I am very much upset. The brilliant destiny awaiting our Albert can not reconcile me to the thought that his country will lose him forever; and, for myself, I lose my greatest happiness. But I think not of myself. The few years I may yet have to live will soon have passed away. May God protect dear Albert, and keep him in the same heavenly frame of mind! I hope the Queen will appreciate him. I have been much pleased that she has shown herself so kind toward me, especially as I am sure I owe it all to the affection of my Albert. And yet I *can not* rejoice. May God spare our Ernest, at least, who will now be our only joy, and the only hope of the country!

"To celebrate the betrothal of dear Albert, I held a reception last Sunday afternoon, in the course of which I showed the lovely portrait of the Queen to the whole assembly. Every body was much moved, for Albert is certainly much beloved both here and in Coburg. I was sorry to hear that he was unwell on Monday, but he was very considerate in making Florschütz write to me the next day to say that he was nearly well again. Thank God for it."

On the 8th of December the official declaration of the intended marriage between the Queen of England and Prince Albert of Saxe-Coburg was made in the most sol emn and formal manner at Coburg.*

Writing to the Queen two days after the ceremony, the Prince thus alludes to what then took place: "The day before yesterday the great ceremony of the Declaration took place, which was really very splendid, and went off well. . . . . The day affected me much, as so many emotions filled my heart! Your health was drunk at dinner, where three hundred persons were present, with a universal cheer.

"The joy of the people was so great that they went on firing in the streets with guns and pistols during the whole night, so that one might have imagined that a battle was taking place. . . . ."

* A copy of the official notice of the ceremonial to be observed in making the Declaration, and of the Declaration itself, will be found in Appendix E.

The more than common affection that united the two brothers, who, till within one short year, had scarcely known what it was to be separated even for a day, has been more than once noticed. We have already seen with what exquisite feeling Prince Albert, in writing to his grandmother, alludes to their first permanent separation on the departure of his brother to enter the Saxon service. The following letter from Prince Ernest, written after the public announcement of the marriage, will be read with no less interest, as giving proof not only of an affection in the writer, rare from its entire and sincere unselfishness, but also of the marked development, even at this early age, of that high moral purpose, and that almost intuitive soundness of judgment, which were to be displayed in the after life of the Prince in so pre-eminent a degree:

PRINCE ERNEST TO THE QUEEN.

"*Dresden, Dec.* 19, 1839.

"MY DEAR COUSIN,—Let me thank you very sincerely for your kind answer to my letter. You are always so good and so kind to me that I really fear I have not thanked you sufficiently.

"Oh! if you could only know the place you and Albert occupy in my heart! Albert is my second self, and my heart is one with his. Independently of his being my brother, I love and esteem him more than any one on earth. You will smile, perhaps, at my speaking of him to you in such glowing terms; but I do so that you may feel still more how much you have gained in him.

"As yet you are chiefly taken with his manner, so

youthfully innocent—his tranquillity—his clear and open mind. It is thus that he appears on first acquaintance. One reads less in his face of knowledge of men and experience, and why? It is because he is pure before the world and before his own conscience. Not as though he did not know what sin was—the earthly temptations—the weakness of man. No; but because he knew, and still knows, how to struggle against them, supported by the incomparable superiority and firmness of his character.

"From our earliest years we have been surrounded by difficult circumstances, of which we were perfectly conscious, and, perhaps more than most people, we have been accustomed to see men in the most opposite positions that human life can offer. Albert never knew what it was to hesitate. Guided by his own clear sense, he always walked calmly and steadily in the right path. In the greatest difficulties that may meet you in your eventful life, you may repose the most entire confidence in him, and then only will you feel how great a treasure you possess in him.

"He has, besides, all other qualities necessary to make a good husband. Your life can not fail to be a happy one.

"I shall be very glad when the excitement of the first days is over and all is again quiet, and when papa shall have left England, to be a distant and unintruding spectator of your new life. But how shall I then feel how much I have lost! Time will, I trust, help me also. Now I feel very lonely. ERNEST."

In the mean time many preliminary arrangements had

been discussed in England. The naturalization of the Prince—the formation of his household—the rank he was to hold—and the income which was to be settled upon him. Nor were these two last points arranged without considerable difficulty, and the occurrence of circumstances productive of much annoyance.

With respect to the precedence which should be given to the Prince, reference was made to the precedent of the marriage of Prince Leopold of Saxe-Coburg (afterward King of the Belgians) with the Princess Charlotte. The Queen mentions, in the Journal kept by her at the time, that Lord Melbourne showed her, on the 25th of November, a copy of the clause inserted in the Bill for the Naturalization of Prince Leopold, empowering the prince regent to give the prince precedence over every one except the princes of the blood. It was now proposed to adopt the same course with respect to Prince Albert, except that, from his different position as husband of the Queen, he should naturally take rank above those princes. It was thought right, however, to endeavor, in the first instance, to obtain the consent of the royal family to this arrangement. After a slight demur on the part of the Duke of Sussex, who spoke in the first instance of the necessity of his considering "the rights and interests of the family," and of "consulting others," both he and the Duke of Cambridge assented to what was proposed. The King of Hanover, however, still withheld his consent, and the Duke of Wellington, when the Naturalization Bill was before the House of Lords, objected to the clause by which it was proposed to give the Prince rank next to the Queen. As it was impossible to carry the clause against the duke's opposition, it was necessarily abandoned, and it was only by the exercise of her own prerogative that the Queen could give to the Prince the precedence which was his due. Many years later, the expediency was discussed of regulating, once for all, by Act of Parliament, the rank and position of a Prince Consort. But, though the leaders of both parties acquiesced in the propriety of such a measure, and though there can be no doubt that it would have only been in accordance with the English sense of what was right—which would have been outraged by seeing the father walk behind his own children—the then government shrank from the opposition with which the proposal might possibly have been met; at all events, they did not feel sufficient confidence in the result to encourage them to persevere in the attempt.

There was also a question as to the Prince's right to quarter the Queen's arms with his own. Garter King-at-Arms, whose special duty it is to make himself acquainted with such subjects, at first gave an opinion against it. It is hardly conceivable that he should have overlooked the very last precedent on the subject—that, namely, of Prince Leopold, who had quartered the Princess Charlotte's arms with his own. He did so, nevertheless; and it was left to the Prince himself to trace and show him the precedent which thus established his own right!

It is needless to follow in detail all the discussions that took place with respect to the formation of the Prince's household. Lord Melbourne wished that Baron Stockmar should come over with full instructions as to the wishes of the Prince and his father on the subject, so that every thing should be settled before the meeting of Parliament; and he drew up a sketch, founded principally on the precedent of that of George IV. when Prince of Wales, of what he thought it should consist of, making, at the same time, several suggestions as to the persons to be appointed to it.*

The King of the Belgians wrote that he thought the best way would be "to name the most needful, 'd'un commun accord,' *now*, and to wait till you can arrange these matters, till you meet." "By letter," he adds, "and at such a distance, it was very difficult to come to an understanding, while a few moments' conversation may settle every thing."

A letter from the Prince himself, on the manner in which his household should be formed, affords a rare proof of sound judgment at a very early age—for he had only completed his twentieth year a few months before—and shows a thorough appreciation of the position which it would become him to occupy in this country after his marriage. It will be seen how steadily and consistently he adhered, under many difficulties, both public and domestic, to the principles of action which he now laid down for himself.

He thus writes to the Queen on the 10th of December, 1839:

". . . Now I come to a second point which you touch upon in your letter, and which I have also much at heart; I mean the choice of the persons who are to belong to my household. The maxim, 'Tell me whom he associates with, and I will tell you who he is,' must here es-

* The Queen's Journal, written at the time.

pecially not be lost sight of. I should wish particularly that the selection should be made without regard to politics; for if I am really to keep myself free from all parties, my people must not belong exclusively to one side. Above all, these appointments should not be mere 'party rewards,' but they should possess other recommendations besides those of party. Let them be either of very high rank, or very rich, or very clever, or persons who have performed important services for England. It is very necessary that they should be chosen from both sides—the same number of Whigs as of Tories; and above all do I wish that they should be well-educated men and of high character, who, as I have already said, shall have already distinguished themselves in their several positions, whether it be in the army, or navy, or in the scientific world. I know you will agree in my views. . . ."

The Queen mentions that the applications for situations in the Prince's household were very numerous; nor, she adds, were the arrangements which were made altogether such as they should have been, and the Prince was a good deal annoyed on the subject.*

* Memorandum by the Queen.

CHAPTER XII.

1840.

Proceedings in Parliament.

On the 16th of January, 1840, the Queen opened Parliament in person, and it being generally known that the proposed marriage would now be formally announced from the throne, the crowds that assembled outside the houses of Parliament, and that lined the route through which the royal procession passed from the Palace, were great beyond all example. The reception of the Queen both going and returning was enthusiastic in the extreme, and the Queen herself records in her Journal that she was "more loudly cheered than she had been for some time."

In the interior of the House every seat was, as usual, filled with the noblest and fairest of the land; and a feeling of more than ordinary interest and sympathy must have thrilled the hearts of all present when their youthful sovereign, only now in her twenty-first year, in her clear voice and distinct articulation, thus announced to the representatives of her people in Parliament assembled her own intended marriage.

"Since you were last assembled, I have declared my intention of allying myself in marriage with the Prince Albert of Saxe-Coburg and Gotha. I humbly implore that the divine blessing may prosper this union, and render it conducive to the interests of my people, as well as to my own domestic happiness; and it will be to me a source of the most lively satisfaction to find the resolution I have taken approved by my Parliament.

"The constant proofs which I have received of your attachment to my person and family persuade me that you will enable me to provide for such an establishment as may appear suitable to the rank of the Prince and the dignity of the crown."

The address in answer to the speech was moved in the House of Lords by the Duke of Somerset, and seconded by Lord Seaford. There was, on all sides, but one language of congratulation and of warm and cordial sympathy in the prospect of domestic happiness and public advantage which the intended marriage held out to the Queen and to the country; and in the House of Commons, where the feeling was equally unanimous, Sir Robert Peel, as leader of the opposition, claimed for himself and for those with whom he acted credit for joining cordially in the congratulations offered by the address. "I do entirely enter," he proceeded, "into the aspirations for the happiness of her Majesty in her approaching nuptials. Her Majesty has been enabled to contract those nuptials under circumstances peculiarly auspicious. It frequently happens that political considerations interfere with such transactions, and that persons in exalted stations are obliged to sacrifice their private feelings to the sense of public duty. Her Majesty, however, has the singular good fortune to be able to gratify her private feelings while she performs her public duty, and to obtain the best guarantee for happiness by contracting an alliance founded on affection. I cordially hope that the union now contemplated will contribute to her Majesty's happiness, and enable her to furnish to her people an exalted example of connubial felicity."*

But the omission to declare that Prince Albert was a Protestant was found fault with in both houses, and the Duke of Wellington, in the House of Lords, "Though entertaining," he said, "no doubt that the Prince was a Protestant," though "he was sure he was a Protestant," and "knew he was of a Protestant family," attributed the omission to the fear on the part of the government to irritate or indispose their Irish supporters. There was much anxiety, he said, on the subject, and he thought that if the House of Lords was "called upon to do any act, or make any declaration on the subject of the marriage, beyond the mere congratulation of the Queen, they should take that course which should give her Majesty's subjects the satisfaction of knowing that Prince Albert was a Protestant, thus showing the public," he added, "that this was still a Protestant state."

The duke consequently moved to insert the word "Protestant" in the address before the word "Prince."

In answer, Lord Melbourne said truly, "The noble duke knows he is a Protestant; all England knows he is a Protestant; the whole world knows he is a Protestant." And Lord Brougham, after expressing his astonishment that the House should have been occupied with the subject for half an hour, pointed out that the world was superfluous, as from the state of the law it could not, in fact,

* Hansard, vol. li., p. 115.

be otherwise. "I may remark," Lord Brougham went on to say, "that my noble friend (Lord Melbourne) was mistaken as to the law. There is no prohibition as to marriage with a Catholic. It is only attended with a penalty, and that penalty is *merely the forfeiture of the crown!*"*

The duke's amendment was, however, agreed to, and the fact of the Prince being a Protestant was recorded in the address.

The King of the Belgians was strongly of opinion that it was injudicious to omit the statement that the Prince was a Protestant in the official declaration of the marriage made to the Privy Council, and had thus expressed himself on the subject in a letter written to the Queen on the 6th of December: "I regret that in your declaration the word 'Protestant' was left out. It could do no harm, and is even perfectly true, and its omission will give rise to a long and interminable growling. On religious matters one can not be too prudent, because one never can foresee what passionate use people will make of such a thing."

The Queen having explained the circumstances under which Lord Melbourne had omitted it, the king again wrote on the 14th of December:

"In the omission of the word 'Protestant' Lord Melbourne was probably right, and it is equally probable that they would have abused him, maybe even more, if he had put it in. There is only this to say, however, the Ernestine branch of the Saxon family has been, there is no doubt, the real cause of the establishment of Protest-

* Hansard, vol. li., p. 11 *et seq.*

antism in Germany, and consequently, in great part, of Northern Europe. This same line became a martyr to that cause, and was deprived of nearly all its possessions in consequence of it.* Recently there have been two cases of Catholic marriages,† but the main branch has remained, and is, in fact, very sincerely Protestant. Both Ernest and Albert are most attached to it, and when deviations took place, they were connected more with the new branch transplanted out of the parent soil than with what now must be properly considered the reigning family."

On the 27th of January the House of Commons resolved itself into a committee to consider the proposal to grant an annual sum of £50,000 to Prince Albert on his marriage with the Queen.

In answer to a question from Mr. Goulburn on the 22d, Lord John Russell had explained that his proposal was founded, not upon any estimate of probable expenses, which would be contrary to all precedent, even if it were possible to form one, but upon what had been usual in "the case of Queen Consorts ever since the time of George II." He found that in the cases of Queen Caroline, Queen Charlotte, and Queen Adelaide, the sum granted for their privy purse had always been £50,000 a year.‡

* In a former chapter it has been seen that the elder or Ernestine branch of the Saxon family lost their birthright, which was transferred to the Albertine or younger branch, after the defeat of of John the Magnanimous at Mühlberg by the Emperor Charles V.

† That of Prince Ferdinand of Saxe-Coburg with the Princess Kohary (see page 4), and the King of Belgium's own marriage with Princess Louise d'Orléans, daughter of Louis Philippe, king of the French.

‡ Hansard, vol. li., p. 494 *et seq.*

This sum was opposed by Mr. Hume, on the usual grounds of economy, with all the often-repeated arguments respecting the severity of taxation, the distress of the country, etc., etc., which distinguished the party to which he belonged. But these arguments met with little response from the House, and the amendment he proposed, to reduce the sum to £21,000, was negatived by 305 to 38.*

Another amendment, however, proposed by Colonel Sibthorpe, to reduce the sum to £30,000, was supported by Sir Robert Peel, Mr. Goulburn, Sir James Graham, Lord Eliot (now Lord St. Germans), etc., on the ground that the position of the Prince differed essentially from that of a Queen Consort. "The status of the latter," Sir James Graham said, "was recognized by the Constitution.† She had an independent station; she had independent officers; and, from her sex, it was indispensably necessary that a large female establishment should be maintained by her." From the small establishment that would be required by the Prince, and from the reductions in the household salaries that had lately been effected, it was argued that £30,000 to him would make the joint privy purse of the Queen and the Prince equal to that of King William and Queen Adelaide.

On a division, the smaller sum was carried by a majority of 262 to 158.‡

It is probable that the mortification which the refusal

* Hansard, vol. li., p. 584.

† Did Sir James mean that a Queen Regnant was not to marry, or that, if she did, the "status" of her husband would *not* be "recognized by the Constitution?"

‡ Hansard, vol. li., p. 633.

of the proposed vote was calculated to occasion to the Queen might have been avoided by proper communications beforehand between Lord Melbourne and the leaders of the opposition, such as in after years, under the guidance of the Prince himself, were frequently had recourse to when the question to be settled was one rather of a personal than a political character.

But party spirit at this time was running very high; the Queen says of herself that she was then actuated by strong feelings of partisanship; and since Sir Robert Peel's failure in the preceding May to form a government, which was attributed by his followers to the intrigues and influence of the ladies of the bedchamber, the language of the opposition had been very violent. We may therefore well believe that if on one side the opposition to the proposed vote may be traced, in part at least, to disappointed hopes of office, the unconciliatory course pursued on the other may have been influenced by the hope, not acknowledged perhaps to themselves, of indisposing the young Prince, on his first arrival, to their opponents, and of seeing the breach widened which already existed between them and the Queen.

It is certain that the inevitable consequence of pressing the vote to a division was perfectly well known. Lord John Russell had informed the Queen that the opposition, as a body, meant to oppose it, and the government whippers-in in the House of Commons had warned Lord Melbourne that if he would avoid defeat, it would be necessary to reduce the amount of income to be proposed.*

* The Queen's Journal, written at the time.

The tone of the debate tended, unfortunately, rather to exasperate than to soften the expected opposition. Nothing, indeed, could be more respectful to the Queen than the language of those who opposed the vote; and Lord Eliot (now Lord St. Germans), who spoke first in support of Colonel Sibthorpe's amendment, was careful to express himself in terms of the most devoted loyalty and attachment to the crown. Unfortunately, however, the language of the opposition out of doors had been widely different, and it was too much in accordance with the spirit in which party warfare was then, and has often at other times been conducted, not to neglect the opportunity thus offered of calling attention to the contrast between the language used in the House and that employed by the same party elsewhere.

"The noble lord," Lord John Russell said, "who stated that he would support the proposition for reducing the vote, made great professions of respect for her Majesty, and of his wishes for her Majesty's domestic comfort. I certainly am bound to give every credit to the noble lord who made those professions; and I wish that such conduct had not been confined to him, or to the speeches of to-night, but had been general among those who maintain the same opinion with himself, and that it had not been reserved for the beginning of the session, but had been continued ever since Parliament separated last year. . . . It appears to me that any member of this House may vote £30,000 a year, or he may vote £50,000 a year, with the same respect for her Majesty. But when professions of extraordinary respect are made, I can not forget that no sovereign of this country has been insulted in such a manner as her present Majesty has been. The extraordinary professions of respect that have been uttered have made it necessary for me to say a word on the subject."*

Lord Eliot having appealed to the House against an attack justified by nothing that had fallen from him, Sir James Graham rose, "he had almost said, with feelings of indignation that a minister of the crown should make an insinuation—for the noble lord dared not directly to make the charge—that in the vote which they were about to give for a smaller sum—that a minister of the crown should insinuate that such a vote was influenced by a want of respect for the sovereign. The noble lord —for he had marked him well—had measured his expressions. He avoided stating that distinctly; but he appealed to the committee whether the insinuation could be misunderstood. . . . . . He, for one, repudiated that insinuation. He felt toward her Majesty that respect which as a loyal subject he owed to her; but, feeling that respect, he also felt that he was sent there as a representative of the people. . . . ." In conclusion, he repeated that "he had not the slightest hesitation in voting with the honorable and gallant member for Lincoln, even though he, and those who sat on the same side of the house with him, might, in doing so, be accused of a want of loyalty,"† etc., etc.

Sir Robert Peel also said that, though he would never shrink from giving his vote on this or any other occasion, yet "he did not know that he should have risen to address the house if it were not for the insinuation of the

* Hansard, vol. li., p. 618–619. † Id. ibid., p. 619–622.

noble lord—an insinuation introduced so unnecessarily, so unjustly, and so contrary to all parliamentary rules and principles—so unworthy, too, as he thought, of the situation which the noble lord occupied, both as a minister of the crown, and as leader of the House of Commons. What right had the noble lord to make the insinuation that he had done? Supposing that he had said that the noble lord's motive in proposing £50,000 was owing to his base subserviency toward the crown . . . . he would have been told at once by the speaker that he had no right to go on imputing motives. Thus he thought it would be base and unworthy of him to be influenced at all by the events of last May; but he also said it would be as unworthy as it would be cowardly in him to shrink from the performance of his duty from the fear that such a motive would be imputed to him. He said it would be puling, effeminate delicacy in him if he acquiesced in a vote which he felt to be wrong, because he feared some honorable gentleman opposite might have said, 'You are acting from a spiteful recollection of the events of last May.' . . . . . I will not," he concluded, "condescend to rebut the charge of want of respect or loyalty. I have no compunctions of conscience on that ground. I never made a concurrence of political sentiment on the part of the sovereign a condition of my loyalty. I never have been otherwise than loyal and respectful toward my sovereign. Not one breath of disloyalty—not one word of disrespect toward the crown or any member of the royal family, however adverse their political sentiments were to mine, has ever escaped my lips; and when performing what I believe to be my duty to this House, and my duty toward the crown, I should think myself unworthy of the position which I hold—of my station as a member of the House of Commons—if I thought that I could not take a straightforward course without needless professions of loyalty, or without a defense against accusations which I believe to be utterly unfounded."*

It is hard to deny that on both sides of the House a spirit was manifested which, on such an occasion, ought not to have existed. If, on the side of the government, that tone of conciliation was wanting which might possibly have spared their sovereign the mortification of what had the appearance of a personal defeat, it is equally certain that, on the other side, the opposition to the proposed vote showed an ungenerous spirit, and betrayed a want of confidence in the Prince that might well have permanently indisposed him toward those who conducted it.

The Prince, however, from the first, rose superior to any thing like personal considerations, and his future relations with the Duke of Wellington, Sir Robert Peel, and other leaders of that party, when called by the turn of events to the councils of the Queen, showed how little his conduct was influenced by what now passed.

It was not only, as I have said, that the Prince was at all times far above being influenced by personal considerations; but he obtained, in a wonderfully short time for a stranger, a clear insight into the nature of political parties in this country, and the mode in which their opposition to each other is conducted; and he soon understood that the opposition to the precedence, and to the

* **Hansard, vol. li., page 625** ***et seq.***

income proposed for him by government, did not proceed (at least in the leaders of the Conservative party) either from want of respect and good-will toward himself, or of loyalty toward the Queen.

The Prince early understood, also, the position which it becomes the sovereign of this great country to hold between conflicting political parties, and the line of conduct which, as the consort of that sovereign, it was right for himself to observe. Although liberal in his political views, and thoroughly imbued with the progressive spirit of the age—though never losing sight of those great principles which he believed to be essential to the good of this country and of the world, nor ever relaxing in his efforts to promote them—he still held himself aloof from all the trammels of party, its jealousies and animosities, and resolutely abstained from even the appearance of political partisanship. And not only so, but the feelings of that nature by which the Queen so candidly admits that she was herself biased at this time, soon ceased to show themselves under the influence of his judicious counsels; and all parties have long borne willing testimony to the cordial and constitutional support which, when charged with the administration of the government, each party in turn received from the Queen, and from the Prince as her natural confidential adviser.

In the further Committee on the Grant, Colonel Sibthorpe, encouraged by his success in effecting a reduction in its amount, proposed an amendment to the effect that, in case the Prince should survive the Queen, he should forfeit the annuity now settled upon him if he remarried a Roman Catholic, or should fail to reside at least six months in each year in the country. This, however, met with no support, and was summarily rejected, Sir Robert Peel declaring it to be most undesirable that such want of confidence should be shown in the Prince.

The King of the Belgians was very indignant at the refusal by the House of Commons of the vote proposed, and expressed himself very strongly on the subject in writing to the Queen. It seemed to him incomprehensible that the party which professed to "uphold the dignity of the crown should treat their sovereign in such a manner," and that, too, upon an occasion "when even in private life the most sour and saturnine people relax and grow gay and are mildly disposed!"

He thought, too, that the Queen being Queen Regnant, "Prince Albert's position was to all intents and purposes that of a Queen Consort; that the same privileges and charges ought to be attached to it which were attached to Queen Adelaide's position; and that the giving up the income which the Queen Dowager came into was, in reality, giving up a thing which custom had sanctioned."

While the government, and, it must be added, the Queen, were sustaining this defeat in the House of Commons, the same want of management and of a conciliatory spirit was subjecting them in the House of Lords to another defeat on a subject on which the Queen was still more sensitive; that, namely, of the precedence to be given to her future husband.

This, too, was a subject on which previous communication between the leaders of government and of the opposition might have been advantageously resorted to, and all the annoyance that arose from the non-settlement of the question possibly avoided.

On the same day (the 27th of January) on which the House of Commons went into committee on the Prince's Annuity Bill, the lord chancellor, in the House of Lords, moved the second reading of that for his Royal Highness's naturalization. In this bill it was proposed to insert a clause having for its objects to give Prince Albert precedence for his life "next after her Majesty in Parliament or elsewhere, as her Majesty may think fit and proper," etc.*

Unfortunately, by an accidental omission, as stated by Lord Melbourne, no mention had been made in the title of the bill of the subject of precedence; and the Duke of Wellington, therefore, on the ground that the House had no previous knowledge of the contents of the bill, and also considering the very large powers which it proposed to confer on the Queen, moved the adjournment of the discussion. In this he was supported by Lord Brougham, who also objected to the mode in which it was sought to give the Prince the desired precedence. "In former bills," he said, "the precise precedence of the Prince was fixed. This bill at once naturalized Prince Albert, and enabled her Majesty to affix him any rank she chose. He had a constitutional objection to such a course. It ought to be taken by Parliament, not by the crown."† He objected, too, to the proposed arrangement, as giving the Prince precedence "not only of the dukes of the blood royal, but of the Prince of Wales. Suppose," he added, "(which God forbid!) that the

* Hansard, vol. li., p. 575–576. † Id. ibid., p. 578.

Queen had paid the debt of nature before any issue of the approaching marriage was born, we should have a king and a Prince of Wales, while Prince Albert would be placed in the anomalous position of a foreign naturalized prince, the husband of a deceased queen, with a higher rank than the Prince of Wales."*

Lord Melbourne and the lord chancellor admitted that the subject of precedence should have been mentioned in the title, and agreed to the postponement of the discussion. It was brought on again on the 31st, when the lord chancellor, with a view to meeting some of the objections urged by Lord Brougham, announced that it was now intended to fix the precedence which the Queen should be empowered to give the Prince "next after any heir apparent to the throne."

This, however, as he refused to add the words suggested by Lord Brougham, in order to limit the precedence thus given to the lifetime of her Majesty, does not appear to have removed the objections which had been taken to the measure. And though the bill was read a second time with little farther discussion (Lord Londonderry only speaking in defense of the interests of the King of Hanover), it was thought expedient, when the House went into Committee on the Bill on the 3d of February, to omit all reference to precedence, and to make the bill what the Duke of Wellington had originally imagined it to be—one of simple naturalization.

Lord Brougham on this occasion pressed for information whether or not it was intended to effect the proposed object by the exercise of the Queen's prerogative;

* Hansard, vol. li., p. 579.

but Lord Melbourne declined to say, and the bill passed in its new shape.

It can not be wondered at if the Queen was, as she herself says,* most indignant at what had occurred, or that the first impression made on the young Prince's mind by the proceedings in both houses should have been a painful one. But, as has been already said, he soon understood the nature of our political parties, and that the proceedings in Parliament were only the result of high party feeling, and were by no means to be taken as marks of personal disrespect, or want of kind feeling toward himself.

* The Queen's Journal.

CHAPTER XIII.

1840.

Departure from Gotha and Arrival in England.

ON the 14th of January, 1840, Lord Torrington and Colonel (now General) Grey left Buckingham Palace with three of the Queen's carriages for Gotha, whence they were to escort Prince Albert to England for his marriage. It had been now settled that this should be celebrated on the 10th of February. They were also bearers of the Garter with which the Prince was to be invested before he left Gotha.

Arriving on the afternoon of the 20th, they were presented the same evening to the duke, by whom and the young princes they were most kindly received. Later in the evening they were presented to the dowager duchess, from whom so many letters have been quoted, at an evening party at her own house. The next morning, after breakfast in their own rooms, the English gentlemen were visited by the two young princes, who remained with them about an hour, impressing them most favorably by the unaffected kindness and cordiality of their manner. Prince Albert was naturally very anxious to hear how the marriage was liked in England—looking forward, as it seemed, with much pleasure, but, at the same time, not without some degree of nervousness, to the change which was about to take place in his position, and expressing a very natural sorrow at the impending separation from all his old associations. At four o'clock there was a great dinner, and in the evening a masked ball at the theatre, to which the duke and duchess, and all the court, went a little after eight.

It had been arranged that the ceremony of investing Prince Albert with the Garter should take place on the 23d. Accordingly, at half past three on that day the whole court assembled, in full uniform, in the throne-room; the duke on the throne, with Prince Albert on his right, supported by his brother, the Prince of Leiningen, etc. The duchess, the Princess of Leiningen, the Princess of Reuss, etc., were in a box on one side of the room; the ladies of the court in a similar one opposite; while the back of the apartment was filled with as many people from the town as it would hold. The fine corridor leading to the throne-room was lined with soldiers; and when every one had taken his place, Lord Torrington was ushered in by the chamberlain and other officers of the court, supported on one side by Colonel Grey, and on the other by Colonel Bentinck, of the Coldstream Guards (a chance visitor at Gotha at the time), bearing on white satin cushions the insignia of the Garter, with which the duke, himself a Knight of the Order, was, by letters patent, authorized to invest his son. Lord Torrington having delivered and read the letters of which he was the bearer, they were again read in German—the patent of election was presented—and Prince Albert was then duly invested with the various insignia; Prince Leiningen, who was also a Knight of the Order, attaching the Garter.

The ceremony of investiture being concluded, the whole court passed in procession before the duke and duchess, Prince Albert, etc., after which there was a general adjournment to the duchess's apartments. A grand dinner followed, to which 180 persons sat down, shortly before which Count Mensdorff, brother-in-law to the duke, arrived with his two sons. The principal table, at which were all the royal personages, and as many of the more distinguished guests as it would accommodate, ran across the top of the room; and at right angles to it, three other tables ran down the room, which were filled to crowding with the more general guests; the doorway, etc., being filled with as many spectators as could find standing room. Toward the end of the first course the duke proposed the Queen's health, which was drunk by all the company standing, accompanied by several distinct flourishes of trumpets; the band playing "God save the Queen," and the artillery outside firing a royal salute. Shortly afterward Lord Torrington, who, with the other English gentlemen, occupied seats at the principal table immediately opposite the duke and duchess, proposed the health of the duke, of Prince Albert, the new-made Knight of the Garter, and the rest of the ducal family, which was received in a similar manner. A third and last toast followed, given by the duke—the rest of the Knights of the Garter—which was similarly received. This last toast might have been attended with serious consequences. In opening the window to give the signal for the salute to the artillery outside, the wind blew the thin muslin curtains into the flame of the candles, and in one instant they blazed up to the top of the room.

Great alarm and confusion ensued for a few moments, caused by people rising from their seats and crowding toward the window. But, fortunately, the curtains were so light and thin that they burnt out almost instantaneously without igniting the wood-work; and the ladies' dresses being, as became the season of the year, mostly of silk and velvet, no mischief followed, and the alarm soon subsided. The dinner being ended, coffee followed in the duchess's apartments, when the company separated for half an hour, again to assemble in order to go in state to the Opera. The theatre is extremely pretty, and being densely crowded, and the audience all in full dress, the effect was very fine when the royal party entered—every one standing up, and receiving Prince Albert with loud and long-continued applause. The performance was the *Freyschütz*, and very good, excepting a little imperfection in the scenery; the acting and singing really excellent. With the opera ended a most exciting and interesting, if a somewhat fatiguing day; but the hours kept are so much better than those in England, that all was over between ten and eleven.*

M. Perthès, under whom the Prince had studied at Bonn, in one of his private letters (published in his Memoirs), thus notices the event which has just been recorded:

"The winter months of this year have been made interesting and exciting by the chapter of history which has been enacted here; for the grand-ducal papa bound the Garter round his boy's knee amid the roar of 101

* The account of the proceedings at Gotha, and of the journey to England, is taken from a journal kept at the time.

cannons. The earnestness and gravity with which the Prince has obeyed this early call to take a European position give him dignity and standing in spite of his youth, and increase the charm of his whole aspect. Queen Victoria will find him the right sort of man; and unless some unlucky fatality interpose, he is sure to become the idol of the English nation—silently to influence the English aristocracy—and deeply to affect the destinies of Europe."

The day following the investiture was devoted to a grand "chasse aux chevreuils," much marred, as a former "chasse aux lièvres" had been, by the severity of the weather. On Saturday there was a luncheon at Reinhardsbrunn, and in the evening a state ball at the Palace. On Sunday the dowager duchess received the English gentlemen in the forenoon, and was much affected by their visit. She was very deaf, but it was really painful to witness her efforts to keep down her grief. She took the gentlemen over her rooms, showed them her pictures, etc.; but the conversation always came back to Prince Albert, and his name was never mentioned without a fresh burst of tears. It was a touching and natural expression of sorrow; for what certainty could the duchess feel that, at her age, she would be permitted again to see her beloved grandson. Monday, the 27th, was the last day the Prince was to spend in his paternal home. The next day he was to turn his back on all the scenes of his youthful associations, and to set out to commence a new career. It was a sad day, for the sorrow at losing their cherished prince was genuine and universal among all classes; yet it was a day of outward festivity and rejoicing. There was again a great full-dress dinner, before which the duke presented the English gentlemen, according to their rank, with the various classes of the family order; and in the evening a full-dress concert. At the end of it, all the ladies and gentlemen passed before Prince Albert to bid him farewell, not a few of them in tears, and the Prince himself very much upset. And could there be a severer trial? However brilliant the prospect before him, could the Prince be otherwise than deeply affected at leaving a country to which he was so warmly attached, and bidding, probably, for the most part, a last adieu to the friends of his youth, and those by whom he was so much beloved?

The next morning, Tuesday, 28th of January, 1840, the journey to England began. The traveling-carriages were sent on about a mile to a small inn called the "Last Shilling;" Duke Ernest of Würtemberg, Prince Reuss, Count Mensdorff and his sons, etc., etc., wishing to accompany the Prince so far before taking a final farewell.

The departure from Gotha was an affecting scene, and every thing showed the genuine love of all classes for their young Prince. The streets were densely crowded; every window was crammed with heads; every house-top covered with people, waving handkerchiefs, and vying with each other in demonstrations of affection that could not be mistaken. The carriages stopped in passing the dowager duchess's, and Prince Albert got out with his father and brother to bid her a last adieu. It was a terrible trial to the poor duchess, who was inconsolable for the loss of her beloved grandson. She came to the window as the carriages drove off, and threw her arms out, calling out "Albert! Albert!" in tones that went to every one's heart, when she was carried away, almost in a fainting state, by her attendants.

Having passed in a long procession through the town, in the duke's carriages, preceded by the carriages of M. Stein, the minister, and others, to the number of more than twenty, the Duke of Würtemberg, Count Mensdorff, etc., took a final leave at the "Last Shilling," and the princes got into one of the Queen's traveling-carriages. The duke, attended by Colonel Grey, went another German mile in his own open carriage to the frontier, where an arch of green fir-trees had been erected, and a number of young girls, dressed in white, with roses and garlands, and a band of musicians and singers, who sung a very pretty hymn, were assembled to bid a final "God speed," as he left his native land behind him, to the young Prince. It was a pretty sight, but bitterly cold. A hard frost, and the ground covered with snow, with a bitter northeast wind, were scarcely in keeping with white muslin gowns and wreaths of flowers! Here M. Stein, the minister, and others who had preceded the royal party so far, took their leave, the duke got into his traveling-carriage, and the journey to England was fairly begun.

The traveling-carriages, with the fourgons, were eight in number. First, the duke's own traveling chariot, in which he was accompanied sometimes by one of his sons, sometimes by one of the English gentlemen, or of his own suite; then the three carriages of the Queen, followed by a couple of britzkas and the two fourgons. The duke and princes were attended, in addition to the three English gentlemen (Lord Torrington, Colonel Grey, and Mr.

Seymour), by Counts Alvensleben, Kolowrath, Gruben, Pöllnitz, etc., etc., and formed altogether a party of twelve.

The travelers stopped at one o'clock at Birschhausen for luncheon, and arrived at Cassel, where they passed the night, a little before eight. The duke and the two princes, on their arrival, paid a visit to the Elector of Hesse, returning to the inn to dine.

The next morning, a little before nine, the party left Cassel to go seventeen German miles to Arnsberg, where they only arrived as the clock was striking ten in the evening. The following night was passed at Deutz, the bridge not having been yet established for the year over the Rhine, which had to be crossed the next morning in boats, a tedious and a cold operation, made more disagreeable by the heavy rain that fell all the time. The party left Cologne about half past nine, dined at Aix-la-Chapelle about three, and arrived at Liège, where they slept, about ten. At Aix-la-Chapelle the Prince heard the news of the rejection of the proposed grant of £50,000, which made a disagreeable impression upon him. It not unnaturally led him to express a fear that the people of England were not pleased with the marriage, an apprehension, however, which was speedily removed by the unqualified cordiality of the reception with which he was every where greeted from the first moment of his entry into this country. Late as it was when the Prince arrived at Liège, the whole city seemed on foot to do him honor. Before crossing the river to enter the city, the governor, accompanied by all the military authorities, met him with an escort of Lancers. A guard of honor was drawn up in the square opposite the hotel (the Pavillon Anglais), and a fine brass band continued playing under the windows till twelve o'clock. Nor was all quiet when they ceased. About one o'clock a large company of peasants took their place, and serenaded the Prince with vocal music till near two in the morning.

Before leaving Liège the next morning the duke received all the authorities, civil and military, who were severally introduced to the Prince. At ten, the carriages having been sent on, the whole party was conveyed, in one large omnibus, to the railroad terminus at Ans, where a special train had been provided, by which they were taken in four hours to Brussels, arriving in that city at three o'clock.

Here they remained, received and treated by the king with the greatest distinction, till Wednesday, the 5th of February. On that day, at half past seven, the journey to England was resumed—by rail as far as Ostend, and thence posting along the coast by Dunkirk and Gravelines to Calais. At Dunkirk the duke and Prince Albert had a narrow escape, in the duke's carriage, of being driven into the ditch of the fortress. The pole of the carriage was broken and other damage done, in consequence of which the duke remained behind for an hour and a half while they were repairing it. At half past eleven the two princes arrived at Calais, where, notwithstanding the lateness of the hour, they found all the officers of the garrison waiting at the hotel to receive them, a guard of honor, etc., etc. The duke did not arrive till half past one. Lord Clarence Paget, who had been sent in the *Firebrand* to escort the Prince over, also met the party at the hotel.

The next morning, Thursday, the 6th of February, the weather was beautiful, with a light air from the N.W. Unfortunately, the tide was too low to admit of sailing before half past eleven, and in the mean time the day changed. A strong breeze freshened up from the S.E., and, before half the passage was made, had increased almost to a gale. The *Firebrand* not being able to get out so soon, the whole party had embarked in the *Ariel*, one of the Dover packets, commanded for the occasion by their well-known commander, Captain Hamilton. But the passage was long (five hours and a half), and the deck of the little steamer was a scene of almost universal misery and sea-sickness. The duke had gone below, and on either side of the cabin staircase lay the two princes, in an almost helpless state. The sea got heavier as the vessel approached the land, and it was by no common effort, as every one who has felt the utter prostration attendant on sea-sickness will readily believe, that Prince Albert, who had continued to suffer up to the last moment, got up as it entered between the piers to bow to the people by which they were crowded. Five minutes later the tide would not have allowed the *Ariel* to enter the harbor. As it was, she grazed the ground in going in.

The resolution and strength of will with which the Prince, on this occasion, shook himself free from the enervating effects of sea-sickness, were at all times distinguishing features in his character. So far from indulging, as most men do, in complaint and pity for himself under every petty ailment, he never gave way, when work was to be done, to feelings of fatigue or indisposition, and would struggle bravely even against severe illness. The most signal illustration, perhaps, of this noble quality was afforded by one of the latest acts of his life. On the 1st of December, 1861, when suffering under the extreme prostration of his last fatal illness, the Prince roused himself to write a memorandum for the Queen on the communication which the government proposed to make to the United States on the affair of the *Trent.** This memorandum was adopted by the Queen, and influencing, as it did, the tone of the government communication, had a material effect in preventing a rupture between the two countries.

Nothing could exceed the enthusiasm of the reception which greeted the Prince when he set his foot on the English shore as the affianced husband of our Queen; and he must have been at once convinced that if the houses of Parliament in their late votes had been actuated by any personal feelings against himself, or against the marriage, those feelings were not shared by the people of England.

The night was spent at Dover, at the York Hotel (it stood on the Esplanade, but now no longer exists), and after a very poor attempt by most of the party at dinner, every one was glad to get to bed before nine o'clock.

It had been arranged that the Prince should not arrive at Buckingham Palace till Saturday, the 8th; a short journey was therefore made the next day to Canterbury, the Prince having first received an address from the

* Except the commencement of a letter to Prince Leopold, which he could not continue after the first line, these were the last words written by the Prince.

mayor and other authorities of Dover, and having held a reception, at which the commandant and officers of the garrison were presented to him. It poured with rain all the morning, but this did not prevent immense crowds from assembling at Dover to see the Prince depart, or from turning out in every village through which he passed on his way to Canterbury, to welcome him with true English and heartfelt cheers.

His reception at Canterbury was no less enthusiastic, and the unfortunate nature of the weather seemed to have no effect in damping the ardor of the multitudes that thronged the streets. The royal party arrived at two, accompanied by an escort of the 11th Hussars, and having received an address from the city authorities, the Prince, with his brother, attended the service of the Cathedral at three. In the evening the city was illuminated, and vast crowds assembled before the hotel, cheering and calling for the Prince, who answered their call by appearing, to their great delight, on the balcony.

From Canterbury the Prince had sent on his valet with his favorite greyhound "Eôs," and the Queen speaks in her Journal of the pleasure which the sight of "dear Eôs," the evening before the arrival of the Prince, gave her.

The Prince had brought this greyhound over with him in 1839. He had himself brought it up and trained it from the time it was a puppy of six weeks old, and a more beautiful, and, at the same time, more sagacious and attached animal could not be imagined. It was jet black, with the exception of a narrow white streak on the nose, and a white foot. It was the dog mentioned by Count Arthur Mensdorff in his recollections of the Prince's youthful days,* and died at Windsor about four years and a half after the marriage of the Queen and Prince. She was buried on the top of the bank above the slopes, and a bronze model of her now marks the spot.†

On Saturday morning, the 8th, after receiving an address from the dean and chapter, the Prince left at ten for London, meeting with the same enthusiastic reception along the whole line of route to Buckingham Palace. Here the party arrived at half past four o'clock, and were received at the hall door by the Queen and the Duchess of Kent, attended by the whole household. At five o'clock the lord chancellor administered the oaths of naturalization to the Prince, and the day ended by a great dinner, attended by the officers of state, Lord Melbourne, etc.; the Queen recording in her Journal, in warm terms, the great joy she felt at seeing the Prince again.‡

On Sunday, the 9th, service was performed by the Bishop of London in the bow room on the ground floor, and was attended by the Queen and Prince, etc.; and in the afternoon the latter drove out, through immense crowds assembled before the Palace, to pay his formal visits to the royal family. On this day the Queen mentions in her Journal that the Prince gave her, as his wedding gift, a beautiful sapphire and diamond brooch, and that she gave him the star and badge of the Garter, and the Garter itself set in diamonds. There was again a great dinner in the evening.§

* See Chap. III., page 68.

† Memorandum by the Queen.

‡ *Ibid.*

§ *Ibid.*

But amid all the hurry and excitement of the journey, and the rejoicings and festivities to which the Prince's arrival in England gave occasion, the grandmother left behind at Gotha, and who had loved him so dearly from his earliest infancy, was not forgotten. The duke had written to her from Brussels to announce their safe arrival thus far, and she thus thanks him for his letter on the 8th of February:

"*Gotha, Feb.* 8, 1840.

"I have really been quite touched, my dear duke, by your kindness in writing to me from Brussels. God be thanked that you arrived safely, in spite of the unfavorable weather. Here we had spring weather for the first week since you went, but we have now more rain. God grant that you may have had a good passage, and that none of you three may have suffered much. My fervent prayers and best wishes have gone with you. I still feel deeply the parting from my angel Albert! You, dear duke, know what he has been to me. May he be as happy as he deserves, and as all his true friends desire that he may be! Though thorns are sure to come in his path, may the roses only prove the more abundant!"

And the Prince himself, on the morning of his wedding-day, sent her these few touching lines:

"Dear Grandmamma,—In less than three hours I shall stand before the altar with my dear bride! In these solemn moments I must once more ask your blessing, which I am well assured I shall receive, and which will be my safeguard and my future joy! I must end. God help me! Ever your faithful Grandson.

"*London, Feb.* 10, 1840."

The marriage had been fixed to take place at the Chapel Royal at one o'clock, and at half past twelve the Queen left Buckingham Palace, with her mother and the Duchess of Sutherland in the carriage with her, for St. James's, wearing the sapphire brooch which the Prince had given her the day before.*

In the Appendix will be found a full description, as given in *The Times* of that day, of all the arrangements for the ceremony, and of the ceremony itself. To that account, which, allowing for such trifling mistakes as it was perhaps impossible to avoid, is generally correct, the reader who wishes to follow the events of this important day in minute detail is referred. He will there find it stated how the several processions of the bride and of the bridegroom, and of the royal personages and others invited to attend the wedding, were formed; how they went to the Chapel, and how they returned from it; the only difference being that the Queen came back with the chosen companion of her life—her husband—by her side; that it was her husband who handed her from the carriage at the Palace door; and that she walked up the grand staircase, in the presence of her court, leaning on her husband's arm!

Then followed the wedding breakfast at the Palace, with a toast to the health of the royal couple; and it is worthy of remark, considering the popular belief in the Queen's luck in weather, that the day, which had been dark and dismal all the morning, with rain and fog, cleared up soon after the return of the bridal procession

* Memorandum by the Queen. See Appendix F. for the account given at the time in *The Times* newspaper of the ceremony.

from the Chapel, and before the departure for Windsor the sun shone forth with all the splendor which distinguishes what is now proverbially called "Queen's weather."

A little before four the Queen and Prince took leave of the Duchess of Kent, and left Buckingham Palace for Windsor Castle. An immense crowd was gathered before the Palace to see their departure, and the road was lined with people anxious to catch a glimpse of their sovereign and her chosen husband nearly the whole way to Windsor.

"Our reception," the Queen says in her Journal, "was most enthusiastic, hearty, and gratifying in every way; the people quite deafening us with their cheers; horsemen and gigs, etc., going along with us." At Eton the whole school had turned out to receive and welcome the royal pair; and the boys in a body accompanied the carriage to the Castle, cheering and shouting as only school-boys can. They swarmed up the mound as the carriage entered the quadrangle, and as the Queen and the Prince descended at the grand entrance, they made the old Castle ring again with their acclamations.

But the sovereigns of this country can not enjoy on such an occasion the privacy which is the privilege and happiness of their subjects.

On the 12th the Duchess of Kent, with the Duke of Coburg and the hereditary prince, attended by the whole court, followed to Windsor. There was dancing there that night and the next; and on the 14th the court returned to London.* Addresses had now to be received

* From the Queen's Journal.

from the houses of Parliament and other bodies both by the Queen and Prince. State visits were paid to the theatres. On the 19th the Queen had a levée, at which the Prince, who led her in, took the place on her Majesty's left hand which he ever afterward occupied. On the 25th (Sunday) the Queen and Prince attended service for the first time at the Chapel Royal, being much cheered as they drove there through the Park; and on the 28th the Duke of Coburg left England. This separation from his father was deeply felt by the Prince. "He said to me," the Queen records in her Journal, "that I had never known a father, and could not, therefore, feel what he did. His childhood had been very happy." "Ernest" (the hereditary prince remained for some time in England after his brother's marriage)—"Ernest, he said, was now the only one remaining here of all his earliest ties and recollections; but that, if I continued to love him as I did now, I could make up for all. He never cried, he said, in general, but Alvensleben and Kolowrath" (they had accompanied the duke to England, and now left with him) "had cried so much that he was quite overcome. Oh, how I did feel for my dearest, precious husband at this moment! Father, brother, friends, country—all has he left, and all for me. God grant that I may be the happy person, the *most* happy person to make this dearest, blessed being happy and contented! What is in my power to make him happy I will do."

How this prayer was answered will best appear as we trace the course of the Queen and Prince's married life in future volumes. In another chapter, which will conclude the present volume, an account will be given of the arrangements that were made immediately after the marriage for giving the Prince precedence next to the Queen, for the formation of his household, etc., as well as a general description of the mode of life now established in its well-regulated division of duties and amusements, from which there was no material deviation in after years.

The Queen was now married to the husband of her choice, amid the sincere and general rejoicings of her subjects. "It is that," Lord Melbourne said to the Queen, "which makes your Majesty's marriage so popular, as they know it is not for mere state reasons."* Heartfelt were the prayers offered up for the happiness of the Queen and Prince, and we can estimate but too well how completely those prayers were granted, writing as we do when all that happiness has passed away.

* From the Queen's Journal.

CHAPTER XIV.

1840.

FIRST YEAR OF MARRIAGE.

The Prince's Position.—Formation of his Household.—Settlement of Precedence.—Freedom from Partisanship.—General Life in London.—At Windsor, Claremont, etc.—Love for the Country.—Attempt on the Queen's Life.—The Regency Bill.—Birth of the Princess Royal.

THE hereditary prince remained in England with the Queen and his brother till the 8th of May, but with his departure the last tie that bound the Prince to his native land seemed to be severed. England was to be henceforth his home. He was to forget his own country and his father's house; or, if not forget—an impossibility to a heart like his—he was at least to act as though he did. Duty now required at his hands an unreserved dedication of himself—of his best energies and abilities—to the land of his adoption; and nobly and unshrinkingly was that duty performed. How great the sacrifice that he was thus called upon to make, few, at that time, could estimate. Many, even now, would admit with difficulty that it could be a sacrifice at all, to exchange the position of a younger son in a comparatively small German dukedom for that of the Consort of the Queen of England. But to any man of warm natural affections, the rending of home ties must, under any circumstances, and however brilliant the future before him, be a sacrifice, and it is now only, when we have had the privilege of reading the letters quoted in the preceding chapters of this memoir, making us acquainted with the intense love he bore to the home of his infancy, and with the feelings of affection and sympathy that bound him to his own family and the friends of his youth,* that we are able, in some degree, to judge of its nature and extent.

To feel that his beloved native land must no longer occupy the first place in his heart—at all events, must be no longer the first object of his thoughts—that, separated from all he had hitherto held most dear, new family ties were to be entered into—new friendships formed—new habits acquired—could a mind, constituted as was the Prince's, reflect upon all this without feeling that, splendid and important as might be the position he would henceforth fill, it was attained at no common sacrifice—that, namely, of all his early ties and most cherished associations! It was a sacrifice, however, which, accepting it as he did in its fullest extent, was not only made supportable by the thought (to a noble nature like the Prince's, of all thoughts the most inspiriting) of the good which it would enable him to do, but was more than compensated by a degree of domestic happiness which the most devoted and confiding love on both sides is alone capable of affording.

We might well enlarge here on the self-denial and single-hearted devotion with which, from this time forward, the Prince applied himself to the discharge of the duties of his new position. But it is not necessary.

* See particularly the letters to the Dowager Duchess of Gotha and to Prince William of Löwenstein.

These qualities will come out in ever bolder relief as this memoir advances. A strong proof, among others, of the spirit in which he entered upon their performance will be found in the fact that, loving his old home as he did, with an intensity of affection that has been rarely equaled, and certainly has never been surpassed, upward of four years elapsed after his marriage before he paid a short and flying visit to the place of his birth.

It must be admitted, however, that, constantly, unostentatiously, and perseveringly as he now gave himself up to the discharge of his new duties, he was exposed, almost during the whole period of his life in this country, to much misconception and much misrepresentation. Not for that, however, did he for one moment relax in his efforts, or allow his zeal to flag, in seeking to promote all that was for the good of the British people. His actions might be misunderstood—his opinions might be misrepresented (of which there was more than one notable instance),* but, supported by his own conscious rectitude, he still pursued the even tenor of his way. Not a complaint—not a murmur—ever escaped his lips; not a single hasty expression did he ever indulge in, even toward those who were most unjust to him. He accepted such injustice as the inevitable lot of one placed, as he was, in high station, trusting surely to the coming of the time when his motives and actions would be better understood and better appreciated by his adopted country.

The principle on which he always acted was (to use

* Note by the Queen.—Especially at the commencement of the Russian War.

his own noble words) "to sink his own individual existence in that of his wife—to aim at no power by himself or for himself—to shun all ostentation—to assume no separate responsibility before the public;" but, making his position entirely a part of the Queen's, "continually and anxiously to watch every part of the public business, in order to be able to advise and assist her at any moment in any of the multifarious and difficult questions brought before her—sometimes political, or social, or personal—as the natural head of her family, superintendent of her household, manager of her private affairs; her sole confidential adviser in politics, and only assistant in her communications with the officers of the government."*

It was not, however, for some time that the position, as described above, was established. For the first year or two the Prince was not, except on rare occasions and by special invitation, present at the interviews of the Queen with her ministers.† Though taking, the Queen says, "great pains to inform himself about every thing;" and though Lord Melbourne expressed much anxiety "that the Queen should tell him and show him every thing connected with public affairs" . . . . "he did not at this time take much part in the transaction of business."‡

Nor were there wanting those who would gladly have kept him perfectly estranged from it; and not only so,

* Letter to the Duke of Wellington, in answer to offer of command of the Army.—*Speeches, etc., of the Prince Consort*, p. 76.

† Note by the Queen.—But this was not from any objection on their part.

‡ Memorandum by the Queen.

but who would have denied him, even in the domestic circle, that authority which, in private families, properly belongs to the husband, and without which, it may be added, there can not be true comfort or happiness in domestic life. The Prince himself early saw the necessity of his asserting and claiming that authority. "In my home life," he writes to Prince Löwenstein in May, 1840, "I am very happy and contented; but the difficulty in filling my place with the proper dignity is, that I am only the husband, not the master in the house."

Fortunately, however, for the country, and still more fortunately for the happiness of the royal couple themselves, things did not long remain in this condition. Thanks to the firmness, but, at the same time, gentleness with which the Prince insisted on filling his proper position as head of the family—thanks also to the clear judgment and right feeling of the Queen, as well as to her singularly honest and straightforward nature—but thanks, more than all, to the mutual love and perfect confidence which bound the Queen and Prince to each other, it was impossible to keep up any separation or difference of interests or duties between them. To those who would urge upon the Queen that, as sovereign, she must be the head of the house and the family, as well as of the state, and that her husband was, after all, but one of her subjects, her Majesty would reply that she had solemnly engaged at the altar to "obey" as well as to "love and honor," and this sacred obligation she could consent neither to limit nor refine away.

From the first, too, the Queen, acting on the advice of Lord Melbourne, communicated all foreign dispatches to the Prince. In August, 1840, he writes to his father: "Victoria allows me to take much part in foreign affairs, and I think I have already done some good. I always commit my views to paper, and then communicate them to Lord Melbourne. He seldom answers me, but I have often had the satisfaction of seeing him act entirely in accordance with what I have said."

And again in April, 1841: "All I can say about my political position is, that I study the politics of the day with great industry, and resolutely hold myself aloof from all parties (*fortfahre mich von allen Parteien frei zu halten*). I take active interest in all national institutions and associations. I speak quite openly with the ministers on all subjects, so as to obtain information, and meet on all sides with much kindness. . . . . I endeavor quietly to be of as much use to Victoria in her position as I can."

Here we have the first announcement of that principle by which the whole of his future life was guided, and to which many years later he gave the noble expression already quoted, of "sinking his individual existence in that of the Queen." Slowly but surely, acting on that principle, did he establish his position; and so entirely was it recognized by the Queen herself, so unreservedly and confidingly did she throw herself upon her husband's support, relying in all questions of difficulty on his judgment, and acting in all things by his advice, that when suddenly bereaved of that support, her sense of the loss which she had sustained as Queen found expression in the pathetic words "that it would now be, in fact, the beginning of a new reign!"

The true nature of the Prince's position, and the noble

and self-sacrificing spirit in which he filled it, will become more apparent as we proceed.

But we must revert now to the events which followed immediately after the marriage, many of which occurred before the departure of his brother.

The first thing to be settled after the marriage was the formation of the Prince's household. It was arranged that it should consist of a groom of the stole, to which office Lord Robert Grosvenor (now Lord Ebury) was first appointed; of two lords in waiting, Lord Boringdon (the late Lord Morley) and Lord George Lennox; two equerries, ultimately increased to four, Colonels, now Lieutenant Generals Bouverie and Wylde; two grooms in waiting, General Sir George Anson, and Captain, now Major General Seymour; and a private secretary, Mr. Anson. The last-named appointment was not made without considerable demur on the part of the Prince, and was reluctantly acquiesced in by him. It was not so much that Mr. Anson was, as it were, imposed upon him, having been selected without his being consulted, but that, having been long private secretary to Lord Melbourne, his appointment to so confidential a post about the Prince's person might seem inconsistent with that entire freedom from partisanship which his Royal Highness had already expressed his determination to preserve, and which he had insisted upon as the principle on which his household should be formed.* By his honest and straightforward conduct, however (which was very conspicuous, the Queen says, on the occasion of the change of government in 1841), the natural accompaniment of a nature some-

* See letter to the Queen, Chap. XI., p. 216.

what blunt and outspoken, but utterly incapable of intrigue, and by his entire devotion to the service and interests of his master, Mr. Anson soon won, and up to the hour of his sudden and lamented death enjoyed, as he deserved to enjoy, not only the confidence, but the friendship of the Prince.*

As regards the other appointments to the Prince's household, the same principle was established as was observed in that of the Queen herself, namely, that those appointments only should be permanent which were held by men entirely unconnected with politics, while those filled by peers or members of the House of Commons should change with the various changes of ministry. This regulation, however, only affected the groom of the stole and one of the lords in waiting. The greater number of those who were now named to the Prince's household remained in his service to the end. At first his Royal Highness had only two equerries, but as they were called upon to perform the same, and even more constant duties than those of the Queen, a third equerry (the late General, then Colonel Sir E. Bowater) was soon added; and in 1854 or 1855, the duties becoming still heavier, the number was increased to four.

It has been seen that the attempt to give the Prince precedence next to the Queen by act of Parliament had failed, and Lord Brougham had, on that occasion, asked if it was intended to effect that object by the exercise of

* Note by the Queen.—The Prince was deeply affected when the news of Mr. Anson's sudden death arrived, and said to the Queen, "He was my only intimate friend. We went through every thing together since I came here. He was almost like a brother to me."

the Queen's prerogative, to which question Lord Melbourne at the time declined to reply. It was now determined, with the concurrence of the leaders of both parties, to adopt this course.

Mr. Charles Greville* wrote a pamphlet, which Lord Melbourne characterized as "clever and well done," to prove that the Queen had the power, if she chose to exercise it, of conferring whatever rank and precedence she pleased upon the Prince by letters patent,† and having submitted his views on the subject to the Duke of Wellington, the latter expressed his concurrence in them, and gave it as his opinion that the Queen might, by letters patent, "give the Prince rank immediately next to herself every where except in Parliament and at the Privy Council."‡

The lord chancellor (the late Lord Cottenham) and Lord Lyndhurst, being consulted, expressed similar opinions; and the Duke of Wellington, on learning this from Lord Lyndhurst, sent Mr. Greville to Lord Melbourne to say that he thought this step might now be taken.§ Lord Melbourne lost no time in communicating these opinions to the Queen, but "Lord Melbourne and I," her Majesty adds, "said, why do this and say this now, when they might so easily and so much better have settled it by Parliament before?"‖ On the 5th of March letters patent were issued, conferring upon the Prince the precedence next to the Queen, which he ever afterward retained.

This was felt, however, not to be so satisfactory a way of effecting the desired object as if the Prince's rank had

* Clerk of the Council. Died January, 1865.

† The Queen's Journal, written at the time. ‡ Ibid. § Ibid. ‖ Ibid.

been definitively fixed by act of Parliament; and many years later, to prevent the scandal which every right-thinking person must feel it would have been, of seeing the father following his own sons, or trusting only to their forbearance to take precedence of them, it was proposed to define at once the position of every prince consort by act of Parliament, and to place him, during the lifetime of his wife, next to the sovereign. From a strange misapprehension, however, of what would have been the feeling of Englishmen on such a subject, this intention was abandoned, and the Prince continued to hold his rank only in virtue of the Queen's letters patent. This subject has, however, been already sufficiently alluded to in a former chapter.

It has also been already stated that the Queen, up to the period of her marriage, had indulged strong feelings of political partisanship. Among the happy consequences of the marriage may be included the gradual extinction of any such feeling. The Prince had already shown, in the discussions and correspondence respecting the formation of his household, his own determination to stand clear from all political parties. Lord Melbourne now, most honorably to himself, supported the Prince in pressing the same course upon the Queen. He told the Prince that he thought the time was come when her Majesty "should have a general amnesty for the Tories;" and on being spoken to by the Queen, to whom the Prince had reported what he had said, repeated that such was his opinion.* On another occasion, the Queen records that Lord Melbourne, speaking of the Prince,

* The Queen's Journal, written at the time.

"said, looking at him with tears in his eyes, 'There is an amazing feeling for him—there is a very favorable impression of him—every one likes him;'" and then adds, "Then, speaking of the Tories, against whom the Queen was very irate, Lord Melbourne said, 'You should now hold out the olive-branch a little.'"*

Levees, drawing-rooms, presentations, addresses, great dinners, state visits to the theatres, etc., etc., followed the marriage in rapid succession. The first levee was held on the 19th of February, on which, as on all other similar occasions for the future, as well as at the opening of Parliament or other state ceremonies, the Prince led the Queen in and stood on her left hand. On one occasion, the 7th of March, the Prince received and personally answered no less than twenty-seven addresses in one day.†

He was at first, the Queen says, a little nervous when addresses were presented to him, to which he had to give answers, though not nearly so nervous, it seems, as many of those by whom the addresses were presented. Mr. Anson, who generally attended the Prince in these ceremonies, used to tell many ludicrous stories about them, but said that nothing could be better or more dignified than the way in which the Prince went through them.‡

The Queen also gave many dinners, often followed by little dances; and they went frequently to the play, of which the Prince was always very fond. Among other plays which they went to see at this time, the Queen mentions six special performances which were got up at Covent Garden, then under the management of Madame

* The Queen's Journal, written at the time.

† Memorandum by the Queen.

‡ Ibid.

Vestris and Mr. Charles Mathews, in which Charles Kemble reappeared in some of Shakspeare's principal characters.* The Prince thoroughly enjoyed and appreciated Shakspeare, and in later years took the greatest interest in the revival of his plays, under the management of Mr. Charles Kean at the Princess's. We may also mention here, in further proof of this, that some years later, when theatrical performances were got up at Windsor Castle, two if not three nights out of the six were devoted to Shakspeare.

But at first the change in his mode of life—the difference of climate—and, above all, the lateness of the hours, were very trying to the Prince. "Victoria and I are quite well," he writes to his grandmother on the 24th of February. "We are very happy and in good spirits, but I find it very difficult to acclimatize myself completely, though I hope soon to find myself more at home. The late hours are what I find it most difficult to bear."

Late hours at night led naturally to late hours in the morning, and, very contrary to the habits afterward established, the Queen mentions that "in these days they were very late of a morning (which was the Queen's fault), breakfasting at ten, and getting out very little, which was very unwholesome."†

The Prince continues in the same letter, which, it will be seen, was written before the departure of his father from England: "I am receiving at present a great number of addresses from different towns and corporations, all of which I am forced to answer personally. To-night we give a small ball.

* Memorandum by the Queen.

† Ibid.

"The royal family are all amazingly kind to me, as is also good Queen Adelaide, whom one must respect for her open straightforward character.

"Alas! dear papa leaves us now in four days! Ernest will then be the only one left of the dear ones from home!"

Again, on the 9th of March: "It is not to be told," he says, "what a quantity of presentations I have, and how many people I must become acquainted with. I can not yet quite remember their faces, but this will come right. After the last levee Victoria gave me the Order of the Bath."

Easter of 1840 was spent at Windsor, when the Queen and Prince took the sacrament together for the first time in St. George's Chapel. "The Prince," the Queen says, "had a very strong feeling about the solemnity of this act, and did not like to appear in company either the evening before or on the day on which he took it, and he and the Queen almost always dined alone on these occasions."* The Queen notes this strong feeling on the part of the Prince more than once in her journal for 1840 and 1841; and on another occasion, a few months later, about Christmas time, when they again took the sacrament in the private chapel at Windsor, she says, "We two dined together, as Albert likes being quite alone before he takes the sacrament; we played part of Mozart's Requiem, and then he read to me out of the *Stunden der Andacht* (Hours of Devotion) the article on *Selbsterkenntniss* (Self-Knowledge)."†

*** Memorandum by the Queen.**

† The Queen's Journal, January, 1841, written at the time.

On Easter Monday, April 20th, the Prince met with a serious, and what might well have been a fatal accident, at the thought of which one still shudders, occurring, too, as it would have done, before the very eyes of the Queen. The stag-hounds were to meet at Ascot, and it had been arranged that the Prince should go out with them, the Queen following to the Heath later in a pony-carriage with his brother the hereditary prince. Before he set out the Prince went to the Queen, and said, jokingly, "I hope we shall meet again."* On leaving the Castle, attended by Colonel Bouverie and Mr. Seymour, his equerry and groom-in-waiting, and by Mr. William Cowper, groom-in-waiting to the Queen, H. R. H., who was mounted "on a handsome but very vicious thorough-bred horse,† called 'Tom Bowling,'" cantered past the window at which the Queen was standing, when the horse, taking the bit between his teeth, suddenly ran away at the top of his speed, and the Prince, after turning him several times, in a vain endeavor to stop him,‡ was at last knocked off by a tree against which he brushed in passing, and fell, most providentially, considering the pace at which he was going, without being seriously hurt. "Albert's horse," the Queen relates in her Journal, written at the time, describing what she saw, "seemed to go very fast and jumped very much. He turned him round several times,‡ and then I saw him run away violently through the trees and disappear. I ran anxiously to Albert's room in hopes of seeing something, but could not. Mr. Cowper

* The Queen's Journal, January, 1841, written at the time. † Ibid.

‡ The Home Park where this happened was not then, as it is now, divided by wire fences.

rode back, and I heard him say Albert was not hurt. Almost immediately afterward I saw dearest Albert ride out of the gate. I sent for Ernest, and he told me Albert had had a fall, but was not hurt!"*

When the Queen arrived at Ascot, "Albert," the Journal continues, "received me on the terrace of the large stand, and led me up. He looked very pale, and said he had been much alarmed lest I should have been frightened by his accident. . . . . He told me he scraped the skin off his poor arm, had bruised his hip and knee, and his coat was torn and dirty. It was a frightful fall, and might (I shudder to think of the danger my dearest, precious, inestimable husband was in) have been nearly fatal." (How naturally the Queen shrinks from admitting, even to herself, the whole extent of the danger escaped.) "The horse ran away from the *very* door, Albert said. He turned him round and round, lost his stirrup, and then he dashed through the trees, and threw Albert violently against a tree, the last near the wall, the force of which brought him to the ground. He scraped his arm and wrenched his hand by holding it up to prevent the tree coming against his side. Oh! how thankful I felt that it was no worse! His anxiety was all for me, not for himself."†

The Queen had never yet been separated from her mother, and since her first arrival in England the Duchess of Kent had never lived by herself. It was now thought expedient that the duchess should have a house

* Note by the Queen.—The horse, which was afterward mounted by one of the grooms, ran away three times in the course of the ride to Ascot!

† The Queen's Journal.

of her own, and accordingly, on the 13th of April, her royal highness removed to Ingestrie House, Belgrave Square, which continued to be her home till in September, after the death of Princess Augusta, she moved to Clarence House, St. James Palace, where she resided, when in London, for the rest of her life. But "she was very much affected," the Queen says, "as it is the first time she has lived alone since she has been in this country." At the same time, Frogmore, which also became vacant on the death of Princess Augusta, was likewise made over to the duchess; but, though she took up her residence there, she continued to dine almost daily with the Queen, and came, besides, constantly to luncheon.*

The Prince's love of music has been already mentioned. In March he was named one of the directors of Ancient Music, the directors taking it in turns to direct the concerts which were held in the Hanover Square Rooms. The Prince's first concert was fixed for the 29th of April, and he took the greatest pains about it, selecting the music to be performed, himself, and attending, with the Queen, a rehearsal of it on the 27th. On these occasions it was customary to give a great dinner to the other directors, after which the Queen and royal family proceeded to the Hanover Square Rooms, where the concert was held, in dress carriages. The Queen was at this time taking lessons in singing from Signor Lablache,† and the

* Memorandum by the Queen.

† Note by the Queen.—He had given the Queen singing-lessons since the year 1836, and was not only one of the finest bass singers, and one of the best actors, both in comedy and tragedy, that we have seen, but a remarkably clever, gentleman-like man, full of anecdote and knowl-

Prince often joined in them, and at other times used constantly to play and sing with the Queen. At Buckingham Palace they used often to play on the organ together in the Prince's drawing-room. The organ at Windsor in the music-room, since converted into a private chapel, was too large for the Queen, but the Prince occasionally played on it by himself.*

On the 9th of May the hereditary prince left England, and it has been already noticed how much the Prince felt his departure. Before he went, the Queen relates that the "two brothers sang a very pretty song together called 'Abschied,' which the students generally sing before they part. Albert was much affected, and when I ran up stairs he looked as pale as a sheet, and his eyes full of tears.... After a little while he said, 'Such things are hard to bear (*Solche Sachen sind hart*),' which indeed they are."†

On the 23d of May the Queen and Prince went to Claremont to keep her Majesty's birthday (24th) in private. It continued to be the custom thus to keep the real day, some other day being fixed for its public observance. In later years, after the purchase of Osborne, it was usually kept there, but, excepting in '46, it was always spent at Claremont till the year '48, when that place was given as a residence to the exiled royal family of

edge, and most kind and warm-hearted. He was very tall, and immensely large, but had a remarkably fine head and countenance. He used to be called "Le Gros de Naples." The Prince and Queen had a sincere regard for him. He died in 1858. His father was a Frenchman and his mother an Irishwoman, and he was born at Naples.

* Memorandum by the Queen.

† The Queen's Journal, written at the time.

France. The Queen was very fond of Claremont, having, she says, "spent many happy days there in her childhood." "The time spent there," she adds, "was always a very happy one, the Prince and Queen being able to take charming walks in the pretty grounds and neighborhood."* How grateful it must have been to the Prince, disliking as he did the dirt and smoke, and still more the late hours, of London, to get away to the freshness and privacy of the beautiful walks of Claremont, and of the charming country round it! His love of the country and of beautiful scenery has been already mentioned; and the Queen records of herself that she now began to share his tastes. In her Journal of the following January she says: "I told Albert that formerly I was too happy to go to London and wretched to leave it, and how, since the blessed hour of my marriage, and still more since the summer, I dislike and am unhappy to leave the country, and could be content and happy never to go to town. This pleased him. The solid pleasures of a peaceful, quiet, yet merry life in the country, with my inestimable husband and friend, my all in all, are far more durable than the amusements of London, though we don't despise or dislike these sometimes."†

Where is the Englishman, if it be indeed true that England is the land where the happiness and comfort of domestic and country life is best understood and appreciated, who will not sympathize with the feeling thus forcibly expressed by the Queen?

* Memorandum by the Queen.

† The Queen's Journal, written at the time.

As years went on, indeed, this preference for the country on the part of the Queen grew stronger and stronger, till residence in London became positively distasteful to her,* and was only made endurable by having her beloved husband at her side, to share with her and support her in the irksome duties of court receptions and state ceremonials.

The Prince himself, though never losing the smallest particle of that intense enjoyment of the country which used to burst forth, as Colonel Seymour relates,† in such expressions as, "Now I am free; now I can breathe," yet sacrificing, as he was ever ready to do, his own inclinations to his sense of duty, was always anxious that the Queen should spend as much time as she could in London. He felt this to be desirable for the convenience of communication with ministers, but perhaps still more from a conviction of the influence for good which the presence of a court, so looked up to and respected as was that of England under the Queen and himself, could not fail to exercise far and wide—far indeed beyond the circle of its immediate neighborhood.

How great a sacrifice this was to him, let the following letters show: "We came here the day before yesterday," he writes to the Duchess of Coburg on the 17th of April, "to spend a week at stately (*herrlichen*) Windsor, and I feel as if in Paradise in this fine fresh air, instead of the dense smoke (*in dem dicken Kohlendampf*) of London. The thick, heavy atmosphere there quite weighs one

* Note by the Queen.—It was also injurious to her health, as she suffered much from the extreme weight and thickness of the atmosphere, which gave her the headache.

† See Chap. IX., page 165.

down (*kann einem ganz nieder beugen*). The town is also so large that, without a long ride or walk, you have no chance of getting out of it. Besides this, wherever I show myself I am still followed by hundreds of people."

Again on the 2d of June, from Claremont:

"You are happily established in the lovely Rosenau, though only for a short time. To me it would be difficult to tear myself from that beautiful place, to which my thoughts still often fondly turn; and particularly so to-day, when we are again come to spend a day at Claremont."

The day before this last letter was written the Prince had presided at a meeting to promote the abolition of the slave-trade, which must be noticed here, because, though he only said a few words, they form the first of that remarkable series of public utterances which has been collected and published under the title of the *Principal Speeches and Addresses of H. R. H. the Prince Consort.* "He was very nervous," the Queen says, "before he went, and had repeated his speech to her in the morning by heart."* In the following letter the Prince gives his own account of his speech, and also mentions a visit he and the Queen had made from Claremont to Epsom races, the only time, her Majesty adds, that she was ever there except as a child:

To the Duke of Coburg.†

"*Buckingham Palace, June* 4, 1840.

"We came back yesterday from Claremont, where we

* Memorandum by the Queen.

† For original of letter, see Appendix C.

have again passed two days. We went there this time in order to be able to go from the neighborhood to the celebrated Epsom races, which were certainly very interesting. The numbers of people there were estimated at from one to two hundred thousand. We were received with the greatest enthusiasm and cordiality. I rode about a little in the crowd, but was almost crushed by the rush of people.

"I had to go to the Anti-Slave-trade meeting, and my speech was received with great applause, and seems to have produced a good effect in the country. This rewards me sufficiently for the fear and nervousness I had to conquer before I began my speech. I composed it myself, and then learned it by heart, for it is always difficult to have to speak in a foreign language before five or six thousand eager listeners.*

"The park near the palace,† of which you speak, is really very pleasant, and I have enlivened it with all sorts of animals and rare aquatic birds." The Queen mentions that in their morning walks in the palace garden it was a great amusement to the Prince to watch and feed these birds.‡

On the 10th of June, as the Queen and Prince were setting out on their usual afternoon drive, a man named Oxford made his well-known attempt on her Majesty's life by firing at her as the carriage was going slowly up Constitution Hill. Full details of the attempt, as well as

* For the speech, see *Speeches and Addresses of the Prince Consort*, p. 81.

† Buckingham Palace Garden, which is certainly more like a park than a garden.

‡ Note by the Queen.—He taught them to come when he whistled to them from a bridge connecting a small island with the rest of the garden.

of the trial and conviction of the man, are given in the *Annual Register* for this year. Oxford himself never denied his guilt; indeed he persisted, in spite of all remonstrances, in pleading guilty; but the extraordinary plea was urged in his favor—extraordinary it would have been in the case of any one, but still more extraordinary when the life attempted was that of the sovereign—that as no bullet was found, the pistols might not have been loaded with ball! Strange to say, too, this plea was so far allowed by the bench that it was left as a point which the jury were to decide; yet it is evident that, standing, as the man was, on a lower level than the carriage, and necessarily giving his pistol an upward direction, the ball, with its tendency to rise on first leaving the pistol, must almost certainly have passed over the garden wall, and what chance could there then be of finding it? The Prince himself gives the following account of this event:

TO THE DOWAGER DUCHESS OF GOTHA,* ETC.

"*Buckingham Palace, June* 11, 1840.

"DEAR GRANDMAMMA,—I hasten to give you an account of an event which might otherwise be misrepresented to you, which endangered my life and that of Victoria, but from which we escaped under the protection of the watchful hand of Providence. We drove out yesterday afternoon, about six o'clock, to pay Aunt Kent a visit, and to take a turn round Hyde Park. We drove in a small phaeton. I sat on the right, Victoria on the left. We had hardly proceeded a hundred yards from the Palace when I noticed, on the footpath on my side, a little

* See Appendix C.

mean-looking man* holding something toward us, and, before I could distinguish what it was, a shot was fired, which almost stunned us both, it was so loud, and fired barely six paces from us. Victoria had just turned to the left to look at a horse, and could not, therefore, understand why her ears were ringing, as from its being so very near she could hardly distinguish that it proceeded from a shot having been fired. The horses started and the carriage stopped. I seized Victoria's hands, and asked if the fright had not shaken her, but she laughed at the thing.

"I then looked again at the man, who was still standing in the same place, his arms crossed, and a pistol in each hand. His attitude was so affected and theatrical it quite amused me. Suddenly he again pointed his pistol and fired a second time. This time Victoria also saw the shot, and stooped quickly, drawn down by me. The ball must have passed just above her head, to judge from the place where it was found sticking in an opposite wall.† The many people who stood round us and the man, and were at first petrified with fright on seeing what happened, now rushed upon him. I called to the postillion to go on, and we arrived safely at Aunt Kent's. From thence we took a short drive through the park, partly to give Victoria a little air, partly also to show the public that we had not, on account of what had happened, lost all confidence in them.

* Lord Melbourne described him to the Queen as "an impudent, horrid little vermin of a man."—*The Queen's Journal.*

† It appears from the trial that the ball was not found. There was a mark in the wall which some believed and others denied to have been made by it.

"To-day I am very tired and knocked up by the quantity of visitors, the questions, and descriptions I have had to give. You must therefore excuse my ending now, only thanking you for your letter which I have just received, but have not yet been able to read.

"My chief anxiety was lest the fright should have been injurious to Victoria in her present state, but she is quite well, as I am myself. I thank Almighty God for his protection. Your faithful grandson,

"ALBERT.

"The name of the culprit is Edward Oxford. He is seventeen years old, a waiter in a low inn—not mad, but quite quiet and composed."

The feeling shown throughout the country on this occasion was intense. Wherever the Queen and Prince showed themselves in public, for many days after the occurrence, they were enthusiastically cheered; and when they went to the opera for the first time after it, "the moment they entered the box," the Queen relates, "the whole house rose and cheered, waved hats and handkerchiefs, and went on so for some time. 'God save the Queen' was sung, ... and Albert was called for separately and much cheered."*

Oxford persisted, Lord Melbourne told the Queen, in having no counsel; and on being pressed by a lawyer of his acquaintance to have one, he said, "The fact is, I am guilty, and I shall plead guilty."† Full details of

* The Queen's Journal.

† "Lord Melbourne, who of course came after the occurrence to see the Queen, and was much affected, said Oxford had asked if I was hurt,

the trial and its result will be found in the *Annual Register* for 1840.

We need not follow in detail the numerous court and fashionable gayeties which the Queen enumerates in her journal as having been shared in by herself and the Prince in this the first year of their marriage. It is more pleasing to turn to the account she gives of their ordinary mode of life. It will be seen that those late hours in the morning, of which the Queen speaks with such regret, were gradually improved under the influence of the Prince—an influence which was farther evident in the judicious and well-regulated division of the hours and occupations of the day, which the Queen describes as follows: "At this time the Prince and Queen seem to have spent their day much as follows: They breakfasted at nine, and took a walk every morning soon afterward. Then came the usual amount of business (far less heavy, however, than now); besides which they drew and etched a great deal together, which was a source of great amusement, having the plates '*bit*'* in the house. Lunch-

and on being answered that, thank God, I was not, stretched out both his arms, as if to say he was very sorry!"—*Queen's Journal.*

* Note by the Queen.—This was done by Miss Skerrett. She was the Queen's first dresser, though she did not act as such. She communicated with the artists, wrote letters to tradespeople, etc. She entered the Queen's service almost immediately after her accession in June, 1837, being recommended to the Queen by the late Marchioness of Lansdowne. She was the niece of a Mr. Mathias, who had been sub-treasurer to Queen Charlotte. Her father was a West Indian proprietor. She is a person of immense literary knowledge and sound understanding, of the greatest discretion and straightforwardness, and was treated with the greatest confidence by the beloved Prince and the Queen, to both of whom she is devotedly attached. She retired from the Queen's service in July, 1862,

eon followed at the usual hour of two o'clock. Lord Melbourne, who was generally staying in the house, came to the Queen in the afternoon, and between five and six the Prince usually drove her out in a pony phaeton. If the Prince did not drive the Queen, he rode, in which case she took a drive with the Duchess of Kent or the ladies. The Prince also read aloud most days to the Queen. The dinner was at eight o'clock, and always with the company. In the evening the Prince frequently played at double chess, a game of which he was very fond, and which he played extremely well."*

At first "the Queen tried to get rid of the bad custom, prevailing only in this country, of the gentlemen remaining, after the ladies had left, in the dining-room. But Lord Melbourne advised against it, and the Prince himself thought it better not to make any change."† The hours, however, were never late of an evening, and it was very seldom that the party had not broken up by eleven o'clock. Comparatively early, too, as the breakfast-hour now was, the Prince had often, particularly in later years, as work got heavier, done much business before it—written letters or prepared the drafts of memoranda on the many important subjects in which he took an interest, or which had to be considered by the Queen.

The Prince was also at this time "much taken up with painting"—an occupation of which he was very fond, but for which, in after years, he had no time—"and began a

having informed the Prince in the summer of 1861 that this was her intention, as she was anxious to pass the remainder of her life with her only sister. She frequently visits the Queen.

* Memorandum by the Queen. † Ibid.

picture of the death of Posa, from Schiller's *Don Carlos*, making first a small sketch for it, which he did beautifully."*

At the beginning of July it was thought expedient to provide for the possible case of the Queen's dying and leaving an heir to the throne, and the question of a regency was therefore considered. Lord Melbourne having consulted the Duke of Wellington, and through him Sir R. Peel and the leaders of the Conservative party, it was unanimously agreed that the Prince was the proper, and, indeed, only person to appoint.† A bill for the purpose was accordingly brought in and passed both houses without a dissentient voice, except from the Duke of Sussex, who recorded his opposition in a speech against the second reading of the bill in the House of Lords.‡

It appears, however, that this unanimity had not been arrived at without some difficulty, and that opposition had only been avoided by the previous communication with the leaders of the Conservative party, which had been so unfortunately neglected on a former occasion. The Prince thus writes on this subject to his father on the 24th of July:

"An affair of the greatest importance to me will be

* Memorandum by the Queen.

† A Council of Regency had been first suggested; but "when Lord Melbourne first spoke to the Duke of Wellington, he immediately answered for himself 'that it could and ought to be nobody but the Prince.'" —*The Queen's Journal.*

‡ The Duke of Sussex had previously written to Lord Melbourne to say "that he must oppose the bill in the House of Lords, and that he must not allow the rights of the family to be passed over."—*The Queen's Journal.*

settled in a few days. I mean the Regency Bill, which will to-day be read for a third time in the House of Lords, after which it will be brought before the House of Commons. There has been much trouble to carry the matter through (*die Sache durchzufechten*), for all sorts of intrigues were at work, and had not Stockmar gained the opposition for ministers, it might well have ended as did the £50,000. There was not a word of opposition in the House of Lords except from the Duke of Sussex."

In the same letter the Prince says, speaking of Lord Melbourne: "He is a very good, upright man, and supports me in every thing that is right." The Prince does not add, which would have been the truth, that it would have been impossible for him to ask or wish for support except in what *was* right.

And again: "The Tories are very friendly to me, as I am also to them."

On the 2d of August the Prince again writes: "The Regency Bill has passed safely through all its stages, and is now conclusively settled (*steht unerschütterlich fest*). . . . It is very gratifying that not a single voice was raised in opposition in either House, or in any one of the newspapers."

And this was the more gratifying, as Lord Melbourne told the Queen it was owing entirely to the golden opinions the Prince had won on all sides since his arrival in the country. "Three months ago," Lord Melbourne said to the Queen, "they would not have done it for him;" adding, with tears in his eyes, "It is entirely his own character."*

* The Queen's Journal.

And well did the Prince deserve that it should be so. From the moment of his establishment in the English palace as the husband of the Queen, his first object was to maintain, and, if possible, even raise the character of the court. With this view he knew that it was not enough that his own conduct should be in truth free from reproach; no shadow of a shade of suspicion should, by possibility, attach to it. He knew that, in his position, every action would be scanned—not always possibly in a friendly spirit; that his goings out and his comings in would be watched, and that in every society, however little disposed to be censorious, there would always be found some, prone, were an opening afforded, to exaggerate, and even to invent stories against him, and to put an uncharitable construction on the most innocent acts.

He therefore, from the first, laid down strict, not to say severe rules for his own guidance. He imposed a degree of restraint and self-denial upon his own movements, which could not but have been irksome had he not been sustained by a sense of the advantage which the throne would derive from it. He denied himself the pleasure—which to one so fond as he was of personally watching and inspecting every improvement that was in progress, would have been very great—of walking at will about the town. Wherever he went, whether in a carriage or on horseback, he was accompanied by his equerry. He paid no visits in general society. His visits were to the studio of the artist, to museums of art or science, to institutions for good and benevolent purposes. Wherever a visit from him, or his presence, could tend to advance the real good of the people, there his horses might be seen waiting; never at the door of mere fashion. Scandal itself could take no liberty with his name. He loved to ride through all the districts of London where building and improvements were in progress, more especially when they were such as would conduce to the health or recreation of the working classes; and few, if any, knew so well, or took such interest as he did, in all that was being done, at any distance east, west, north, or south of the great city—from Victoria Park to Battersea—from the Regent's Park to the Crystal Palace, and far beyond. "He would frequently return," the Queen says, "to luncheon at a great pace, and would always come through the Queen's dressing-room, where she generally was at that time, with that bright, loving smile with which he ever greeted her, telling her where he had been—what new buildings he had seen—what studios, etc., he had visited. Riding for mere riding's sake he disliked, and said, 'Es ennuyirt mich so (It bores me so).'"

There were some, undoubtedly, who would gladly have seen his conduct the reverse of all this, with whom he would have been more popular had he shared habitually and indiscriminately in the gayeties of the fashionable world—had he been a regular attendant at the racecourse—had he, in short, imitated the free lives, and even, it must be said, the vices of former generations of the royal family. But the country generally knew how to estimate and admire the beauty of domestic life beyond reproach, or the possibility of reproach, of which the Queen and he set so noble an example. It is this which has been the glory and the strength of the throne in our day, and which has won for the English court the love and veneration of the British people, and the respect of the world. Above all, he has set an example for his children, from which they may be sure they can never deviate without falling in public estimation, and running the risk of undoing the work which he has been so instrumental in accomplishing.

On the 11th of August the Queen prorogued Parliament in person, the Prince accompanying her for the first time, and thus mentioning the subject in a letter to his father: "The prorogation of Parliament passed off very quietly (*ging ganz ruhig vorüber*). I went with Victoria, and sat in the House in an arm-chair placed next to the throne."

It appears that some difficulty had been expected on the part of the Duke of Sussex* as to the place the Prince should occupy on this occasion, and it is to this the Prince alludes when he says every thing went off quietly. "I told you it was quite right," the Duke of Wellington said to the Queen a few days later at Windsor. "Let the Queen put the Prince where she likes, and settle it herself; that is the best way."†

The next day the court left London, to the great joy of the Prince. "We leave town," he had written to his father on the 2d, "on the 14th, and take up our residence at Windsor, at which I rejoice greatly. If you come here again I hope to be able to give you some tolerable shooting. I am now forming also a pretty little

* NOTE BY THE QUEEN.—Not only the Duke of Sussex: there were other people, who shall be nameless, who pretended that he could not drive with the Queen in the state carriage, or sit next to her in the House of Lords.

† The Queen's Journal.

stud of all the Arab horses which Victoria has received as presents.

"The new stables and the riding-school will be magnificent. The long green space below the terrace where the old trees stand, not under, but on the top of the hill, is to be laid out in pleasure-grounds, with plants, etc., and I shall occupy myself much with it. It gave me much trouble to get this settled, as it did before to save the existence of the fishing temple and George IV.'s cottage, which were to have been taken away. These are now safe."

And one who remembers what the home park at Windsor was at the time of the Queen's marriage—the public road winding round it under a high brick wall that divided it from Frogmore—with its fashionable "Frying Pan" walk, and the low public houses opposite—the footpath leading across the park close to Adelaide Cottage, and totally destructive of all privacy, to the old Datchet bridge—and the slopes so overgrown with trees, dark, gloomy, and damp—will readily admit how much Windsor, as a residence for the Queen, owes to the Prince. His talent in laying out grounds was really most remarkable;* and he has left enduring remembrances of his extreme good taste, not only at Windsor, where every improvement that has been effected since the Queen came to the throne is his doing, but still more at Osborne and Balmoral, both of which, beautiful and enjoyable as they are, are his entire creation.†

* Note by the Queen.—An inheritance from his father.

† The Queen writes in her Journal at Balmoral, October 13, 1856: "Every year my heart becomes more fixed in this dear Paradise, and so

On the 27th of August the Prince wrote to his father with reference to his birthday the day before. . . . . . "This is the first time that I have not heard these good wishes from your own lips!" . . . . "My thoughts yesterday were naturally much at the Rosenau"—the place of his birth, and the much-loved home of his infancy and youth.

"To-morrow," he goes on, "I shall have to encounter much fatigue. I go to the city; first, to the corporation of the Fishmongers,* into which body I am to be received as a member; and thence to the Guildhall, where, besides addresses, I am to receive the freedom of the city. After that I have to attend a banquet of four hours' duration at the Mansion House.

"Yesterday evening all London was illuminated in honor of my birthday, and they say it was very brilliant."

On the 6th of September, writing to his grandmother, the Dowager Duchess of Gotha, he gives the following description of the manner in which this, the first birthday he had ever passed out of his native country, was kept:

"Dear Grandmamma,—Your last letter, written on the 26th, gave me great pleasure. It is very dear and good of you to take so much interest from afar in what concerns me. You wish to know how we spent the birthday, and I will briefly give you a description of it.

much more so now that *all* has become my dearest Albert's *own* creation, own work, own building, own laying out, as at Osborne; that his great taste, and the impress of his dear hand, have been stamped every where." —*Leaves from Journal*, page 56.

* In the course of the summer the Prince had also been made a member of the Goldsmiths' Company.

"In the morning I was awoke by a reveillé.* We breakfasted with all the family, who are here, at Adelaide Cottage, which lies at the foot of the hill on which Windsor stands. Féodore's† children were dressed as Coburg peasants, and very funny they looked. In the afternoon I drove Victoria in a phaeton in the park. The weather favored the day very much. In the evening there was rather a larger dinner than usual."

There was now a succession of visitors at Windsor. The King and Queen of the Belgians had arrived a few days before the court left London. Princess Hohenlohe and her children arrived a day or two after it had moved to Windsor, and remained for a fortnight. Among others, too, the queen dowager, who was always most kind and affectionate to the Queen and Prince,‡ spent a few days at Windsor, and the Prince also received a visit, which gave him much pleasure, from the three princes of Hohenlohe-Schillingfürst, who had been fellow-students with him at Bonn.

To study and make himself thoroughly acquainted with the institutions of the land of his adoption was a task to which the Prince resolutely applied himself from the moment of his first establishment in England. And the summer of 1840 was scarcely over before he had begun regular readings in the English laws and Constitution with Mr. Selwyn, a highly distinguished barrister, at

* Note by the Queen.—It consisted of a German chorale, interwoven into a sort of quick-step, composed by Walch of Coburg.

† Princess Hohenlohe, the Queen's sister.

‡ Memorandum by the Queen.

that time treasurer of Lincoln's Inn.* "The lessons with Mr. Selwyn," he writes to Baron Stockmar on the 12th of September, "have begun, and can not fail to be of use. He is a highly educated and learned man, and, in particular, a good classical scholar, and has a clear and agreeable mode of teaching. The only fault I have yet to find with him is a want of method. He is preparing himself now for the Magna Charta, while I and Prætorius† are working out a sort of programme of studies, in order to lay it before him. Should he not approve of it, this will force him to make another."

"Mr. Selwyn," his son‡ relates, "always spoke in the highest terms of his Royal Highness's quick intelligence and diligent attention, and of his readiness in seizing the points of resemblance between English and German jurisprudence.

"And he often related the following anecdote, as one among the many proofs of the Prince's kindness of heart:

"Two days after the birth of the princess royal, Mr. Selwyn came, according to appointment, and the Prince said, 'I fear I can not read any law to-day, there are so many constantly coming to congratulate; but you will like to see the little princess;' and, finding that her royal highness was asleep, he took Mr. Selwyn into the nurs-

* Mr. Selwyn published, in 1806, the first part of the valuable work "*Selwyn's Nisi Prius*," which has run through thirteen editions, and has been a sort of lawyer's manual for nearly half a century. The 10th edition was published in 1840, and was dedicated by him,

"*Alberto Principi, legum Angliæ studioso.*"

Mr. Selwyn died in 1855.

† Librarian and German secretary to the Prince when he first came over.

‡ Dr. Selwyn, one of the Queen's chaplains.

ery, and taking the little hand of the infant, he said, 'The next time we read, it must be on the rights and duties of a princess royal.'"

On the 11th of September the Prince was made a member of the Privy Council. "Yesterday," he writes to Baron Stockmar in the letter above quoted, "I was introduced into the Privy Council. Lords Melbourne, John Russell, Clarendon, Holland, and Minto were present. The thing in itself is an empty form (*eine leere Form*), but from a distance it appears very grand."*

Princess Augusta was very ill all this time at Clarence House, and suffered terribly. On the 22d of September she died. The Prince visited her more than once during her illness, and, after her death, accompanied the Queen on the 1st of October to Claremont, in order to be out of the way at the time of the funeral, which the Prince did not attend on account of the Queen's health.†

On their return to Windsor the Queen records that she and the Prince read Hallam's *Constitutional History* together.

She also mentions that the Prince, who had been lately appointed to the colonelcy of the 11th Hussars, used occasionally to go in the park with a squadron of the 1st Life Guards, then commanded by Colonel Cavendish, in order to become acquainted with the English system of drill and the words of command.

The mode of life at Windsor did not differ materially from that observed elsewhere, except that on three, and

* Note by the Queen.—By this the Prince meant that no political or other discussion took place there, as was formerly the custom.

† Memorandum by the Queen.

occasionally four days in the week, at this season, there was shooting from eleven to two. In the afternoon there were drives, as in London; and in the evening, dinners and occasional dances.

On the 13th of November the court returned to Buckingham Palace, where, on the 21st, the princess royal was born. The Prince, writing to his father on the 23d, says, "Victoria is as well as if nothing had happened. She sleeps well, has a good appetite, and is extremely quiet and cheerful. The little one is very well and very merry. . . . I should certainly have liked it better if she had been a son, as would Victoria also; but, at the same time, we must be equally satisfied and thankful as it is. . . . The rejoicing in the public is universal."

"For a moment only," the Queen says, "was he disappointed at its being a daughter and not a son." His first care was for the safety of the Queen,* and "we can not be thankful enough to God," he writes to the Duchess of Gotha on the 24th, "that every thing has passed so very prosperously."

"During the time the Queen was laid up, his care and devotion," the Queen records, "were quite beyond expression."

He refused to go to the play or any where else, generally dining alone with the Duchess of Kent till the Queen was able to join them, and was always at hand to do any thing in his power for her comfort. He was content to sit by her in a darkened room, to read to her, or write for her. "No one but himself ever lifted her from her bed to her sofa, and he always helped to wheel her on her bed or sofa into the next room. For this purpose he would

* Memorandum by the Queen.

come instantly when sent for from any part of the house. As years went on and he became overwhelmed with work" (for his attentions were the same in all the Queen's subsequent confinements), "this was often done at much inconvenience to himself; but he ever came with a sweet smile on his face. In short," the Queen adds, "his care of her was like that of a mother, nor could there be a kinder, wiser, or more judicious nurse."*

During the Queen's illness the Prince also saw the ministers, and transacted all necessary business for her.

When the Queen was well enough to move the court returned to Windsor, where Christmas was passed in the manner ever afterward observed. It was the favorite festival of the Prince—a day, he thought, for the interchange of presents, as marks of mutual affection and good-will. Christmas-trees were set up in the Queen and Prince's rooms, a custom which was continued in future years, when they were also set up in another room for the young princes and princesses, and in the oak-room for the household. The ladies and gentlemen in waiting were summoned to the corridor on Christmas-eve. The Queen and Prince, accompanied by the royal family, pointed out the presents for each, inviting them afterward to go through the different rooms to see what they themselves had mutually given and received.

The princess royal's christening took place on the 10th of February, 1841, the first anniversary of the Queen's happy marriage; but the account of this, as well as the other events of that year, must be reserved for another volume.

* Memorandum by the Queen.

APPENDICES.

APPENDIX A.

REMINISCENCES OF THE KING OF THE BELGIANS.

In the preceding chapters little has been said of the Prince's family. The wish has been to confine this memoir to what more immediately concerned the Prince himself; and therefore, beyond the slight allusion to them in the opening chapter, no mention has been made of any members of the family except those—his father, grandmothers, and brother—with whom his own early life was naturally identified.

Yet his immediate ancestors for two, if not three generations, had been so mixed up with the stirring events which marked the close of the last and the opening of the present century, that some notice of them from one who has himself borne a prominent part in the European history of these latter times will not be out of place here. The Prince's great-grand-uncle, the Field-marshal Prince Friedrich of Saxe-Coburg, had commanded with distinction and success in the Netherlands at the commencement of the French Revolutionary War; his father commanded a corps toward its close; while his uncle Leopold, after greatly distinguishing himself in the latter campaigns against Napoleon, has for the last four-and-thirty years, as King of Belgium, earned for himself, by the consummate ability and prudence with which he has passed through times of the greatest difficulty and danger, the character of the most sagacious as well as the most enlightened sovereign of Europe.*

In 1862, with a view to this memoir, the Queen applied to the king for some account of his recollections of the Prince and of his family; and his majesty, responding to that appeal, has related his reminiscences in the following letters.

* It will be seen that this was written while the king was still alive

Though they extend back to times long anterior to the Prince's birth, and his memoir has, therefore, properly no concern with them, yet they will be read with interest, and no apology is made for giving them almost at full length:

"My recollections," the king writes, "go as far back as the Urgrossvater, Herzog Franz Josias. He was very much looked up to. A tall, powerful man. He had lost an eye at tennis, formerly much played on the Continent. His wife was a Princess of Schwarzburg Sondershausen. I am, however, not quite certain about it. These people I, of course, never saw. The children of this Duke Francis Josias were: Ernest Friedrich, who became the reigning duke — Prince Christian, who served in the Austrian army, but retired and lived at Coburg, where he died—and Prince Friedrich Josias, who entered the Austrian army rather young, and served in the Seven Years' War. He was shot through the hand during that war when he was colonel of the Anspach Cuirassiers. He was liked and protected by the Empress Maria Theresa, and important commands were confided to him. He made himself a great name during the Turkish campaign. The Emperor Joseph, who commanded in person a strong army in the direction of Servia, failed completely, and lost also great part of his army by sickness. Prince Friedrich commanded a comparatively small army of some 20,000 men in Moldavia and Wallachia, when he was joined by a small Russian force under Suwaroff. They beat the Grand Vizier, and conquered both principalities. For this very brilliant campaign he was made a field-marshal, and got the Grand Cordon of Maria Theresa.

"At this time the French attacked the Netherlands, where Duke Albert of Saxe Teschen* (the Prince's godfather) commanded, Heaven knows, very indifferently, and lost, with the battle of Jemappes, the whole of the Netherlands. Prince Friedrich was now sent there, and gained one of the most important battles of modern history—that of Neerwinden, near Tirlemont. Poor King Louis Philippe commanded a division there under Dumouriez. This battle forced the French to evacuate the Netherlands, and disorganized them

* He was married to the Archduchess Maria Christina, daughter of the Empress Maria Theresa, and built the Palace of Laeken when Governor of the Netherlands. The line of Saxe Teschen is extinct.

so much that, after the junction of the English and Dutch auxiliaries, the Allies might have marched to Paris, as was done after Waterloo. Unfortunately, the English government took it into its head to try to conquer Dunkirk, an object of very secondary importance. The Duke of York, never successful in war, was beaten by General Houchard. This discomposed matters a good deal. The Prince Friedrich was for peace, seeing the difficulties of the position; but the Austrian minister, Count Mercy d'Argenteau, opposed this rather wise idea. Things got worse, and Prince Friedrich, declining the responsibility, retired to Coburg. A Colonel Witzleben wrote recently, at my expense, a life of the field-marshal, which must be in your library. There was a fourth brother. I can not recollect his name now. He served in the Saxon army, and was killed, very young, in the Seven Years' War. He seems to have been romantic. There existed somewhere an inscription by him: 'Tout par amour, rien par force.' For some time one could not learn what had become of him, as he was not recognized on the field of battle. There were two sisters; the Margravine of Anspach, very handsome, but not very happy with her flighty husband, having no child; and the Duchess of Mecklenburg Schwerin, mother of all the generations of Schwerin. She lived long and much beloved. Duke Ernest Friedrich was a good-natured, easy, and well-meaning man, who must have been good-looking in his younger years. He married a Princess of Braunschveig Wolfenbuttle, who, in a great monarchy, would most certainly have played a great part, perhaps not of the mildest, like her sister Queen Ulrique of Denmark.* She ruled every thing at Coburg, and treated that little duchy as if it had been an empire. She was very generous, and in that respect did much harm, as she squandered the revenues in a dreadful manner. The duke stood very much in awe of his imperious wife. I dare not say any thing against her, having been her great favorite. The duke died in 1800, and she in 1801. The children were our dear and benevolent father, Prince Ludwig, and Princess Caroline.

"In our family," the king says in another letter, "a prominent character was my grandmother. She was of the old Brunswick stock, sister of Duke Ferdinand and of the Queen

* A third sister was married to Frederick the Great.

Ulrique of Denmark, and of the mother of Frederick William the Second. Her niece was the distinguished Duchess of Weimar, some years regent for her son, the first grand-duke. She was, in fact, too great a person for a small dukedom; but she brought into the family energy and superior qualities above the minute twaddle of these small establishments.

"My poor father, suffering comparatively early in life from bad health, was the most amiable and humane character—benevolence itself. Stockmar was always so struck with it. His great love and knowledge of every thing connected with the fine arts was inherited by Albert. No one else in the family possessed it to the same degree.

"My beloved mother* was in every respect distinguished; warm-hearted, possessing a most powerful understanding, she loved her grandchildren most tenderly.

"Without meaning to say any thing unkind of the other branches of the Saxon family, ours was more truly intelligent and more naturally so, without affectation, or any thing pedantic about it."

Continuing in subsequent letters his account of the family, the King of the Belgians goes on to say, that in his grandfather's time, "owing to the love of display, and the generous disposition of the duchess, the affairs of the duchy had already become a good deal involved. . . . His father succeeded in 1800, when the events consequent on the French Revolution had driven most of the principal people of the adjacent states into emigration; and the hospitality which was extended to them under the somewhat old-fashioned management of the Ober-marshal von Wangenheim, a man much resembling George IV. in his love of display, soon exhausted the resources of the duchy. A Mons. de Kretschmann, who had a high character as an administrator, was consequently brought from Beireuth to manage the duchy matters. He certainly effected great improvements; but he also caused much trouble and agitation—not forgetting his own interests—one consequence of which was, to produce a quarrel between the duke and his uncle the field-marshal, as well as with his brother Louis, both of whom for some time refused to attend the court. All this was a source of much

* She was Augusta Caroline Sophia, eldest daughter of Henry XXIV., reigning Count Reuss Ebersdorff.

vexation to the duke—the kindest and most benevolent of men—and for some years seriously affected his health."

About this time the king's eldest brother Ernest (the father of our Prince) went to Berlin, and there formed a lasting friendship with Frederick William III. and his queen. It was also in the course of the same year (1803?) that the next brother Ferdinand, "who had already for some years held honorary rank in the Austrian service, joined somewhat unwillingly Rosenberg's regiment of light horse."

Of his sisters the king says that, in 1795, the Empress Catharine, "being anxious for the marriage of the Grand-duke Constantine, procured through M. de Budberg, distinguished both as a minister and a general, a visit from the three princesses of Saxe-Coburg, who were all undoubtedly very handsome. The grand-duke fancied most Julie, the youngest of the three, very pretty, but still a mere child, being only fifteen years of age." "How strangely," the king proceeds, "do things often come to pass! If the grand-duke's choice had fallen on Antoinette (the second sister), she would have suited that position wonderfully well. I know much of all this from Constantine himself. He told me that the empress-mother, looking to the two younger sons, did not wish the 'ménages' of the two elder brothers to succeed. He himself was dreadfully 'taquin;' and, 'comme surcroît de malheur,' the then Grand-duke Alexander and his wife were Aunt Julie's great friends, and supported her in the little domestic squabbles. Without the shocking hypocrisy of the empress-mother, things might have gone on. The grand-duke admired his wife extremely; and with an amiable husband, generous-hearted as she was, she would have been an excellent wife. She felt unhappy, and ended, without a formal separation, by leaving Russia in 1802. He always wished for a reconciliation, and went with me in January, 1814, to Elfenau, near Berne, but she could not bring herself to consent to this reconciliation. The consequence was, finally, a divorce much approved of by the empress-mother."

The grand-duchess, however, felt painfully, the king adds, the neglect to which she was subjected for many years afterward.

Antoinette, the second sister, married, in 1798, Duke Alexander of Würtemberg. She is described by the king as having been clever, amiable, and possessed of a "great esprit de conduite." Her elder sister Sophia was much attached to her, and lived with her a great deal at Fantaisie, near Baireuth, which at that time was the resort of many Bavarian families, as well as of French emigrants. It was here that the Princess Sophia made the acquaintance of Count Mensdorff, whom she afterward married, after refusing many very eligible matches of her own rank. The greatest intimacy and friendship existed in youth between her sons—all distinguished in the Austrian service—and their cousin Prince Albert.

"My poor father's health," the king continues, "was sinking very fast when the war with Austria broke out in 1805, and Napoleon nearly destroyed Austria. Your uncle Ferdinand" (the letter is addressed to the Queen) "was then in the ——— Husaren; served well, but had much to suffer. Your uncle Ernest, and myself only fifteen years old, left Coburg to join the Russian army in Moravia; but Austerlitz put an end to it. We went to Berlin, where we met the Grand-duke Constantine, and returned afterward to Coburg. In 1806 the war with Prussia became evident. There was still a great notion that the Prussians, who spoke with great contempt of the Austrians, would do wonders. Toward the end of September my brother joined the King of Prussia. My parents, Aunt Sophia Mensdorff, little Hugo, and myself, went to Saalfeld, hoping that perhaps, owing to the Thuringerwald, we should remain perfectly quiet. Poor Prince Louis Ferdinand of Prussia, however, took an absurd position near Saalfeld, which clearly, once the fact known that the French were in great force, could only lead to his destruction. So we who went to Saalfeld to be out of the way, got into the very midst of a battle; Coburg having only had the passage of the French, but no other inconvenience.

"We returned, 'tant bien que mal,' to Coburg. Toward the end of November and the first days of December, our beloved benevolent father sank very fast, and died on the 9th of December, 1806. The situation was a sad one. The French had occupied but not yet seized Coburg, as our father was present. But after his death the question was immediately put: 'Where is the new duke?' Hearing that he was with the King of Prussia, Coburg was taken possession of, and a military intendant took every thing in hand. He was not an agreeable person: a M. Vilain, bearing well that name.

"To complicate matters still more, there was a very ill-timed sort of insurrection against M. de Kretschmann. The French believed it partly directed against themselves. It was put down by military intervention. Soon after a new intendant arrived, a M. Dumolart, Auditeur du Conseil d'Etat. Nearly all the young men of good families, who did not serve in the army, were utilisés as Auditeurs du Conseil d'Etat. Molé, Duc de Broglie, etc., were all in this position, and generally employed in the administration of conquered countries. At the same time Colonel Parigot was named military commandant. My good mother and all of us had no means of existence but what was clandestinely given by our employés, and a little tolerated by the intendant.

"Our mother, in the hope of obtaining the means of getting your uncle back, and also to make Coburg enter into the Rheinbund which the other Saxon houses were going to obtain, went to Berlin, and was ready to go to Warsaw to see the great man. She got, however, not beyond Berlin, Napoleon not being very fond of those visits. General Clerke, duc de Feltre, the Governor of Berlin, was very kind to her. I am sorry to say that our cousins behaved very badly, particularly la Duchesse de Meiningen, whose plenipotentiary was the famous Baron Erfa. Their wish was to get Coburg excluded, and thereby of course destroyed. During the time my poor brother was ill at Königsberg, and when it became necessary to leave it for Memel, he was thrown, crossing the ice, into the river. He had typhus, and though there are examples of cold baths saving the patient, he remained ill for some time, recovering but slowly. My poor mother returned to Coburg, and we remained 'une possession Française.'

"At the end of April, 1807, my brother arrived by way of Austria, but not at Coburg. He went to a quiet place near Baireuth to meet us, and then to Egra, Franzensbrunnen, where I went with him.

"The Peace of Tilsit, as one of its clauses, 'réintégra le Duc de Saxe-Cobourg,' and then only he returned to Coburg and took possession.

"In September, 1807, it was considered right to pay a vis-

N 2

it to Napoleon at Paris. The two Mecklenburgs, also réintégrés by the peace of Tilsit, went also there. We were kindly treated. The Duke Alexander and Antoinette had gone to Russia in 1803, where they were entirely settled. After our return from Paris in the spring of 1808, I nearly died of a typhus fever. My brother went to Petersburg to claim some increase of territory, and also to claim the hand of the Grand-duchess Anna Paulowna, which was promised to him when he was still too young; but the engagement was positive. Antoinette had come to Coburg, and my mother, Antoinette, and for some time your mamma, went to Carlsbad and Töplitz, in Bohemia. I recovered very slowly. At the beginning of October I was summoned by the Emperor Alexander and the Grand-duke Constantine to Weimar and Erfurth, that famous Congress. Aunt Antoinette was also called upon. I saw then a good deal of Napoleon, and should have succeeded in getting for my brother some territory if the Emperor Alexander had had more energy, and that my dear brother always asked a little too much.

"In 1809 was the Austrian war, in which Uncle Ferdinand served as Obrist von E. H. Ferdinand Husaren, and was wounded, and Mensdorff was also wounded.

"The years 1810 and 1811 were quiet enough. I had the disappointment of being prohibited to serve in Russia; Napoleon rendering my brother responsible, as he knew that I could not otherwise be prevented. It was a dangerous moment out of which to get, as he wished me to enter the French service. However, it succeeded. Queen Hortense was then very friendly, and aided me to escape the emperor's propositions. Old Joséphine was also always very kind to us and the Mecklenburgs.

"In 1811, in the summer, not being yet twenty-one, I got my brother a very good treaty with Bavaria, by which Bavaria consented to divide with Coburg possessions which they had acquired in 1805! and which had been Reich's '*unmittelbar.*' Feo (Princess Hohenlohe) will explain this; only imagine that the Bavarians had Füllbach and another village* opposite!

"In 1812 the Russian war broke out, and at the same time the marriage with the Grand-duchess Anna, that had been

* Villages about four miles from Coburg.

getting more and more doubtful, the empress-mother not being sincere in it, was finally broken off.

"Napoleon's excuse for engaging in this war was, that Russia, by permitting trade with England, was destroying his system of Continental blockade. Germany was ruined by the passage of innumerable masses of troops, which were gradually pushed toward Poland. In May, Napoleon invited the German sovereigns to Dresden. The Emperor of Austria, and the Empress, the King of Prussia, the King of Bavaria, the King of Würtemberg, the Queen of Westphalia, and all the minor German princes, went there. All the ministers of these various princes went there also. The Duke of Coburg and his brother Ferdinand went also to Dresden. The younger brother, Leopold, did not think it safe to appear, as the Emperor Napoleon had, in 1811, expressed a wish to employ him. He went to Vienna and then to Italy, to be quite out of the way.

"Germany was, at the beginning of 1812, in the lowest and most humiliating position; Austria and Prussia sunk to be auxiliaries; every body frightened and submissive, except Spain, supported by England!

"The two elder brothers were chiefly at Coburg. The Mensdorffs came also; as well as Victoire, the Princess of Leiningen.

"All the news that reached Germany were favorable to the Emperor Napoleon. In November only there came vague reports of non-success in Russia. In December there appeared the famous bulletin which told the end of the disastrous campaign in Russia. The Duke of Coburg went to Berlin to act upon the mind of the King Frederick William III., who was known, though dreadfully maltreated, to come with great reluctance to any decision, and who took in general gloomy views of every thing. The enthusiasm of Germany can not be described. After seven years of slavery a ray of hope animated again the people.

"The first of January, 1813, saw Germany happier than it had been for a very long time. The Duke of Coburg had returned from Berlin, where he left the king much perplexed. After some stay at home he made a second voyage there. Prince Ferdinand went to Vienna to ascertain the sentiments there. Prince Leopold went to Munich at the beginning of

February to see the Crown Prince of Bavaria, afterward King Louis, with whom he was on terms of great friendship, and who was ardently devoted to the 'Befreiung' of Germany from the French tyranny. The Duke of Coburg exercised a useful influence on the King of Prussia, contributing to decide him to go to Breslau. At Berlin he had been surrounded by the French corps of Marshal Augereau, who had not been in Russia, but left behind pour surveiller Prussia. The king might at any moment have been arrested at Berlin. At Breslau he was surrounded by his own troops and a very devoted population. Prince Leopold went from Munich to Breslau, where he was joined by Prince Ferdinand, who brought favorable news from Vienna.

"The duke, being still completely in the hands of France, was forced to return to Coburg, where great efforts were made to keep secret the journeys of the two princes. Prince Ferdinand returned to Vienna, and soon took the command of some Austrian troops again. Prince Leopold left Breslau for Kalisch in Poland, where the Emperor Alexander had his head-quarters. He was the first German prince who joined the liberating army. On the demand of the Grand-duke Constantine, his brother-in-law, who commanded the Guards, he was attached to his staff. The emperor having reserved the rank of major general, he found himself one of the older generals.

"The Russian army had been much weakened by the fatigues of the winter campaign. The King of Prussia, coming to Kalisch, expressed to Prince Leopold his apprehension that the Russian army would not be strong enough when the French reorganized army should advance. The prince shared the king's misgivings on that subject. The army advanced toward Dresden, where it arrived in the latter days of April. After a short stay it moved on toward the Saal. The battle of Lutzen took place on the 2d of May. If the dispositions had been made as they ought to have been, it ought to have been a decisive victory, owing to the great superiority in number and quality of the allied cavalry.

"As it was, the ground was kept by the army, which retired toward the Elbe, and afterward to the neighborhood of Dantzic, where, on the 20th and 21st of May, a second battle*

* Bautzen.

was fought. The allied army was too weak, and, though again not beaten, it was forced to retire into Silesia. An armistice was then concluded at the beginning of June, which lasted till the middle of August. Negotiations had been carried on at Prague. Napoleon could not bring himself to accept the most moderate propositions of the three Powers. The Emperor of Austria feared the breaking out of a war, and, to the last moment, expressed the hope that Napoleon would give way.

"Prince Leopold remained the whole time at Prague, much in the society of the negotiators, Prince Metternich, Baron Humboldt, Baron Austedt, the Russian plenipotentiary, Chevalier Gentz, etc. He was the only person admitted to see the Emperor Francis of Austria. During the armistice the Emperor Alexander had wished to see his sister-in-law, the Grand-duchess Anna Feodorowna. Prince Leopold arranged the meeting, which took place at Blasdorff, in Silesia, in a pretty château. The emperor had gone there quite alone, and it was interesting to see him so. He was extremely amiable.

"On the 26th of August most of the troops composing the Bohemian allied army had already crossed into Saxony and marched toward Dresden. The cavalry of the Guard, and part of the reserves, were on the better higher road, when the Prince Eugene of Würtemberg, who commanded the extreme right wing of General Wittgenstein, was attacked, on the 26th of August, by General Vandamme, with very superior forces. The prince begging to have some cavalry sent to him, Prince Leopold was detached to his assistance, and enabled him to leave a position in which he had been much exposed. The advance of General Vandamme threatening the communications with Bohemia, the first division of Foot Guards, the Hussars of the Guard, and other troops, were sent to protect the right wing, under Generals Ostermann and Germoloff, Prince Leopold taking the command of all the cavalry present. The allied army retiring to Bohemia in the night of the 27th to the 28th of August, Count Ostermann's little corps had to force its way through Vandamme's corps to regain the principal road leading to Töplitz. Prince Leopold was, of all the generals, the only one who knew the country, which proved of great importance. The 29th was devoted to hard fighting. On the 30th General Vandamme and most of his corps were taken prisoners. Prince Leopold received on the morning of the 30th, on the field, the Third Class of the Military Order of St. George of Russia, and later the Cross of Maria Theresa of Austria, and the Iron Cross of Prussia.

"After some delay the allied army went into Saxony in October, and on the 16th, 17th, and 18th of October, battles took place at Leipsic, finally liberating Germany.

"From Weimar, at the beginning of November, the Grand-duke Constantine of Russia went with Prince Leopold to Coburg, where he wished to see the family. There were present the duke, the dowager duchess, Princess Sophia, and Field-marshal Prince Frederick Josias. The grand-duke remained a week at Coburg. He joined the army again at Frankfort, where soon all the allied sovereigns were united. He paid, with Prince Leopold, a visit to the Princess of Leiningen, at Amorbach. At Frankfort the duke, Princes Ferdinand and Leopold, remained some time. It was at that period that there were some negotiations about a marriage of the duke with Princess Herminie of Anhalt Schaumburg, who afterward married the archduke palatine. The duke did not follow up that plan, as a more advantageous marriage seemed possible.

"In December great part of the allied army took the direction of Switzerland. The Grand-duke Constantine and Prince Leopold paid a second and longer visit at Amorbach. The duke remained at Frankfort to take the command of a German corps d'observation, which was to blockade, and, if possible, to take Mayence, where a considerable French force had remained. Prince Ferdinand, after some demonstrations against Mayence, went with the Austrian army to Switzerland, and afterward to Franche-Comté, in Eastern France, where he remained. The great head-quarters of the Emperor of Russia and the King of Prussia occupied Bâle on the 12th of January, 1814. The Grand-duke Constantine went with Prince Leopold to Elfenau, near Berne, the residence of the Grand-duchess Anna Feodorowna. His ardent wish was a reconciliation. Unfortunately, it did not take place. The great army struggled on in France, political difficulties preventing its going after the battle of Brienne, on the 2d of February, to Paris, which might easily have been done. Only.

on the 30th of March the attack of Paris took place. On the 31st the allied army entered Paris. Prince Leopold entered it at the head of the cavalry he commanded, and remained at Paris; the duke, after an armistice with Mayence, settled its evacuation by the French, and came to Paris. Prince Ferdinand came there also. In the middle of June the duke went to Germany—Prince Ferdinand also. Prince Leopold accompanied the Emperor Alexander to England. The events which took place then are known. The Duke and Duchess of York were most friendly, so was the Duke of Kent. The regent was much irritated, first, by Princess Charlotte refusing the Prince of Orange; afterward by her flight to her mother. The majority of the public were favorable to Prince Leopold—even ministers—particularly the Wellesley family, Lord Castlereagh, etc.

"At the end of July Prince Leopold left London. Before that he was graciously received by the regent, who had verified that no unfair intrigue had taken place. He assisted at a splendid ball at Carlton House, which closed the season, and where he received demonstrations of kindness from the whole family. The prince opened the ball with Princess Mary, not yet Duchess of Gloucester. The Duke of Sussex and the Duke of Gloucester were not at that time received by the regent or his ministers. Prince Leopold went through Holland to Amorbach, where the Prince of Leiningen had died unexpectedly. He assisted the Princess to settle her guardianship. The three brothers met at Amorbach, and afterward at Coburg.

"At the end of August the duke and Prince Ferdinand went to Vienna, where the Congress had begun its sittings. Prince Leopold, who had remained with his beloved mother, joined them there toward the end of September. The duke intrusted a good deal of the management of what he hoped to obtain to Prince Leopold.

"Good results were to be obtained, but the duke interfering in the great affairs in a way which was disagreeable to the Emperor of Russia, his chief protector, his affairs declined. Prince Leopold again took their direction, but made the condition that the duke would not interfere in any way. The result was not so good as what Prince Leopold had originally almost already obtained; still it was important for the house of Coburg. Prussia showed great hatred to the duke, owing to his having been against her plan concerning the King of Saxony. If Chevalier Gentz had not kindly informed the prince that the Prussians had prevented the arrangement for Coburg from being in the treaty, which was to be signed the following day, the hopes of Coburg would have been wrecked at the last moment; as it was, the prince got the Russian and Austrian ministers to put into the treaty the paragraph concerning Coburg, to the great displeasure of Baron von Humboldt. From that moment the Prussians showed the utmost hostility to Coburg, and never executed the part of their engagement by which they were bound to exchange the territories which had been assigned to Coburg on the Rhine, against some detached territories in Saxony, which were most desirable for Coburg.

"During the Congress Prince Ferdinand gained the heart of the blooming heiress of the house of Kohary. The Duke of Wellington, and Lord Castlereagh, and all the English, showed a marked kindness to Prince Leopold. The Duke of Kent was so kind as to favor some communications with Princess Charlotte, who expressed her determination to remain firm in her plans. I forgot to mention a subject which has been since told as a proof of the great poverty of Prince Leopold when he was in England in 1814. He came with the Emperor Alexander, and as long as the emperor remained himself in England, the lodgings of the persons who had come with him were paid by him. The Russian embassador, Count Lieven, had the charge of locating the suite, and as they lived in Harley Street, they lodged the people near it, and had taken a rather indifferent lodging for Prince Leopold in High Street, Marylebone. The prince had nothing to do with the choice of that lodging, and as soon as the emperor had left, he lodged himself in Stratford Place, in a house where General Count Beroldingen, the Würtemberg minister, lodged, and where he remained till he left London. He might have explained these things before, but he had not thought it worth while.

"The final conclusion of the Congress of Vienna took place in June, 1815. After the return of Napoleon from Elba, the Allies were occupied in collecting their armies. The Duke of Coburg received the command of a corps d'observation, which remained in Alsace, and was composed of the royal Saxon contingent. The battle of Waterloo decided the fate of Napoleon. An Austrian army occupied the south and east of France. The German troops of the Confederation occupied eastern France. A Russian army advanced, but reached France only in July and August. Prince Leopold, whose division of light cavalry did not go as far as France, went to Paris with the approbation of the Emperor Alexander in July. He remained there occupied with political affairs, and obtained for his brother an augmentation of territory. He was treated with marked kindness by the English. The Duke of Kent was so kind as to facilitate, through an officer devoted to him, communications with Princess Charlotte. The princess and her friends wished the prince to go to England. He was, however, of opinion that the princess's father should not be braved (*bravé*), as it would render things but more difficult. The princess thought this an excess of discretion, and was not pleased; but after events proved that the forbearance had been wise.

"Prince Ferdinand married young Princess Kohary at the beginning of 1816. The duke went to Vienna to be present at this marriage. Prince Leopold, by his brother's desire, went to Berlin to effect the exchange which Prussia had engaged by treaty to make; which, however, with remarkable bad faith, it eluded to execute. It was in January, at Berlin, that Prince Leopold received the invitation of the prince regent to come to England, and also an explanation from Lord Castlereagh. He was forced to wait for his brother's arrival from Vienna, and then left in fearfully cold weather for Coburg. He caught an inflammatory cold, which retained him, to his great dismay, at Coburg, receiving the most pressing letters from England to hasten his arrival. It was painful to be quite unable to set out, and only in February could he leave Coburg. At Calais he was detained by stormy weather. In London he found Lord Castlereagh, with whom he went to Brighton, to be presented to the prince regent, who received him graciously, though suffering from gout. He spoke about the Princess Charlotte and his plans about her. Soon Queen Charlotte and the Princesses Augusta, Elizabeth, and Mary arrived, and in their society Princess Charlotte; her friends being mostly of the opposition, they had inspired her with the apprehension that the prince would be too subservient to the regent, and she expressed this apprehension rather warmly.

"There were no formal fiançailles, but the marriage was declared as being fully decided. The princesses left Brighton at the beginning of March for Windsor; Princess Charlotte for Cranbourn Lodge,* where she resided with the Dowager Lady Ilchester, Mrs. Campbell, Colonel Addenbrook, and Dr. Short. Prince Leopold remained at Brighton; made, however, a visit to Windsor, where Princess Charlotte came, and also at Cranbourn, which the regent did not approve.

"The marriage was to have been in April, but, after many delays, it took place on the 2d of May. The public showed the most affectionate interest. The young couple spent a fortnight at Oatlands, the Duke of York's residence. Great demonstrations took place during the summer.

"Claremont, the property of Mr. R. Ellis, was selected by Prince Leopold after having seen other places. In September the prince and princess established themselves there. Unfortunately the season was uncommonly rainy. In December a visit was paid at Brighton, when the whole family was united except the Duchess of York, who rarely went to these reunions, living generally at Oatlands. The duchess came often to Claremont, and was also frequently visited. The Orleans family came to Claremont, and were visited at Twickenham.

"The princess's health was liable to be a little deranged. Her nerves had suffered much during the last few years. She improved, however, visibly at Claremont.

"From March there began to be hopes. The princess's health was in a satisfactory state. She gave, however, up walking too much, which proved pernicious. November† saw the ruin of this happy home, and the destruction at one blow of every hope and happiness of Prince Leopold. He has never recovered the feeling of happiness which had blessed his short married life.

"The Duke of Coburg had, after some difficulty, succeeded in securing the last offspring of the house of Gotha, Princess

* In Windsor Park. One tower alone now remains, where a keeper lives.

† She died on the 5th in childbed, a few hours after the birth of a still-born son. Had she been skillfully treated her life at least would have been saved.

Louise. The Duke of Kent had offered his hand to the Princess of Leiningen, but her position as guardian of her children created delays. Princess Charlotte, who loved tenderly her uncle, the Duke of Kent, was most ardently desirous of this union, and most impatient to see it concluded. 1818 was passed in retirement by Prince Leopold, who only saw some members of the royal family. The Duke and Duchess of Kent resided most of the time at Claremont. In September Prince Leopold went by Switzerland to see his sister to Coburg, where he remained till the beginning of May, 1819, when he returned by Paris to England, where his sister had been happily confined.

"The regent was not kind to his brother. At every instant something or other of an unpleasant nature arose. The duke and duchess resided repeatedly at Claremont. Prince Leopold made in August an excursion to Scotland and through various parts of England. He received every where the most enthusiastic welcome. The regent was not pleased with this journey. The Duke and Duchess of Kent came to Claremont after the prince's return, and remained there till he went to Sidmouth, where the duke hoped to escape the winter which had set in with unusual severity, even in November, when thick ice was every where to be seen. 1820 Prince Leopold was at Lord Craven's, when the news arrived that a cold which the duke got at Salisbury, visiting the Cathedral, had become alarming. Soon after the prince's arrival the duke breathed his last.* The duchess, who lost a most amiable and devoted husband, was in a state of the greatest distress. It was fortunate that Prince Leopold had not been out of the country, as the poor duke had left his family deprived of all means of existence. The journey to Kensington was most painful, and the weather, at the same time, very severe. It had been the opinion of many people that the duchess ought, first of all, to have taken possession of Kensington. King George III. died almost at the same moment as his son. King George IV. showed himself, at the first moment, very affable to Prince Leopold, which line of conduct was in view of what might happen concerning the now Queen Caroline. The Duchess of Kent resided with

* On the 23d of January.

the princesses* a good deal at Claremont. Queen Caroline's arrival in June threw the whole country into confusion. Prince Leopold's position became unbearingly distressing between the king and the Queen Caroline. A severe illness of his mother, the Dowager Duchess of Coburg, would have given a color to his leaving England, to keep out of the painful struggle which was going on; it was much wished by the king, who employed Lord Lauderdale in this sad affair; but how abandon entirely the mother of Princess Charlotte, who, though she knew her mother well, loved her very much. The prince determined not to interfere till the evidence against the queen should be closed, so that whatever he might do could not influence the evidence. This decision was evidently the most honest and the most impartial. He waited till the evidence was closed, and then paid a visit to his mother-in-law at Brandenburg House. She received him kindly; looked very strange, and said strange things. The country was in a state of incredible excitement, and this visit was a great card for the queen. It had an effect on the Lords which it ought not to have had, as it could not change the evidence; but it is certain that many lords changed, and ministers came to the certainty that the proceedings could not be carried farther. They proposed that the measure should be given up. The king, who had been, it must be confessed, much maltreated during this sad trial, was furious, and particularly against Prince Leopold. He never forgave it, being very vindictive, though he occasionally showed kinder sentiments, particularly during Mr. Canning's being minister. He, of course, at first declared that he would never see the prince again. However, the Duke of York arranged an interview. The king could not resist his curiosity, and got Prince Leopold to tell him how Queen Caroline was dressed, and all sorts of details.

"After the coronation, in July, 1821, Prince Leopold went to Coburg. He arranged for his mother, the Duchess of Coburg, a residence for the winter at Genoa, which did benefit her health extremely. He remained some time with her, and afterward went to Florence, Rome, and Naples. In the spring of 1822 the duchess returned to Coburg. The Duke

* The infant Princess Victoria, and her eldest daughter, Princess Feodore of Leiningen, now Princess Hohenlohe.

Auguste of Gotha died during the summer. His brother, Duke Frederick, succeeded him. His health was in a most deplorable state.

"Prince Leopold went at the beginning of September to Vienna to see the Emperor Alexander. The late Lord Londonderry (Charles) did all he could to get the prince unkindly received. Prince Metternich did the same, but from other motives. He fancied the prince had intentions upon Greece, which was not the case. The Duke of Wellington arrived afterward and put a stop to Lord Londonderry's calumnies, who had wished to recommend himself by it to George IV. The prince, far too good-natured, ought to have avenged himself on Lord Londonderry.

"The prince went in October to Coburg, where he remained some time with his family, going in December to Paris, and in January to England. The Duchess of Kent and her children came to Claremont. Later in the year took place the first séjour at Ramsgate of the duchess, her children, and Prince Leopold.

"In 1824 the duchess repeatedly spent some time at Claremont.* Prince Leopold arrived too late in August to prevent some painful events at Coburg. He returned by Paris to England, where he arrived in January, 1825. At Coburg there were still the consequences of the sad events of 1824. The young princes, Ernest and Albert, prospered. The health of Prince Albert was more delicate than that of his brother. He suffered occasionally from an affection of the bronchia. The Dowager Duchess of Coburg came at the end of August to England, and the united family spent a very beautiful autumn at Claremont. Princess Victoria was then seriously unwell, and alarmed the family very much. The dowager duchess returned to the Continent at the beginning of October. The royal family lived tolerably quietly this year.

"1826. In the course of the summer Duke Frederick of Gotha died.† This created considerable discussion among the three remaining branches of Ernest the Pious's children. It was finally decided that Meiningen should receive Hildburghausen and Saalfeld — Hildburghausen, the rich and

* Note by the Queen.—These were the happiest days of the queen's childhood.

† This must be a mistake. He seems to have died in 1825. The arrangement for the division of his inheritance was only completed in 1826. See Chapters I. to III.

beautiful dukedom of Altenburg, and Coburg Gotha. The loss of Saalfeld with its very pleasant environs, on the banks of the Saal, grieved some members of the family. Gotha had, besides, the inconvenience of being entirely separated from Coburg.

"Prince Leopold went to Carlsbad for his health. He afterward spent some time at Coburg, and gave his assistance to the arrangements which resulted from this new order of things. Later in the year he went to Italy, and spent the winter at Naples. Since 1825 overtures had been made to Prince Leopold about Greece. Mr. Canning would not listen to these overtures, saying that Prince Leopold would be much more useful in England.

"At Naples Prince Leopold was dangerously ill of fever. He returned in the spring of 1827 to England. The Duchess of Kent and Princess Victoria visited Claremont, afterward Tunbridge and Ramsgate. The dowager duchess spent the winter at Genoa.

"Early in 1828 Princess Feodore married the Prince of Hohenlohe Langenburg. Prince Leopold went for a short time to Paris. Charles X. was always most kind to him. Some of the Legitimists spoke of the advantages which might result from a marriage of the Duchess de Berri with Prince Leopold, who, however, felt no partiality for their plans.

"The Duke of Coburg was much occupied with his new and splendid possession of Gotha. Prince Leopold went to Silesia to meet King Frederick Guillaume III. of Prussia. His chief object had been to see then the best friend he ever had, Prince William* of Prussia, the king's youngest brother. The then crown prince of Prussia made Prince Leopold promise to join him at Naples, which he did in November. In March, 1829, he returned by Paris to England. The propositions concerning Greece had now already taken a more prominent tournure. Russia and France were particularly favorable, and desirous to see the prince accept. In England matters were also now progressing. Great political events took place in England. The Duke of Cumberland had, at that time, great influence with the king, and opposed the Duke of Wellington's administration most bitterly. He took also a violent part in Greek affairs, engaging the king

* Maternal grandfather to Prince Louis of Hesse, husband of Princess Alice.

to prefer the candidature of Duke Charles of Mecklenburg Strelitz, the brother of the Duchess of Cumberland. Ministers pressed the king to accept Prince Leopold, and were even forced to threaten to resign. This was most unfortunate for the Greek affairs, as it rendered it impossible for Prince Leopold to press upon a cabinet that staked its existence on the question those measures which many sensible people in England thought necessary for the existence of Greece.

"Prince Metternich had from the beginning wished to ruin the young Greek state. Not succeeding in this, he used the influence he had with the duke and Lord Aberdeen to propose a frontier which was quite unacceptable, and of which . . . . ."

The king's notes break off here, but in a Memorandum which he wrote in answer to the misstatements contained in a history of these transactions, and of which he sent a copy to the Queen in 1862, he says that as the Porte had left the question of frontier entirely in the hands of the London Conference, and France and Russia were not unfavorably disposed, it might have been settled in a satisfactory manner, without serious opposition, had the English government been equally well inclined. But there seems also to have been a question of the annexation of Candia as well as of the Ionian Islands to the new Greek state. Prince Leopold himself pressed for the former, and says that in England both Parliament and the public were also in favor of the latter in case he accepted the Greek throne. The English government seems, however, to have set its face against the cession of either. The Duke of Wellington declared that Candia must belong to the possessors of the Dardanelles; and, though in the face of public opinion, the cession of the Ionian Islands could not be openly opposed, it was easy to interpose delay, which proved as effectual in defeating the proposal; for before any final decision had been come to on this point, the whole arrangement, as far as Prince Leopold was concerned, had come to an end on the question of frontier.

In the course of 1830, by a visit to Paris and great personal exertions, the prince had obtained the assent of the three Powers to a guaranteed loan of 60,000,000 of francs,* with-

* The French and Russian governments, the king says, came readily into this arrangement, that of England not without some difficulty.

out which the government of the new State of Greece (the country itself being entirely without credit) could not have been carried on. But when the frontier came to be discussed with a view to its final settlement, Lord Aberdeen, who conducted the business in the name of the English government, would admit of no modification of the line proposed by them, and which the king describes as having been utterly impossible. He had himself, with a view to a compromise which might be accepted by the Greeks, proposed a line running from the Gulf of Volo to that of Arta. But Lord Aberdeen asserted that it was a question of an arrangement to be declared, not one subject to negotiation. And as Prince Leopold had made his acceptance of the government dependent on the acceptance of the frontier line he had proposed, there was nothing left for him after this but to withdraw altogether from the affair.*

The king adds in his Memorandum that the Conference then determined upon sending out a commission to consider the question of frontier on the spot, and that, as the result of their labors, in 1831, a line such as he had himself suggested was agreed to, and is, in fact, now the northern frontier of Greece.

APPENDIX B.

CONFIRMATION OF THE PRINCES.

Coburg, April 13th, 1835.

THE confirmation of the two princes Ernest and Albert took place at Coburg on the 11th and 12th inst. Both parts of the country, Coburg as well as Gotha, would have taken the liveliest interest in this event, even if it had been celebrated quietly in the circle of the family, as the two promising young princes are looked up to with the warmest affection by all the inhabitants of the duchy. But the duke, regarding himself as the head of the great family of his subjects, wished to be surrounded by them on this joyful occasion, and to enable them to take part in his happiness. Invitations were

* The Queen well remembers her joy when this took place, as she adored her uncle, and was in despair at the thought of his departure for Greece.

consequently sent to all the authorities; and all heads of departments, as well as deputations from the Diet, the clergy, the towns, and villages attended.

On the first day, the 11th of April, the public examination of the princes took place in the "Giants' Hall" of the castle, in presence of the duke, her highness the Duchess Dowager of Gotha-Altenburg, their serene highnesses the Princes Alexander and Ernest of Würtemberg, Prince Leiningen, Princess Hohenlohe-Langenburg, and Princess Hohenlohe-Schillingsfürst. The household, the ministry, the members of the government offices, the various deputations, and a great number of persons of all classes were also present. An altar, simply but appropriately decorated, had been placed at the end of the hall. The chaplain of the court, Dr. Jacobi, who had prepared the princes for the confirmation, having taken his place before the altar, with the two princes standing to his right and left, the choir began the service by singing the first verse of the old hymn, "Come, Holy Ghost," etc. Dr. Jacobi then spoke some introductory words and proceeded to the examination. The dignified and decorous bearing of the princes, their strict attention to the questions, the frankness, decision, and correctness of their answers, produced a deep impression on the numerous assembly. Nothing was more striking in their answers than the evidence they gave of deep feeling and of inward strength of conviction.

The questions put by the examiner were not such as to be met by a simple yes or no. They were carefully considered, in order to give the audience a clear insight into the views and feelings of the young princes. One of the most touching moments was when the examiner asked the hereditary prince whether he intended steadfastly to hold to the Evangelical Church; and the Prince answered not only yes, but added in a clear and decided tone, "I and my brother are firmly resolved ever to remain faithful to the acknowledged truth." All present were deeply moved at these words, especially as they proved how sincerely he associated his brother with himself in the inmost folds of his heart. The examination, which touched on all the most important articles of the faith, having lasted for an hour, was followed by some concluding remarks of the examiner, and by a short prayer; the second verse of the above-mentioned hymn was then sung, the blessing pronounced, and the service brought to a conclusion by the singing of the third verse.

The princes stepped down from the altar and were fondly embraced by their father and by their venerable grandmother.

On the following day, Palm Sunday, the confirmation of the princes took place in the chapel of the castle. The service commenced with a chorus accompanied by the organ. A hymn followed; after which the act of confirmation was solemnly performed by the first chaplain of the court, the superintendent general, Dr. Genzler, of Coburg. The princes pronounced the Creed with firm and audible voice, and, kneeling before the altar, received the blessing. A short hymn having been sung, Dr. Genzler preached the sermon, and read the confession and the prayer of consecration. The Holy Communion was then received by the duke, the duchess dowager, the princes, a considerable number of government officers, and many inhabitants of Coburg. The whole service was performed by Dr. Genzler in the most solemn manner, and produced in all present the feeling of humility and thankfulness toward God.

At half past one o'clock a special service was performed in the Cathedral, to which the court drove in procession. The spacious church was filled with thousands of the inhabitants of the town, and of strangers, but every where devout silence was observed. The procession, having passed through the streets densely crowded with people, was received by the clergy at the principal entrance of the church. Solemn music was performed and an appropriate sermon preached by Archdeacon Henkel. This ended the solemnities on the part of the Church. In the afternoon the princely personages dined with the ducal family; the numerous strangers present dined with the household.

On the day following, April the 13th, the court received congratulations in the throne-room, and afterward a grand banquet took place in the "Giants' Hall."

His highness the duke showed his satisfaction by bestowing numerous marks of favor, especially on those who had taken part in the education and instruction of the two princes. The town of Coburg presented the tutor of the two princes, Councilor Florschütz, with a diamond ring as an acknowledgment of his services. His greatest reward, however, for having spent the best years of his life in the education of the princes, will be found in his having been able to present the pupils committed to his charge to their father, healthy and sound in body as well as in mind and heart.

One thing only caused sincere regret on this joyful occasion, viz., that her highness the duchess was prevented from being present, as she could not venture on the journey from Gotha to Coburg at this inclement season. But her best wishes undoubtedly attended her sons.

The kindness with which the people of Gotha were received by the inhabitants of Coburg deserves especial acknowledgment; but chiefly to the duke are hearty thanks due for the care taken by his highness, that their visit to Coburg should be made as agreeable as possible to his subjects of Gotha.

APPENDIX C.

THE PRINCE'S LETTERS.

To Dr. Seebode. (See *Translation*, pp. 114 *et seqq.*)

Verehrtester Herr Consistorialrath,—Trotz allen den Zerstreuungen, welche das Leben hier in Gotha uns bietet, trotz einer Anzahl von Besuchen, trotz dem Heulen des Sturmwindes, trotz dem Lärm der Wache unter unsern Fenstern, habe ich doch endlich die Disposition zu dem Aufsatze „über die Anschauungsweise der Deutschen" vollendet, und schicke sie Ihnen hierbei zur Durchsicht, mit der Bitte, die vielerlei Mängel, welche Ihr kritischer Blick ohne Zweifel entdecken wird, nicht allzu streng zu rügen. Sie erhalten meine Arbeit ohne Kopf und Schwanz. Ich habe deßhalb zu der Einleitung und dem Schluß kein Skelett entworfen, weil ich es für unnöthig hielt; ich will nämlich den Culturgang der Deutschen in dem Verlaufe der Geschichte verfolgen bis auf unsre jetzigen Zeiten, und werde mich dabei in allgemeinen Umrissen der Eintheilung bedienen, welche der Abhandlung zu Grunde liegt. Der Schluß sollte einen Rückblick auf die Mängel unserer Zeit geben und die Aufforderung enthalten, daß ein Jeder sich beeifern möge, jene Mängel zuerst aus seinem eignen Benehmen zu verbannen, und so mit dem guten Beispiele voranzugehen.

Sollte Ihnen, Herr Director, dieser Gedanke nicht gefallen, so bitte ich Sie, mir es zu schreiben, ich werde mich dann bemühen, einen andern Schluß aufzufinden.

Gotha, Febr. 5, 1836.

Verehrtester Herr Consistorialrath,—Mit großem Bedauern hörten wir von dem Unfalle, welcher Sie getroffen hat. Ich wollte es Anfangs nicht glauben, Ihr Brief jedoch bestätigte es. Ich will wünschen, daß Sie recht bald sich wieder wohl und gesund befinden mögen.

Die Arbeiten in der deutschen Literaturgeschichte gehen bei unsern Gothaischen Verhältnissen nur langsam von Statten. Empfangen Sie noch meinen herzlichsten Dank für die Correctur meines letzten Aufsatzes. Die Punkte, bei welchen Sie einige Bedenken hegen, werde ich bei der Ausführung verändern und mildern.

Der Zeitpunkt unserer Abreise nach Brüssel rückt zwar immer näher, steht aber doch noch so weit vor uns, daß wir auf jeden Fall vorher noch einmal nach Koburg kommen werden, und das wahrscheinlich gegen Ostern. Dann werden wir Sie gewiß einmal in Ihrer Behausung heimsuchen, und dort hoffentlich vollkommen wieder hergestellt antreffen.

Gotha, März 12, 1836.

Verehrtester Herr Consistorialrath,—Empfangen Sie meinen herzlichsten Dank sowohl für Ihren freundlichen Brief, als auch für das schöne Geschenk, mit welchem Sie ihn begleiteten. Sie hätten mich mit Nichts mehr erfreuen können, als mit diesem erhabenen Werke. Ich bin soeben im Begriffe es zu studiren und dem großen Klopstock in seinen Tiefen nachzudenken, was mir jedoch meist mißlingt.

Ich denke oft mit der größten Freude an die interessanten Stunden zurück, welche wir mit Ihnen in Koburg zubrachten. Gern lauschte mein Ohr Ihren Lobpreisungen deutscher Meister. Hier, wo man nur von fremder Literatur umgeben ist, nur in fremder Literatur lebt, hier lernt man den wirklichen Werth unsrer eignen deutschen erst recht kennen. Es ist jedoch schmerzlich zu sehen, welchen geringen Begriff Franzosen und Belgier und selbst die Engländer von unsrer deutschen

Literatur haben; aber man tröstet sich hierüber, wenn man bemerkt, daß diese Geringschätzung aus einer völligen Unfähigkeit, die deutschen Werke zu verstehen entstanden ist. Um Ihnen einen leisen Begriff von dieser Unfähigkeit zu geben, lege ich diesem Briefe eine französische Uebersetzung von Göthe's Faust bei, welche im eigentlichen Sinne des Worts die Haare zu Berge steigen macht. Aus solchen Arbeiten freilich können die Ausländer den tiefen Geist unsrer Literatur nicht fassen, und es ist erklärlich, warum ihnen so Manches schwach und lächerlich unter uns erscheint.

Sie werden mich für undankbar halten, daß ich Ihnen so spät auf Ihren freundlichen Brief antworte. Zu meiner Entschuldigung kann ich Ihnen nur sagen, daß die Zeit uns sehr kurz zugemessen ist, und eine sehr ausgedehnte Correspondenz noch die wenigen Augenblicke, welche uns zur freien Arbeit übrig bleiben, verschlingt. Wenn wir wirklich auch hier die Zeit mit möglichster Sorgfalt benutzen, so giebt es doch auch mancherlei Zerstreuungen, die mit einem Hofe immer unvermeidlich verbunden sind.

Unser Aufenthalt in Brüssel wird bis Ostern währen. Wohin wir dann ziehen werden, um neue Weisheit zu suchen, wissen wir noch nicht. Nach Coburg zuerst, denn dahin zieht die Liebe. Dann wahrscheinlich auf eine deutsche Universität, auf welche? ist noch unbestimmt.

In der Hoffnung, Sie recht bald wohl und heiter in der Heimath wieder zu sehen, verbleibe ich

Ihr dankbarer

Albert.

Brüssel, Dec. 18, 1836.

To the Duchess of Coburg. (See pp. 118, 122.)

London, Juni 1, 1836.

Liebe Mama—Nehme meinen und Ernst's herzlichsten Dank für Deinen lieben freundlichen Brief. Ich würde Dir schon früher geantwortet haben, wenn ich nicht mehrere Tage an einem Gallenfieber laborirend krank gewesen wäre. Das hiesige Clima, die verschiedene Küche und die späten Stunden wollen mir gar nicht zusagen; ich bin jetzt wieder ganz auf den Beinen.

Mein erster Ausgang war ein außerordentlich langes und ermüdendes, jedoch sehr interessantes Levee beim Könige; des Abends am selbigen

Tage speisten wir bei Hofe und des Nachts war ein sehr schönes Concert, bei welchem wir bis 2 Uhr zu stehen hatten. Sonnabend am folgenden Tage wurde der Geburtstag des Königs gefeiert. Wir fuhren des Mittags zu einem Drawingroom in St. James's Palace, wo an 3800 Menschen beim Könige, der Königin und den übrigen hohen Herrschaften vorbeidefilirten, um ihre Glückwünsche darzubringen. Des Abends war wiederum große Tafel und dann Concert bis um 1 Uhr. Daß ich bei diesen nächtlichen Freuden manchen harten Kampf mit dem Schlafe zu bestehen habe, kannst Du Dir wohl denken. Vorgestern, am Montag, gab die Tante hier in Kensington einen außerordentlich glänzenden Ball, bei welchem die Herrn in Uniform und die Damen in sogenannten Fancy-dresses erschienen; wir blieben bis um 4 Uhr. Von den Gästen werden Dir vielleicht interessant sein—der Herzog Wilhelm von Braunschweig, der Prinz von Oranien mit seinen beiden Söhnen, der Herzog von Wellington, zc. — Gestern waren wir in Sion beim Herzog von Northumberland und jetzt wollen wir nach Claremont fahren.

Du wirst daran sehen, daß wir unsere Zeit sehr zusammen nehmen müssen, nur um einiges von den Merkwürdigkeiten London's zu sehen.

Die liebe Tante ist sehr gütig gegen uns, und thut alles, was uns nur irgend Freude machen kann; auch die Cousine ist außerordentlich freundlich mit uns. Wir wohnen hier zwar etwas beschränkt; aber doch sehr angenehm. — Ich hoffe Dir aus Brüssel ausführlichern Bericht abzustatten.

Brüssel, 30sten Juni 1836.

Liebe Mama — Ich benutze die Gelegenheit, daß Papa zurück nach Koburg geht, um Dir endlich einmal wieder zu schreiben. Wenn ich in Paris nur irgend Zeit dazu gehabt hätte, so würde ich Dir von dort aus schon einige Zeilen gesandt haben. Das Hotel des Princes, in welchem wir in Paris wohnten, war für uns alle ein fürchterlicher Aufenthaltsort, da man vor Lärm auf der Straße kaum sein eignes Wort verstehen konnte. Ernst Würtemberg hatte kurz vorher in demselben Hause gewohnt. Während unsres Aufenthaltes in Paris haben wir nicht nur die Stadt und ihre Merkwürdigkeiten kennen gelernt, sondern haben auch mehrere sehr hübsche Ausflüge in die nähern Umgebungen gemacht. Wir besuchten St. Cloud, Meudon, Montmorency, Neuilly, Versailles,

T r i a n o n, 2c., und bewunderten überall die herrliche Gegend, in welcher Paris liegt. Bei Hof wurden wir mit der allergrößten Artigkeit und Höflichkeit empfangen, und wir müssen alle im höchsten Grade dem großen Lobe beipflichten, das man der königlichen Familie zollt.

Nun, nach allen Fatiguen und allen Zerstreuungen sind wir in eine neue Heimath eingezogen, und sind froh ein geregeltes, ruhigeres Leben wieder führen zu können. Wir bewohnen ein kleines, aber recht freundliches Haus, mit einem kleinen Gärtchen davor, und sind hier obgleich in einer großen Stadt, doch ganz abgeschieden von dem Lärmen der Straßen.

Die Lehrer, welche für uns bestimmt sind, sollen ganz vortrefflich sein, so daß sich alles vereint, um unsere Studien zu fördern, denn an unserm Fleiß wird es hoffentlich nicht fehlen. Onkel Leopold wird erst am 15ten hier eintreffen; bis er kommt, wird alles schon im besten Gange sein. Wir haben uns bis jetzt schon vollkommen eingerichtet, werden die nächsten Tage zu den nöthigen Visiten verwenden, und dann in der nächsten Woche unser neues Leben beginnen.

Wenn Du diese Zeilen erhalten wirst, stehest Du auch gerade im Begriff ein neues Leben zu beginnen. Deine Reise nach dem Seebade, hörte ich, willst Du am 10ten schon antreten. Ich wünsche, daß diese Cur Dich in allem zufrieden stellen möge. Mir hat die Reise nach England einen totalen Abscheu gegen die See verursacht, so daß ich gar nicht gern nur daran denke.

To the Duke of Coburg. (See pp. 124, 131, 138.)

Brüssel, am 15ten August 1836.

Wir begleiteten den Onkel ins Lager von Beverloo, ein Lager welches in einer ungeheuren Ebene liegt, auf welcher in zehn Stunden Umfang kein Haus zu sehen ist. Das Lager selbst mag eine Stunde im Umfang haben, und ist mit der allergrößten Eleganz erbaut, die Baracken und Ställe werden besser eingerichtet, als in den meisten Casernen der Fall ist. Wir hatten zur Wohnung eine recht hübsche kleine Baracke, neben der Königlichen, auf welcher eine belgische und eine sächsische Flagge wehte. Alle Tage war ein anderes militairisches Schauspiel zu sehen, unter welchen sich aber besonders zwei Manöver auszeichneten. Besonders das zweite war außerordentlich schön, und soll dem Ausspruche aller erfahrenen Officiere nach, ein treues Bild des wirklichen Krieges gewesen sein.—Die gewinnende Armee wurde von den Generälen Goetals, Magnan und Marneff commandirt, die verlierende von den Generälen d'Olivier und Lime; weil diese aber aus ihrer bedrängten Lage sich nicht zu helfen wußten, leitete der Onkel selbst den Rückzug.—Nach den ermüdenden Parthien unterhielten sich die Soldaten mit verschiedenen Spielen, bei welchen wir zugegen waren, wie Wettläufe, Klettern auf hohen Stangen, Sackhüpfen, Fechten, Ringen, 2c.,—in welchen sie viel Geschicklichkeit zeigten. Im Ganzen zeigten sich die Truppen auf eine so vortheilhafte Weise, daß wir alle darüber erstaunt waren. — Gegen Abend war zuweilen eine vortreffliche Musik, zusammengesetzt aus allen Regimentsmusiken, in welcher an 160 Musiker mitwirkten.

Bonn, 30sten Juli 1837.

Lieber Papa—. . . . . Onkel Leopold hat mir sehr viel über England und das Treiben daselbst geschrieben. So sehr sich im Lobe der jungen Königin alle Partheien vereinigen, so sehr intriguiren und manövriren sie mit und gegen einander. Die Kabalen und Intriguen sollen sich von allen Seiten her durchkreuzen und gegen einander ankämpfen. Alle Partheien sollen in unverständigem Wesen gegen einander stehen! . . . .

Bonn, 12 November 1837.

Lieber Papa—. . . Das vorige Semester war uns verflossen, noch ehe wir recht daran denken konnten. In das neue haben wir uns schon ganz gestürzt.

Dieser Winter wird für uns ein angestrengter werden (da wir mit Collegien und Ausarbeitungen ganz überhäuft sind). Hauptgegenstand unserer jetzigen Beschäftigungen ist das Römische Recht, das Staatsrecht, und die Staatswissenschaftslehre, mit Finanzwissenschaft.

Daneben hören wir noch zwei historische Collegien bei Löbell und A. W. von Schlegel, und ein philosophisches bei Fichte (Anthropologie und Philosophie), und werden zugleich an unserm Eifer von den neueren Sprachen nicht ablassen.

An die verwittwete Herzogin von Sachsen-Gotha.

(See p. 139.)

Bonn, 19ten November 1837.

Vorgestern erhielt ich einen Brief von Onkel Leopold, in welchem er den Wunsch ausspricht, uns in der Weihnachtswoche in welcher keine Collegien gehalten werden, bei sich in Brüssel zu sehen. Du wirst Dir leicht denken können, liebe Großmama, wie sehr uns dieser kleine Besuch freut. Mir ist es darum besonders angenehm, weil wir nun deutlicher auch des Onkels Meinung über die uns bevorstehende Trennung unserer Einheit im kommenden Frühjahre hören können, und ihm dann auch die unsrige expliciren können.

Jener Moment steht in seiner trüben Gestalt ganz vor mir. Darum wollen wir, so lange es noch Zeit ist, alles thun um ihn uns zu erleichtern, um die Pille zu vergolden.

To the Duke of Coburg. (See p. 139.)

Bonn, 24sten November 1837.

Lieber Papa—Das Thema, welches jetzt hier und in der Umgegend die ganze Welt beschäftigt, ist die Gefangennehmung des Erzbischofs von Köln. Die Katholische Partei ist ganz wüthend, und droht allen Preußen und Protestanten den Tod und den Untergang. Gestern, am Clemenstage, erwartete man einen Aufstand in Aachen und Köln; aber es scheint, daß aus Furcht vor militärischen Ausrüstungen Alles ruhig geblieben ist.

Du wirst wissen, wie sich der Erzbischof in Bezug auf die Hermesianischen Lehren gegen die Universität Bonn benommen hat, daß er den Professoren verboten hat zu lesen, daß er das hiesige Seminarium aufgelöst hat, und offnen Krieg gegen die Preußische Regierung geführt.

Hierauf hat der König den Minister Rochow nach Köln geschickt, um mit dem Erzbischofe zu unterhandeln, welcher jenen jedoch nicht aufnahm, und auch keinem Professoren oder Geistlichen erlaubte vor ihm seine Grundsätze zu rechtfertigen.

Neuerdings widersetzte sich der Erzbischof offen gegen die Einsegnung der gemischten Ehen, wenn nicht alle Kinder katholisch werden sollten.

Einer Aufforderung seine Stelle niederzulegen, von Seiten des Königs, erwiderte er, der König habe in Geistlichen Angelegenheiten gar keine Stimme, worauf denn die geheime Verhaftung und nächtliche Entführung des Erzbischofs erfolgte.

Ein reicher angesehener Katholik hier äußerte :—„Man muß mit „uns regieren, denn gegen uns kann man nicht regieren, es muß noch „so weit kommen als es in Belgien ist; nehmen sich die Preußen in „Acht, daß sie nicht mit Dreschflegeln aus dem Lande gejagt werden."

To the Dowager Duchess of Gotha. (See p. 141.)

Bonn, am 26sten December 1837.

Liebe Großmama—Tausend tausend Dank für das schöne Weihnachtsgeschenk, welches mir der Herr Rath in Deinem Namen bescheerte. Wenn man an einem solchen Tage so weit getrennt von der Heimath und den Seinigen ist, so ist es überaus wohlthuend durch ein Andenken in ihren Kreis zurückgerufen zu werden. In Gedanken ging ich alle verflossenen Weihnachtsabende durch, deren wir die meisten bei Dir verlebten, und von Dir immer so glänzend beschenkt wurden. Doch auch an diesem Weihnachtsabend war ich in Deiner Nähe, wenigstens im Geiste.

Das Glas ist wirklich ganz wunderschön und mit der hübschen Weste hoffe ich mich bald zu schmücken.

Wir gedachten, wie Du weißt, liebe Großmama, die Weinachtswoche in Brüssel zu verleben, daran hat uns mein einfältiges Knie verhindert, welches zwar fast ganz wieder heil ist, aber noch nicht stark genug ist, eine ähnliche Reise und die dortigen Anstrengungen ohne Folgen auszuhalten. Es thut uns außerordentlich leid auf diese Freude verzichten zu müssen. Doch, auf der andern Seite, haben wir nun um so mehr Zeit und Muße die Collegien und Arbeiten zu repetiren und die ruhige Erholung meines Fußes abzuwarten.

Zugleich, liebe Großmama, erlaube mir Dir meine herzlichsten Glückwünsche zu Füßen zu legen. Möge aller Segen des Himmels auch im kommenden Jahre auf Dir ruhen. Möge der Himmel Dir stets Gesundheit und ungetrübte Heiterkeit verleihen. Mir erhalte auch im nächsten Jahre die Liebe und das Wohlwollen deren ich mich jetzt erfreute.

Noch bin ich Dir vielen Dank für zwei Briefe schuldig, die ich bis jetzt nicht beantworten konnte,, da vor herankommenden Ferien, die Arbeiten sich so häufen, daß sie den ganzen Tag in Anspruch nehmen.

Wie freute es mich zu hören daß Du wieder vollkommen wohl und gesund bist.

Von dem lieben Bonn habe ich Dir nichts zu erzählen. Der Streit der Meinungen über die hannövrischen Angelegenheiten und die mit dem Erzbischof von Köln, bilden den Mittelpunkt und Wunderpunkt der hiesigen Conversationen.

Nun lebe wohl, liebe Großmama, und behalte in liebevollem Andenken

Deinen treuen Enkel,

Albert.

To the Duke of Coburg. (See p. 142.)

26sten December 1837.

Wir gedachten Deinen Geburtstag in Brüssel mit dem lieben Onkel zu feiern; allein der einfältige Stoß an mein Knie hat uns um diese Freude gebracht. Ich bin zwar wieder total hergestellt, aber muß doch noch das Bein etwas schonen, und hätte einerseits darum auch den Fatiguen Brüssel's mich nicht unterziehen können, anderseits wollte ich auch dort nicht als Hinkender herumsteigen. Wir sind darum im stillen Bonn geblieben, wo wir mit der Repetition der Collegien beschäftigt sind. . . . Du wirst auch bestimmt Antheil an den Cölner Ereignissen genommen haben. Hier ist es die Lebensfrage geworden und zeigt sich sehr deutlich, daß die vielgepriesene Anhänglichkeit der Rheinlande erstaunlich locker ist. „Preuß und Lutherischer Ketzer" sind gewöhnliche Schimpfreden. Wie es scheint, ist die Priesterpartei außerordentlich stark; sie findet ihre Hauptstütze in dem Adel und den Landleuten. Namentlich der Adel ist hier sehr bigott.

Dein treuer Sohn

Albert.

To the Dowager Duchess of Gotha. (See p. 151.)

Liebe Großmama—Ich habe schon wieder lange gesäumt ehe ich Dir schreibe; aber wenn man ein Mal im Nichtsthun sich vertieft hat, so ist es schwer daraus sich hervorzuarbeiten.

Aus Deinem lieben Brief an Ernst ersah ich, daß es mit Deinem Befinden doch besser geht und daß Du in Deinem schönen jetzt wieder mit neuem Glanze gezierten Winterpalais eingezogen bist. Wie vergänglich solcher Glanz ist, haben wir gestern recht deutlich empfunden, wo wenn Gott seine schirmende Hand nicht über uns gehalten hätte, wohl das ganze Schloß ein Raub der Flammen geworden wäre, und wir beide in keiner Weise hätten entrinnen können.

Alle Morgen wird in unsren Stuben etwas geheizt, damit wenn wir zuweilen des Mittags in die Stadt kommen wir nicht ganz kalte Zimmer finden. Zufälliger Weise waren wir vorgestern Abend nach dem Theater in der Stadt geblieben, um uns bei dem Zurückfahren auf die Rosenau nicht zu erkälten. Am andern Morgen erwachte ich von einem unangenehmen Geruche; ich sprang aus dem Bette, um zu sehen ob nicht an einem der Oefen vielleicht vergessen worden war die Klappe aufzumachen; ein immer dickerer Rauch kam mir entgegen, doch konnte ich nichts entdecken; als ich in die vierte Stube kam schlugen mir die hellen Flammen entgegen, sie stand ganz in Feuer. Ich schrie Feuer! Feuer! worauf Ernst und Kart aus seinem Zimmer zu Hülfe kam. Außer uns Dreien war keine Seele in dem Flügel des Schlosses, es war auch zu früh daß auch Niemand in der Nachbarschaft auf war. Du kannst Dir unsern Schrecken denken. Wir hielten nicht lange Rath, sondern schlossen alle Thüren zu, und sperrten uns mit dem Feuer ein. Es standen uns nur zwei Krüge mit Wasser und eine Kanne mit Camillenthee zu Gebote, die wir nach Möglichkeit verwendeten. Ernst ergriff meinen und seinen Mantel und warf sie oben auf die Flammen, ich trug mein ganzes Bett herbei und große Decken und Matratzen gegen die brennende Wand, Kart schwang mit einer unglaublichen Kraft einen marmornen Tisch in die Höhe und schleuderte ihn auf ein in Flammen stehendes Bücherbrett, welches hierauf in sich zusammenstürzte. Nachdem wir in dieser Weise Herr über das Feuer geworden waren, konnten wir erst daran denken um weitere Hülfe zu flehen.

Ernst stürzte wie er aus dem Bette gekommen war die Treppen hinunter zur Schildwache, die nun den Feuerruf erschallen ließ, während ich und Kart noch oben arbeiteten; die Hitze und der Qualm waren so ungeheuer, daß alle Fenster hinaus geplatzt waren, daß selbst die Gläser die auf Bildern unter Rahmen standen sprangen, und die Bilder hinein gedrückt waren, daß der Firniß an der Thüre ganz verkohlt ist.

Jetzt kam eiligst Hülfe von allen Seiten, eine Menge von Arbeitern kamen mit Wasser herauf und löschten die nur gedämpfte Gluth. Verbrannt sind ein Bücherbrett mit vielen Büchern und unseren sämmtlichen Kupferstichen, zwei Stühle, ein Tisch, ein Spiegel, 2c.

Es ist weiter gar kein Unglück geschehen als daß Kart und ich uns die Fußsohlen verbrannt haben, da wir barfuß in Kohlen gerathen waren.

Das Unglück war dadurch entstanden daß ein unkundiger Einheitzer in einem Ofen geheizt hatte welcher nicht dazu bestimmt war, und auf welchem Bücher und Kupferstiche standen, gegen den eine Menge von Mappen gelehnt waren. Das einzige Bild welches unversehrt geblieben ist, ist eine Abbildung von dem Brand des Palais in Gotha.

Nun lebe wodl, liebe Großmama. Erhalte Deine Liebe

Deinem treuen Enkel,

Albert.

Rosenau, am 18ten Oct. 1838.

P.S.—Das versprochene Gemälde werde ich bald abschicken können.

To Prince William of Löwenstein. (See p. 154.)

Koburg, 26ten October 1838.

Lieber Löwenstein—Empfange tausend tausend Dank für Deine lieben, freundlichen Zeilen, die uns ein Zeichen sind, daß Du noch zuweilen Deiner treuen Freunde gedenkst. Ich glaube, für immer werden mir die heitern Tage, welche wir zusammen theils in nützlicher Beschäftigung, theils in froher Unterhaltung zubrachten, als die glücklichsten meines Lebens erscheinen. Trotz der großen Ungenirtheit und den vielen Neckereien herrschte stets die vollkommenste Harmonie. Wie schön waren unsre Winterconzerte, unsre theatralischen Versuche, Spaziergänge nach dem Venusberg, die Schwimmbahn, der Fechtboden! Ich darf gar nicht an Alles zurückdenken!

Ernst geht nun nach Dresden, um sich dort dem Mars zu opfern, er will sich dort ganz in's militairische Wesen stürzen. Meine italienische Reise werde ich in Kurzem beginnen. Ich werde Dir zuweilen von verschiedenen Punkten aus, Nachricht geben; Du mußt mir aber auch schreiben, ich will Dir immer Punkte angeben, wohin. In 10 bis 12 Tagen werde ich schon die Heimath im Rücken haben. Ich will nicht eher abreisen, als bis auch Ernst sein Schiff flott macht, damit er nicht allein zurückbleibt: die Trennung wird uns fürchterlich schwer werden; wir waren bis jetzt, so lange wir denken können, keiner noch einen Tag ohne den andern. Ich mag mir den Augenblick gar nicht vergegenwärtigen.

TO THE DOWAGER DUCHESS OF GOTHA. (See p. 156.)

Jetzt bin ich ganz allein. Ernst ist über alle Berge, ich bin zurückgeblieben und noch umgeben von so vielen Dingen die mir immer vorspiegeln, er müsse in der Nebenstube sein. Zu wem kann ich mich besser wenden und meinem Herzen Luft machen, als zu Dir, liebe Großmama, die Du immer so vielen Antheil nimmst an Allem was uns begegnet; die Du uns beide auch so ganz kennst und verstehst. Wir begleiteten Ernst noch bis nach Lobenstein, wo wir noch einen Abend und den folgenden Morgen zusammen bei der guten alten Großtante zubrachten. Sie war sehr erfreut uns wieder einmal bei sich zu sehen, vielleicht zum letzten Male; denn sie ist schon 80 Jahre alt, und sehr kränklich geworden; auch die beiden Cousinen waren sehr freundlich gegen uns. Wir waren noch den Abend recht vergnügt. Der andere Morgen brachte dann den Schmerz des Abschieds. Wir blieben nur noch bis Mittag und fuhren dann (dießmal ohne Ernst) wieder der Heimath zu, wo wir fast zu Eis gefroren, Abends um 10 Uhr anlangten. Wir waren, wie gewöhnlich, wieder auf einer offnen Droschke gefahren und hatten in dem lieblichen Frankenwalde eine Kälte von 16 Graden zu überstehen. Nunmehr hat Ernst die erste Nacht in Dresden durchschlafen. Es wird ihm der heutige Tag doch auch etwas leer vorkommen. Ich schrieb ihm heute und erwarte morgen oder übermorgen ein paar Zeilen von ihm, ich will sie Dir sogleich zuschicken, wenn es Dir recht ist.

Wenn ich Dir lange nicht schrieb, so geschah es, weil wir in den letzten Tagen wirklich noch sehr Vieles zu besprechen und zu besorgen hatten. Du wirst es mir bestimmt nicht übel nehmen. Das „Wir" werde ich mir nun wohl abgewöhnen müssen und mich immer des so egoistisch und kalt lautenden Ich's bedienen müssen. In Wir klang Alles viel weicher, denn das Wir drückt die Harmonie mehrerer Seelen aus, das Ich drückt mehr den Widerstand des Einzelnen gegen die äußeren Kräfte aus, jedoch auch das Vertrauen auf eigene Stärke.

Ich muß fürchten, Dich mit meinem Geschwätz zu langweilen, doch ist es mir bei der jetzigen Stille eine Wohlthat schwätzen zu können.

Koburg, am 29 Novbr. 1838.

Tausend Dank für Deinen letzten gnädigen, so liebevollen Brief. Wie wohl thut es zu wissen, daß Jemand die Gefühle die uns beseelen mitfühlt. Ich habe einen Brief von Ernst erhalten, da er aber früheren Datums ist als der Deinige, so sende ich ihn Dir nicht. Es hat mir viele Freude gemacht so öfters von ihm zu hören.

Koburg, am 5ten Decbr. 1838.

To Prince William of Löwenstein. (See p. 166.)

Florenz, 25sten Februar 1839.

Lieber Löwenstein.—Schon längst drängte es mich Dir ein Paar Zeilen zu schreiben und Dir für Deinen lieben Brief vom 3. Januar zu danken, den ich von Gotha zugeschickt erhielt; allein Du weißt, daß die besten Vorsätze immer am seltensten ausgeführt werden; so komme ich denn recht spät.

Ach, Florenz, wo ich mich seit zwei Monaten aufhalte, vereinigt herrliche Kunstschätze in sich; ich bin oft ganz trunken von Genuß, wenn ich aus einer der Galerien komme. Auch die Gegend um Florenz hat außerordentliche Reize. Ich habe mich die Zeit her ganz in den Strudel der Gesellschaften gestürzt. Ich habe getanzt, dinirt, suppirt, Complimente gemacht, mich und mir präsentiren lassen, französisch und englisch parlirt, alle Phrasen über das Wetter erschöpft, den Liebenswürdigen gespielt, kurz "*bonne mine à mauvais jeu*" gemacht. Du kennst meine Passion für dergleichen, mußt also meine Charakterstärke bewundern, daß ich mich nie entschuldigt habe, nie vor 5 Uhr des Morgens in meine Behausung zurückgekehrt, den Carnevalsbecher bis auf den Boden geleert habe.

Mein Verweilen in Florenz wird nicht mehr lange währen. Ich gehe am 10. März nach Rom, wo ich 3 Wochen bleiben werde; dann eile ich Neapel zu, und vor dem Eintritt der allzugroßen Hitze suche ich wieder die weißen Häupter der Alpen im Gesicht zu haben.

Nun muß ich Dir wieder Lebewohl sagen, lieber Löwenstein.

To the Duke of Coburg. (See pp. 167 *et seqq.*)

Rom, 17ten März 1839.

Gestern Abend sind wir in dem weltberühmten Rom angekommen; ich setzte mich sogleich nieder, um Dir Nachricht davon zu geben.

Wir haben 4 Tage zu unserer Reise hierher verwendet, da wir einige merkwürdige Punkte der Gegend noch besahen, wie den berühmten Wasserfall bei Terni, der wirklich großartiger ist, als man irgend etwas in der Schweiz sieht, den See Trasimene, die Brücke des Augustus bei Narni, &c. Gestern habe ich noch mit Mr. Seymour einen Spaziergang durch die Straßen Rom's gemacht; es fällt mir entsetzlich schwer mich zu überzeugen, daß ich in Rom bin; es könnte—einige prachtvolle Paläste abgerechnet—eben so gut jede Stadt Deutschlands sein.

Ich glaube, daß wir bis gegen den 1. April alles Sehenswürdige hier gesehen haben werden, und dann in den ersten Tagen des nächsten Monats unsere Reise nach Neapel fortsetzen können . . .

Rom, 31sten März 1839.

. . . Einen einzigen Moment nehme ich aus; das ist der, in welchem der Papst vom Balcon des Vaticans herab dem in Massen zuströmenden Volke die Benediction ertheilt; es geschieht unter Glockengeläute, Kanonendonner von der Engelsburg und militairischer Musik. Das ist wirklich eine ergreifende Scene. Der Rest ist gar zu lang und gedehnt, und gibt zu sehr das Bild vom Götzendienst. Am vergangenen Dienstag habe ich die Ehre gehabt seiner Heiligkeit aufzuwarten. Der alte Herr war sehr freundlich und höflich. Ich blieb fast eine halbe Stunde bei ihm in einer kleinen Stube eingeschlossen, wir unterhielten uns auf Italienisch über den Einfluß der Aegyptier auf die griechische Kunst, und dieser auf die römische. Der Papst behauptete die Etrusker hätten den Griechen als Vorbilder gedient. Trotz seiner Infallibilität, wagte ich es zu behaupten, daß dieses Volk seine Kunst erst von den Aegyptiern entnommen habe.

Neapel, am 11ten April 1839.

. . . Ich bin nun ohngefähr 5 Tage hier und mit dem Sehen der inneren Merkwürdigkeiten beschäftigt, deren Neapel nicht viele aufzuweisen hat. Man ist hier auf die schöne Natur angewiesen, die auch wirklich reizend sein muß. Noch habe ich sie nicht recht genießen können, da ihr der südliche Anstrich ganz abgeht; die Berge und selbst der Vesuv sind mit Schnee bedeckt, und Himmel und Meer so grau und düster, daß man sich an die Nordsee versetzt glaubt. Man erwartet zum Mondwechsel, welcher in wenigen Tagen eintritt, das Beste. Vorgestern habe ich mich dem Könige und der Königin präsentiren lassen. . . .

Neapel, am 25ten April 1839.

Nehme tausend Dank für Deinen letzten Brief, der mich von Deinen Reiseplänen in Kenntniß setzt. Ich reise morgen frühe von Neapel ab, und werde nun Schritt für Schritt, doch ohne einen längeren Aufenthalt an irgend einem Orte zu machen, an der Westküste Italiens hinaufwandern, und gedenke dann gegen Ende des nächsten Monats in Turin zu sein. Wie sehr wird es mich freuen Dich auf dem Boden Italiens oder in den Schweizer Bergen wieder zu sehen! Du wirst auf jeden Fall in Mailand einen Brief von mir vorfinden, "poste restante," in welchem ich meinen näheren Reisebericht abstatten werde.

Mein Aufenthalt in Neapel war äußerst interessant, ich habe ihn auch recht benutzt um Alles zu sehen. Was mich besonders angesprochen hat ist Pompeji, ein durch und durch merkwürdiger Punkt. Von den umliegenden schönsten Theilen der Gegend habe ich den Vesuv, Pästum, Sorrent und die Insel Capri besucht.

Pisa, am 5ten Mai 1839.

Ich schreibe diese Zeilen in der Hoffnung, daß sie Dich gesund und wohlbehalten in Mailand treffen mögen, um Dir Rapport über unseren Reisezustand abzustatten. Wir haben Neapel am 26sten verlassen und sind direct nach Rom gegangen, wo ich mich 2 Tage aufhielt, den e i n e n, um noch eine allgemeine Uebersicht der Sachen zu bekommen, die ich während meines längeren Aufenthalts daselbst im Einzelnen gesehen hatte; den a n d e r n, um Tivoli zu sehen. Wir sind nun über Viterbo und Siena direct hierher, ohne Florenz zu berühren. Heute werde ich hier bleiben, morgen nach Livorno gehen und wieder hierher zurückkommen, dann werde ich über Lucca nach Genua meinen Weg nehmen, wo ich also gegen den 9ten anlangen werde. Mein Aufenthalt daselbst wird sich auf 2 bis 3 Tage beschränken, so daß ich bestimmt am 13ten dort abreisen werde. Dann werde ich auf der Straße von Novi dem Norden zusteuern. Erhalte ich bis dahin von Dir bestimmte Nachricht aus Mailand, so werde ich mich beeilen dort einzutreffen. Höre ich nichts bestimmtes, so werde ich nach Turin gehen, um mich dort einige Tage aufzuhalten. Dann würde ich über den Bernhard und Lausanne nach Bern mich wenden, und Dich dort auf alle Fälle erwarten.

TO PRINCE WILLIAM OF LÖWENSTEIN. (See p. 172.)

Koburg, 30sten Juni 1839.

Lieber Löwenstein,—Du hast mir durch Deine lieben Zeilen aus Berlin große Freude gemacht, denn ich hatte recht lange gar nichts von Dir gehört. Du bist also wohl und vergnügt und trägst Dein Schicksal, Bewohner der Berliner Sandsteppe zu sein, mit viel Fassung und Geduld! Uebrigens kann ich mir denken, daß die Universität und die vielen ausgezeichneten und berühmten Männer, welche daran wirken, eine reichliche Entschädigung bieten. Wenn ich das Wort Universität ausspreche, und mich dabei aller der guten Vorsätze erinnere, die ich dort mir vorhielt, so schäme ich mich fast meines jetzigen Lebens, welches doch hauptsächlich in einem Herumschleudern und Complimenten Machen besteht. Doch muß ich gestehen, daß diese letzte italienische Reise von großem Nutzen für mich war; sie hat nicht sowohl im Einzelnen, als durch ihren Gesammteindruck auf mich gewirkt. Mein Gesichtskreis hat sich fast um das Doppelte erweitert und das richtige Urtheil wird sehr davon unterstützt, gesehen zu haben. Italien ist wirklich ein höchst interessantes Land und unerschöpfliche Quelle der Belehrung; von dem Genuß jedoch, den man sich von dort verspricht, bekommt man außerordentlich wenig zu kosten. Das Land bleibt in vielen, vielen Beziehungen weit hinter dem zurück, was man davon erwartet. Das Klima, die Gegend, das Kunststreben sind Dinge, in denen man sich sehr unangenehm getäuscht fühlt.

Mein Leben im Ganzen war höchst angenehm. Die Gesellschaft eines so höchst ausgezeichneten Mannes, wie des Herrn von Stockmar, war mir sehr theuer und werth, dann begleitete mich auch ein junger, sehr liebenswürdiger Engländer, Mr. Seymour, mit dem ich sehr vertraut wurde. Ueberhaupt herrschte unter uns eine völlige Harmonie, was so nothwendig ist, um das Leben irgend genießen zu können.

Am 21. Juni feierten wir hier Ernst's Geburtstag, und zwar seinen 21sten, an welchem er mündig wurde. Ich hatte die große Freude, auch am selben Tage, durch ein Ministerialpatent volljährig erklärt zu werden, und bin nun Herr über mich selbst, was ich hoffe stets und in jeder Beziehung zu sein. In Folge dieses Ereignisses hatten wir hier große Feste, an welchen das ganze Land mit viel Herzlichkeit Theil nahm.

Am 13. werde ich Ernst nach Dresden begleiten und ungefähr 14 Tage bei ihm bleiben; dann muß ich nach einem mir bis in den Tod verhaßten Ort, das liebenswürdige Karlsbad, wo Papa die Kur braucht und sehr wünscht mich um sich zu haben. Hoffentlich wird dieser Feldzug bis Mitte Augusts beendet sein.

Daß ich mich sehr gefreut habe, Ernst und das liebe Koburg wieder zu sehen, kannst Du Dir wohl denken. Herrn Rath habe ich verheirathet wiedergefunden; Wiechmann fand ich in Genf, bei meiner Tante, der Großfürstin. Ach! könnte ich Dir einmal bald irgend wo über den Weg rennen; es würde mich sehr freuen nur ein Paar Stunden mit Dir zusammen sein zu können. In diesen Gedanken vertieft schwätze ich Dir ein Paar Stunden weg und bedenke nicht, daß Du mehr zu thun hast als mein Geschmier zu lesen! Darum ein kurzer Abschied! Lasse bald von Dir hören und vergiß nicht

Deinen, 2c. 2c.

TO CONCERT-MASTER SPAETH. (See p. 175.)

Mein bester Herr Conzertmeister,—Sie werden durch den Geheimen Assistenzrath Florschütz die letzte Sendung der Beiträge zu dem Singverein erhalten haben, welche ich noch in Gotha eintrieb.

Heute schicke ich Ihnen den ersehnten, heißgeliebten Preis der Tonkunst von Beethoven. Er war hier nur stückweise zu haben, weshalb ich erst nach Leipzig schreiben lassen mußte, darum erhalten Sie auch die Musikalien erst jetzt. Die ausgesetzten Instrumentalstimmen sind dabei und durch einen glücklichen Irrthum der Handlung die Singstimmen sogar doppelt. Das Ganze kommt doch theurer, als ich es Anfangs glaubte, es wird sich die Summe ohngefähr anf 60 Gulden belaufen; das zeigt, daß wir mit unsren Fonds keine sehr greßen Acquisitionen werden machen können. Diese Cantate können Sie nun der Bibliothek des Singvereins einverleiben, nur den Klavierauszug würde ich mir wieder zurückerbitten, wenn das Conzert vorüber sein sollte.

Ich melde mich zu der Solo=Baß=Stimme in der Cantate, die, wenn sie auch nicht bedeutend ist, mir doch recht interessant erscheint. erscheint. Zwei Soprane gut zu besetzen wird Ihnen vielleicht einige Mühe machen. Zu der obligaten Violinstimne, die ausgezeichnet schön ist, wird sich Eichhorn sehr gut eignen.

Nun leben Sie wohl, bester Herr Conzertmeister, lassen Sie mir doch nach Karlsbad einige Nachricht über die Proben des Händel und Nencini zukommen.

Immer Ihr Ihnen gewogner

Albert.

Dresden, am 23sten Juli 1839.

To Baron Stockmar. (See pp. 187, 193.)

Ich schreibe Ihnen heute an einem glücklichsten Tage meines Lebens und die freudigste Nachricht, die ich Ihnen mittheilen kann . . . Sie ist so gut und freundlich gegen mich, daß ich oft gar nicht glauben kann, daß mir solche Herzlichkeit werden soll. Ich weiß, Sie nehmen Theil an meinem Glück, darum schütte ich mein Herz vor Ihnen aus! . . . Mehr und ernster kann ich Ihnen nicht schreiben, dazu bin ich in diesem Augenblick zu confus; denn

„Das Auge sieht den Himmel offen,
„Es schwimmt das Herz in Seligkeit." .

Windsor, 16. Oktober 1839.

Bester Herr von Stockmar,—Haben Sie tausend, tausend Dank für Ihren so lieben, freundlichen Brief. Ich dachte mir, Sie würden bestimmt vielen Antheil an einem Gegenstande nehmen, der für mich so wichtig ist, den Sie vorbereiteten. Ihre Voraussage hat eingetroffen; der Event hat uns überrascht, ehe wir ihn erwarten konnten und nun thut es mir doppelt leid, daß ich den letzten Sommer, den ich noch zu vielen nützlichen Vorbereitungen hätte anwenden können, durch verwandtschaftliche Rücksichten und die widersprechende Ansicht derer, die auf die Eintheilung meines Lebens wirkten, verloren habe. Ihre freundschaftlichen, wohlwollenden Rathschläge zur wahren Begründung meines zukünftigen Glücks habe ich recht beherzigt und sie stimmen ganz mit den Grundsätzen überein, die ich im Stillen mir darüber gemacht habe. Eine Persönlichkeit, ein Charakter, der die Achtung, die Liebe und das Vertrauen der Königin und der Nation erweckt, muß die Grundlage der Stellung sein. Jene Persönlichkeit bürgt für die Gesinnung, die den Handlungen zu Grunde liegt, und sollten auch Mißgriffe geschehen, so werden sie leichter jener Persönlichkeit zu gute gehalten, als oft die großartigsten schönsten Unternehmungen eines Mannes unterstützt werden, zu dem man Vertrauen zu fassen nicht im Stande ist. Bin ich also ein edler Fürst im eigentlichsten Sinne des Wortes, wie Sie mir zurufen, so wird mir besonnene und kluge Handlungsweise um so leichter und deren Resultate um so segensreicher. Ich will den Muth nicht sinken lassen, mit kräftigem Vorsatz und wahrem Eifer kann es nicht fehlen in Allem edel, männlich, fürstlich zu bleiben. Zum Handeln bedarf es erst guten Rathes, den Sie mir am besten geben könnten, wenn Sie sich entschließen wollten das erste Jahr wenigstens meines Hierseins, Ihre Zeit mir zu opfern.

Ich habe Ihnen noch so viel zu sagen und muß doch jetzt schließen, da der Kurier nicht länger säumen kann. Ich hoffe dann mündlich in Wiesbaden mehr mit Ihnen mich darüber zu unterhalten.

In der Hoffnung Sie dann dort recht wohl und gesund zu finden, bleibe ich

Ihr treuer
Albert.

Windsor, 6. November 1839.

(P.S.)—Noch muß ich Ihnen sagen, was ich dem Onkel zu schreiben vergaß: daß es nach unsrer Abreise durchaus nothwendig sein wird, eine Kurierkette zwischen Koburg, Wiesbaden, Brüssel, London zu organisiren, um im Stande zu sein, rasch, oft und sicher schreiben zu können. Ich bitte, sprechen Sie mit dem Onkel darüber.

To the Dowager-Duchess of Gotha. (See pp. 196, 199.)

Liebe Großmama,—Ich zaudre indem ich die Feder ergreife, da ich befürchten muß, daß, was ich Dir zu sagen im Begriffe stehe, zugleich auch einen Gedanken in Dir errege, der schmerzlich sein muß, und ach! es mir auch so sehr ist: nämlich den der Trennung. Der Gegenstand, der in der letzten Zeit uusre Aufmerksamkeit auf sich gezogen hatte, ist zum Schlusse gekommen.

Die Königin hat mich vor mehreren Tagen ganz privatim zu sich kommen lassen, und erklärte mir in einem wahren Ergusse von Herzlichkeit und Liebe, ich habe ihr ganzes Herz gewonnen, und ich könne sie überglücklich machen, wenn ich ihr das Opfer bringen wolle, mit ihr mein Leben zu theilen, denn als ein Opfer sähe sie es an; das Einzige was sie besorgt machte, wäre, daß sie meiner nicht werth wäre. Die freudige Freimüthigkeit mit der sie mir dieß sagte, hat mich wirklich ganz bezaubert und hingerissen, ich konnte nicht anders als ihr beide Hände reichen, die sie mit Zärtlichkeit an sich riß.

Sie ist wirklich gar gut und liebenswürdig, und ich bin fest überzeugt, der Himmel hat mich in keine schlechten Hände gegeben und wir werden glücklich zusammen sein.

Seit jenem Augenblicke thut Victoria alles, was sie mir nur an den Augen absehen kann, und wir unterhalten uns viel über die Zukunft, die sie mir so glücklich zu machen verspricht als nur möglich.

Ach die Zukunft! bringt sie nicht auch den Augenblick, wo ich von der lieben, lieben Heimath, wo ich von Dir Abschied nehmen muß. Daran darf ich gar nicht denken, ohne daß eine tiefe Wehmuth mich ergreift.

Schon am 15ten October geschah es daß V. mir die Erklärung machte, und bis jetzt habe ich angestanden Dir es mitzutheilen, doch was kann das Säumen helfen?

Der Zeitpunkt unserer Vermählung liegt schon nahe; die Königin und die Minister wünschen durchaus die ersten Tage des Februars, was ich auch nach den von ihnen angegebenen Gründen zugestehen mußte. Wir haben darum unsre Abreise auf den 14ten dieses festgesetzt, um noch soviel Zeit als möglich zu Hause zu gewinnen.

Wir folgen darum diesem Briefe dicht auf der Ferse.

Meine hiesige Stellung wird dadurch sehr angenehm, daß ich alle mir beantragten Titel abgelehnt habe, ich behalte meinen Namen und bleibe was ich war. Dieß wird mich sehr selbstständig erhalten, und macht es mir auch leicht, hie und da rasch einen Sprung nach der Heimath zu machen, um alle theuren Verwandten zu sehen. Doch ist es schmerzlich ein Meer zwischen sich zu wissen.

Nun nehme ich wieder Abschied von Dir. Victoria schreibt Dir selbst, um Dir ihren Wunsch zu erkennen zu geben.

Ich bitte zu einem so wichtigen und entscheidenden Schritte meines Lebens um Deinen großmütterlichen Segen, der mir ein Talisman sein wird gegen alle Stürme, die die Zukunft mir noch vorbehalten mag. Lebe wohl, liebe Großmutter, und entziehe mir Deine Liebe nicht.

Der Himmel wird alles gut machen.

Albert.

Liebe Großmama—Wie sehr dankbar bin ich Dir für Deinen lieben gnädigen Brief, den ich gestern erhielt, ich mußte ihn mehrmals durchlesen um ja recht die herrlichen Gesinnungen ganz zu fassen die Du darin aussprichst.

Jedes Wort ist ein Ausfluß Deines lieben Charakters. Gewiß, liebe Großmama, die theure Heimath, das theure Vaterland, wird mir immer werth sein, und mein Herz wird ihm ein Freund sein, der mich oft daran erinnern wird. Für das Wohl meines zukünftigen neuen Vaterlandes zu leben, sich aufzuopfern, schließt ja nicht aus, dem Lande wohl zu thun, von dem man selbst so viele Wohlthaten empfangen hat. Ich werde neben unermüdlichem Streben und Arbeiten für das Land, dem ich in Zukunft angehören soll, und wo ich zu einer hoher Stellung berufen bin, nicht aufhören, ein treuer Deutscher, Koburger, Gothaner zu sein. Die Trennung wird mir noch recht weh thun. Ich freue mich recht auf die Paar Tage, die ich noch im Stande sein werde, bei Dir zuzubringen, es sind nur wenige, aber wir wollen sie recht genießen. . . .

Deinen treuen Enkel,

Albert.

Koburg, 28ten November 1839.

To Prince William of Löwenstein. (See p. 201.)

Koburg, 6ten December 1839.

Lieber Löwenstein — Obgleich ich von einem Wust von Geschäften und Arbeiten aller Art überhäuft bin, so muß ich doch ein paar Minuten zu erübrigen suchen, um Dir, einem treuen Freunde, persönlich Kunde von meinem Glück zu geben. Ich bin also wirklich Bräutigam und soll schon gegen den 4ten Februar mit der, die ich liebe, mich verbunden sehen. Du weißt, wie die Sachen standen, als ich Dich zuletzt hier sah. Seitdem verfinsterte sich der Himmel immer mehr. Die Königin erklärte meinem Onkel von Belgien, sie wünsche, daß die Verhandlungen als abgebrochen betrachtet sein möchten, und vor 4 Jahren werde sie an gar keine Verbindung denken. Ich ging ruhig und mit dem festen Vorsatz hinüber, zu erklären, daß auch ich des Hingehaltenwerdens müde mich von der Sache ganz zurückziehen würde. Doch dies war nicht im Rathe der Götter beschlossen, denn schon am 2ten Tage nach unsrer Ankunft gelangten die freundlichsten Demonstrationen an mich, und 2 Tage darauf ward ich im Geheim zu einer Privataudienz beschieden, in welcher mir die Königin Hand und Herz anbot. Nun bedurfte es des strengsten Geheimnisses, nur Ernst wußte darum; erst bei unserer Abreise durfte die Verlobung der Mutter mitgetheilt werden.

Ich glaube sehr glücklich zu werden, denn Victoria besitzt alle die

Eigenschaften, die eine glückliche Häuslichkeit verbürgen, und scheint mir mit ganzer Seele zugethan. Mein künftiges Loos ist hoch und glänzend, doch auch reichlich mit Dornen besetzt. An Kämpfen wird es nicht fehlen, schon der Monat März scheint Stürme zu erwarten.

Der Abschied von der Heimath, von dem lieben Koburg, von so vielen Freunden wird mir recht schwer. Wann werde ich Dich wiedersehen, lieber Löwenstein?

Ich bitte, zeige diesen Brief Niemanden, ich schrieb Dir einige Details, auf Deine Verschwiegenheit rechnend, da ich Deine Freundschaft kenne. Lebe nun wohl und denke zuweilen an Deinen

Albert.

To the Duke of Coburg. (See p. 271.)

Buckingham Palace, 4ten Juni.

Wir sind gestern von Claremont zurückgekommen, wo wir abermals zwei Tage zubrachten. Wir gingen diesmal dahin um ganz aus der Nähe zu den berühmten Pferderennen von Epsom kommen zu können, die auch wirklich sehr interessant waren. Die Masse der anwesenden Menschen wurde auf ein- bis zweihundert Tausend geschätzt. Wir wurden mit großem Enthusiasmus und Herzlichkeit empfangen. Ich ritt etwas in der Masse herum, um einzelne Pferde zu sehen, bin aber fast von der anströmenden Menge erdrückt worden.

Ich habe richtig noch zu dem Meeting wegen des Sclavenhandels gehen müssen, und meine Rede ist mit großem Applaus aufgenommen worden, und scheint einen guten Effect in London gemacht zu haben.

Dies belohnt mich hinreichend für die Angst und Beklommenheit, die ich überwinden mußte, ehe ich die Rede beginnen konnte, die ich selbst ausgearbeitet und dann auswendig gelernt hatte. Denn es ist immer schwer in einer fremden Sprache vor 5–6000 gespannten Zuhörern sprechen zu müssen.

Der Park am Palast, von dem du sprichst, ist wirklich sehr angenehm, und ich habe ihn noch mit allerhand Thieren und seltsamen Wasservögeln belebt.

To the Dowager Duchess of Gotha. (See p. 273.)

Liebe Großmama.—Ich beeile mich, Dir von einem Evenement Nachricht zu geben, das Dir vielleicht sonst auf unrechte Weise berichtet wird, das mein und Victoria's Leben gefährdete, dem wir aber, durch die wachende Hand der Vorsehung geschützt, entgangen sind. Wir fuhren nämlich gestern Abend um 6 Uhr aus, um der Tante Kent einen Besuch und eine Tour um den Hyde Park zu machen. Wir fuhren in einer kleinen engen Droschke. Ich saß rechts, Victoria links. Als wir kaum 100 Schritte vom Palast gekommen waren, bemerkte ich neben mir auf dem Fußwege einen unansehnlichen kleinen Menschen etwas gegen uns haltend, und noch ehe ich unterscheiden konnte, was es war, fiel ein Schuß, der uns beide fast betäubte, so stark war er, und nur kaum auf 6 Schritte auf uns gefeuert. Victoria hatte sich gerade links nach einem Pferde umgesehen, begriff darum gar nicht warum ihr die Ohren so klangen, weil sie in der großen Nähe kaum unterscheiden konnte, daß es die Folge eines Schusses war. Die Pferde erschracken und der Wagen hielt darum an. Ich ergriff Victoria's Hände und fragte sie, ob der Schreck ihr nicht geschadet habe; allein sie lachte über den Vorfall.

Darauf sah ich mich wieder nach dem Menschen um, der noch auf derselben Stelle stand mit verschränkten Armen, in jeder Hand ein Pistol, und in einer höchst affectirten theatralischen Stellung, so daß es mich lächerte. Auf einmal zielt er wieder und schießt zum zweiten Male; dießmal sah auch Victoria den Schuß und bückte sich rasch, von mir niedergezogen. Die Kugel muß grade über ihrem Kopfe hingeflogen sein, nach der Stelle zu urtheilen, wo man sie in einer gegenüberstehenden Mauer stecken fand. Die Menge Leute, die um uns und um den Menschen herum standen und bis jetzt vor Schreck versteinert die Sache mitangesehen hatten, fielen nun über ihn her. Ich rief dem Postillion zu fortzufahren und wir langten glücklich bei der Tante an, und machten noch von dort aus eine kleine Spazierfahrt durch die Parks, theils um Victoria etwas an die Luft zu bringen, theils auch um dem Publikum zu zeigen, daß wir dadurch nicht alles Vertrauen zu ihm verloren haben.

Heute bin ich recht müde und caput von den vielen Besuchen, Fragen und Beschreibungen. Du mußt darum verzeihen, wenn ich hier schließe und Dir nur meinen Dank für Deinen Brief sage, den ich eben erhalten habe, aber noch nicht lesen konnte.

P

Meine Hauptsorge war, daß der Schreck Victoria in ihrem jetzigen Zustande schaden möchte. Sie ist jedoch recht wohl, ich auch.

Ich danke Gott dem Allmächtigen für seinen Schutz!

Dein treuer Enkel,
(gez.) Albert.

Buckingham Palace, den 11. Juni 1840.

Der Uebelthäter heißt Edward Oxford, und ist 17 Jahre alt, ein Kellner in einem schlechten Wirthshause, nicht verrückt, und ganz ruhig und gefaßt.

APPENDIX D.

LIST OF MEMBERS OF THE PRIVY COUNCIL PRESENT AT THE DECLARATION.

[*Those marked with an asterisk are since dead.*]

Duke of Cambridge.*
Archbishop of Canterbury.*
Lord Chancellor (Earl of Cottenham).*
Lord President (Lord Lansdowne).*
Lord Privy Seal (Lord Clarendon).
Duke of Norfolk.*
Devonshire.*
Montrose.
Wellington.*
Marquis of Salisbury.
Anglesey.*
Normanby.*
Lord Chamberlain (Lord Uxbridge).
Earl of Surrey.*
Albemarle.*
Jersey.*
Erroll.*
Tankerville.*
Minto.*
Howe.
Amherst.*
Durham.*
Ripon.*
Viscount Castlereagh.
Strangford.*
Palmerston.*
Melbourne.*
Viscount Beresford.*
Ebrington.*
Lord John Russell.
Burghersh.*
Willoughby d'Eresby.*
Holland.*
Ellenborough.
Hill.*
Bexley.'
Lord Bloomfield.*
Wharncliffe.*
Lyndhurst.*
Cowley.*
Wynford.*
Brougham.
Denman.*
Abinger.*
Ashburton.*
Hatherton.*
Langdale.*
Monteagle.*
Bishop of London.*
The Speaker.*
Hon. J. P. Courteney.*
H. Pierrepoint.*
Sir R. Peel.*
G. Ouseley.*
Mr. Goulburn.*
Lord C. J. Tyndal.*
Sir W. Alexander.*
G. Cockburn.*

Mr. S. Lushington.
    Herries.*
The Vice-Chancellor.*
Sir G. Murray.*
    H. Hardinge.*
    R. Adair.*
    B. Taylor.*
Hon. J. Erskine.*
Sir Hyde Earl.*
    J. Hobhouse.
Mr. Tennyson d'Eyncourt.*
    E. Ellice.*
Baron Parke.*
Sir A. Johnstone.*
Mr. Justice Bosanquet.*
Sir E. Knatchbull.*
Mr. Planta.*
    Wm. Peel.*
    Labouchere.
Hon. G. Byng.
Dr. Lushington.
Sir G. Grey.
Sir F. Baring (Chancellor of the Exchequer).
Mr. Macaulay.*

APPENDIX E.

A COPY OF THE OFFICIAL NOTICE OF THE CEREMONIAL TO BE OBSERVED IN MAKING THE DECLARATION, AND OF THE DECLARATION ITSELF.

"*Coburg*, 8 *Dec.*, 1839.

"Divine service in the Court Chapel, at which the reigning duke and duchess, Prince Albert, the whole court, the states, the chief authorities of the duchy of Coburg and Gotha, and all persons belonging to the nobility, will be present at four o'clock. The court, and the persons on a visit to the duke, the ministers, etc., etc., all in full dress, will assemble in the large drawing-room—the ladies in the room. They will then proceed to the throne-room, and take their several places; and, when every thing is ready, the two chief officers of the court, the grand marshal and the master of the household, will proceed to the apartments of the duke and duchess, and conduct them, with Prince Albert, to the throne-room." Having all taken the seats appointed for them, "the minister of state will proclaim the happy event as follows:

"DECLARATION.

"His serene highness the reigning Duke of Saxe-Coburg and Gotha, our gracious duke and master, fully convinced of the sincere interest his faithful subjects always take in any events concerning H. S. H.'s house, finds it necessary to assemble the nobles of the land, as well as the chief authorities and persons in office, in order to communicate to them the most joyful news of the betrothal of his second son, H. S. H. Prince Albert, to her most gracious majesty the Queen of Great Britain and Ireland.

"H. S. H. feels the greatest satisfaction in expressing at the same time his sincere conviction that, considering her Majesty's noble qualities, both of heart and mind, this alliance will, under the protection of Divine Providence, prove a real happiness to his beloved son, who will henceforward devote his whole life to his new country, but who, though separated from his native land, will preserve for it his present feelings of attachment and affection."

"As soon as the proclamation shall have been made, the cannon of the fortress will announce the same to the town and country.

"Prince Albert will then receive the congratulations of all present.

"The ceremony being concluded, their serene highnesses will proceed in procession to the Giants' Hall, where having taken their seats, the chaplain will say grace.

"In the course of the dinner, the Queen and Prince Albert's healths will be first drunk, then those of the duke and duchess. In the evening, Cherubini's opera, *Le Deux Journées*, will be performed."

APPENDIX F.

CELEBRATION OF HER MAJESTY'S MARRIAGE WITH HIS ROYAL HIGHNESS PRINCE ALBERT OF SAXE-COBURG AND GOTHA.

(From the "Times" of February 11, 1840.*)*

THIS most important and national event took place yesterday at noon, at the Chapel Royal, St. James's; and since the marriage of her royal highness, the late Princess Charlotte of

Wales, there has been no occurrence connected with the royal family of England which excited so great an interest. It was known throughout the metropolis in the course of the last week that the celebration of the marriage would take place at noon, instead of an advanced hour of the evening, as was heretofore the custom with respect to royal marriages. The knowledge of this fact brought many, many thousands from all sides of London into the Park at an early hour. Never did St. James's Park present such an extraordinary display—never was such an immense multitude assembled there since the rejoicings at the visit of the allied sovereigns in 1814. As early as nine o'clock considerable numbers had arrived in order to secure a good place from which to see the royal *cortège* pass from Buckingham Palace to St. James's. By that hour the vicinity of Buckingham Palace, and all the avenues leading to both palaces, were thronged. As the day wore on to noon, the assemblage between the back of Carlton Terrace and the foot of Constitution Hill had increased to a dense mass of very many thousands, through which it was difficult to keep open the carriage-way for that portion of the company who had the privilege of the *entrée*. The very lowering aspect of the weather seemed to have no terrors for the visitors, male and female, young and old, who continued to arrive in masses, by which the space already described became, before eleven o'clock, thronged to most distressing pressure. Nor was this pressure diminished to any important extent by the smart showers which came down at intervals. As each successive group of visitors arrived, they of course thickened the broad line of crowd at each side of the carriage-way between the two palaces. Those whose stations were in the rear of this line soon got an opportunity of over-looking those in front by hiring standing-room on some one of the many hundred chairs, tables, or benches, which were let out at various prices, from 1*s.* 6*d.* to 5*s.* each person. Many who could not afford, or would not pay for such a luxury, succeeded in getting on the branches of the trees as well out of as in the line of the expected procession. The numbers who sought these commanding positions were so great in some of the trees that the branches gave way, and the parties came, not immediately to the ground, but on the heads and shoulders of the dense masses beneath them. We did not hear, however, that any persons were seriously hurt by those accidents. Many of them excited roars of laughter, from the efforts of those who had resorted to them to keep their places on the falling branches, or to secure more firm positions on the boughs above them. In the course of the morning the crowds in that part of the Park situate between the back of Carlton Terrace and Marlborough House were much amused by a marrow-bone and cleaver concert, got up in honor of the royal nuptials, and we must do justice to those engaged by saying that the effect of this rude music was by no means disagreeable. Soon after the firing of the guns, announcing the most important part of the ceremonial, the placing the ring on her Majesty's finger, the whole mass of the visitors who had not obtained fixed stands rushed almost simultaneously toward Buckingham Palace, in order to have a view of her Majesty and the Prince on their return. The pressure here became so great that it required the united and incessant efforts of the police and the Horse Guards Blue to keep the carriage-way open. The necessary but disagreeable part of their duty was performed with much good temper, and in general was received with good humor even by those who appeared to suffer a little from it. The police regulations in this part of the Park, and, indeed, in every part that we had an opportunity of observing, were admirably well arranged by the Commissioners Rowan and Mayne, and their directions were carried out by the force-officers and men under their command with great judgment and good temper. They had in some parts of the line an arduous and difficult task to perform; but we think that a great deal of their labor might have been saved by the erection of a strong barricade on each side of the line from Buckingham Palace to St. James's.

BUCKINGHAM PALACE (INTERIOR).

The officers of the household and the attendants on her Majesty began to arrive at Buckingham Palace about half past ten o'clock. The Earl of Uxbridge, the Earl of Belfast, the Earl of Surrey, the Earl of Albemarle, Colonel Cavendish, Lord Alfred Paget, Sir George Anson, the lord in waiting, ladies in waiting, maids of honor, bedchamber women, gentlemen ushers, etc., were all assembled at eleven o'clock. After some little time had elapsed, the ladies of her Majesty's suite were summoned by the master of the horse, and handed into four of the royal carriages by Colonel Cavendish (clerk marshal) and Lord Alfred Paget, and dispatched to St. James's Palace.

At half past eleven the six gentlemen composing the foreign suites of his Royal Highness Prince Albert and the Duke of Saxe-Coburg-Gotha mustered in the grand hall. They appeared in dark blue or green uniforms, and three of them took their departure in a royal carriage for St. James's, accompanied by two gentlemen ushers of the Queen's household, to be in readiness to receive Prince Albert.

At a quarter to twelve, the royal carriages having returned, notice was given to the royal bridegroom that all was in readiness for his departure. The Prince immediately quitted the private apartments of the palace, and passed through the state rooms, into which a very few spectators were admitted. His Royal Highness was dressed in the uniform of a British field-marshal, and wore no other decoration than the insignia of the Order of the Garter, viz., the collar, with the George appended, set in precious stones, the star of the order set in diamonds, and the Garter itself, embroidered in diamonds, round his knee. The Prince was supported on one side by his father, the Duke of Saxe-Coburg-Gotha, and his brother, the hereditary prince. The duke was dressed in a dark green uniform, turned up with red, with military boots similar to those worn by the Life Guards. His serene highness wore the collar of the Order of the Garter, and the Star, and the Star of the Order of Coburg-Gotha. Prince Ernest wore a light blue cavalry uniform, with silver appointments, carrying a light helmet in his hand. His serene highness wore the insignia of a Grand Cross of an Order of Knighthood. His Royal Highness Prince Albert was preceded by the lord chamberlain, the vice-chamberlain, the treasurer and controller of the household, Lord Torrington (who wore the insignia of a Grand Cross of the Order of Saxe-Coburg-Gotha, with which he had been lately invested), the clerk marshal, equerries, gentlemen ushers, etc., the remaining portion of the foreign suite bringing up the rear. On descending the grand staircase, the favored few occupying the grand hall behind the Yeoman Guard received the prince with a loud clapping of hands, which his Royal Highness acknowledged in the most gracious manner.

Indeed, to a group of ladies stationed close to the entrance, who were testifying their satisfaction, the Prince made his acknowledgments with an air of the most courteous gallantry. The Prince entered the carriage amid the sound of trumpets, the lowering of colors, the presenting of arms, and all the honors paid to the Queen herself. His Royal Highness, with his father and brother, occupied one carriage, and the attendants two other royal carriages. A squadron of Life Guards escorted the Prince to St. James's Palace. On the return of the lord chamberlain six of the royal carriages were assembled, and his lordship informed her Majesty that all was ready. The Queen then left her apartment, leaning on the arm of the Earl of Uxbridge as lord chamberlain, supported by the Duchess of Kent, and followed by a page of honor. Her Majesty was preceded by the Earl of Belfast, the Earl of Surrey, Lord Torrington, the Earl of Albemarle, Colonel Cavendish, Sir George Anson, Lord Alfred Paget, Mr. Byng, and several other officers of the household. Her Majesty carried her train over her arm.* The royal bride was greeted with loud acclamations on descending to the grand hall, but her eye was bent principally on the ground, and a hurried glance around, and a slight inclination of the head, was all the acknowledgment returned. Her Majesty wore no diamonds on her head, nothing but a simple wreath of orange-blossoms. The magnificent veil did not cover her face, but hung down on each shoulder. A pair of very large diamond earrings, a diamond necklace, and the insignia of the Order of the Garter,† were the principal ornaments worn by the Queen.

The Duchess of Kent and the Duchess of Sutherland rode in the same carriage with her Majesty, and the royal *cortège* left the Palace at a slow pace, under a strong escort of the Household Cavalry.

BUCKINGHAM PALACE (EXTERIOR).

This morning, at an early hour, every public approach to the Palace was crowded by numbers of her Majesty's loyal subjects, anxious to obtain, if possible, a view of the bridal procession, and testify by their vociferous applause their perfect commendation of her Majesty's choice of a Royal Con-

* A mistake: she did not.

† She wore the collar.

sort. The court in front of the Palace was occupied by the band of the Regiment of Blues, and one or two companies of the Grenadier Guards, and the whole of the line thence to the garden-entrance of St. James's Palace was lined with Horse Guards and a strong corps of the police. The immediate road for the procession was kept clear with great difficulty, so numerous were the attempts from the pressure without to break in on the line, and secure a position where a sight of the royal pair might be better had. The police, however, notwithstanding these ebullitions of "popular feeling," conducted themselves with great temper, and maintained order without any violent exercise of their supreme authority. Anxiously did the assembled multitude look for some signal of her Majesty's departure from Buckingham Palace, and as carriage after carriage rolled down the Mall, carrying some of the honored spectators to the chapel, the more impatient they became for the passing of the procession. Twelve o'clock at length arrived, and his Royal Highness Prince Albert, attended by a small escort of Horse Guards, and accompanied by his father, the Duke of Saxe-Coburg and Gotha, and his brother, the hereditary prince, then left the Palace and proceeded to St. James's; but, from the windows of the carriages being closed, the royal party were only partially recognized, and passed along with but slight applause. At a quarter past twelve, however, the band in front of the Palace struck up the national air of "God save the Queen," and by the tremendous shouts which resounded through the Park, it was proclaimed that her Majesty had entered her carriage and was then proceeding to St. James's to plight her troth to his Royal Highness Prince Albert of Saxe-Coburg and Gotha. As her Majesty passed down the line she was most enthusiastically cheered, and appeared highly gratified by the loyalty which her subjects expressed, one or two ludicrous incidents among the crowd also exciting her smile; but her countenance was extremely pale, and appeared to betoken considerable anxiety. The *cortège* of her Majesty was attended by a full guard of honor, but the carriages were drawn by only two horses each, and without the rich caparison which they usually wear on state occasions. The order of the carriages was thus:

FIRST CARRIAGE.

Two Gentlemen Ushers.
Exon of the Yeomen of the Guard.
Groom of the Robes.

SECOND CARRIAGE.

Equerry in Waiting, Hon. C. Grey.
Two Pages of Honor.
Groom in Waiting, Hon. Major Keppel.

THIRD CARRIAGE.

Clerk Marshal, Hon. H. F. Cavendish.
Vice-Chamberlain, Earl of Belfast.
Keeper of the Privy Purse, Sir H. Wheatley.
Controller of the Household, Right Hon. G. Stevens Byng.

FOURTH CARRIAGE.

Bedchamber Woman in Waiting.
Captain of the Yeomen of the Guard, Earl of Ilchester.
Master of the Buckhounds, Lord Kinnaird.
Treasurer of the Household, Earl of Surrey.

FIFTH CARRIAGE.

Maid of Honor in Waiting.
Duchess of Kent's Lady in Waiting, Lady Charlotte Dundas.
Gold Stick, Lord Hill.
Lord in Waiting, Viscount Torrington.

SIXTH CARRIAGE.

Lady of the Bedchamber in Waiting.
Master of the Horse, Earl of Albemarle.
Lord Steward, Earl of Errol.
Lord Chamberlain, Earl of Uxbridge.

SEVENTH CARRIAGE.

THE QUEEN.
The Duchess of Kent.
Mistress of the Robes, Duchess of Sutherland.

By about ten minutes past twelve o'clock the whole of these carriages, with their respective occupants, had reached

ST. JAMES'S PALACE.

THE THRONE-ROOM.

On the arrival of the Queen at St. James's Palace, her Majesty was conducted to her closet, immediately behind the throne-room, where she remained attended by the maids of honor and trainbearers until the summons was received from the lord chamberlain, conveying the intimation that every thing was duly prepared for the Sovereign's moving toward the Chapel.

In this room the formal procession may be said to have been formed and marshaled.

PRESENCE CHAMBER.

In this room the principal individuals who were to fall into the different processions were congregated.

QUEEN ANNE'S DRAWING-ROOM.

Round the southern side of this room a gallery was erected, consisting of several rows of seats, each capable of accommodating a considerable number of visitors. Through this room the procession passed into

THE GUARD OR ARMORY-ROOM,

in which a gallery on a smaller scale was raised. The procession progressed from this into the vestibule, and from that down the

GRAND STAIRCASE,

opposite to which a gallery had been put up capable of containing about 150 persons.

THE COLONNADE.

Shortly after nine o'clock the seats in the colonnade began to be taken possession of, and ere many minutes had elapsed there remained but few of the seats unoccupied, although there was an occasional arrival down to eleven o'clock.

At this hour the appearance which the scene presented was one of extreme animation, inasmuch as by far the greater portion of the assembled company was composed of elegantly, and, in some instances, brilliantly dressed ladies. It were a matter of impossibility to enter upon an attempt to give any thing like a minute detail of the attire either of the one sex or of the other, for it comprised every known color, and embraced every description of style of make. The most conspicuous dresses were of light blue relieved with white, light green also intermingled with white, amber, crimson, purple, fawn, stone, and a considerable number of white robes only. Every lady exhibited a wedding favor, some of which were admirable specimens of a refined taste. They were of all sizes, many of white satin ribbon tied up into bows, and mixed with layers of rich silver lace, others merely of ribbon intermixed with sprigs of orange-flower-blossom, while were here and there to be seen bouquets of huge dimensions of ribbon and massive silver bullion, having in their centre what might almost be termed a branch of orange-blossoms. Large as they were, however, they were not more so than the apparent devotion of their owners, if the anxiety with which they watched every movement of the officials passing to and fro, from the instant they entered the colonnade until the last of the "men of state" had quitted the scene, may be taken as a criterion.

It was remarked that "favors" did not form a very general appendage with the male branch of the spectators, notwithstanding there were many who had not failed to furnish themselves with this distinguishing emblem of the occasion. Some gentlemen there were, also, who did not even pay the respect to their sovereign of providing court dresses. There appeared, nevertheless, to have been a unanimity of feeling with regard to the total banishment of black, except in a rare instance where a shawl or scarf of that hue was to be discovered.

The colonnade through which the procession passed to the Chapel was not only excellently arranged, but was admirably lighted from the lanterns above and the windows behind. The seats, which were separated from the pillared colonnade by a dwarf railing, were covered with crimson cushions with gold-colored borders and fringe. All the remainder of this temporary structure had the semblance of having been constructed of solid masonry. The floor of the colonnade was covered with rich Brussels carpet, which extended into the vestibule, up the grand staircase to the armory, through the presence-chamber to Queen Anne's drawing-room, and thence to the antechamber and throne-room, where her Majesty and Prince Albert's portions of the procession were marshaled. The seats erected for the accommodation of the spectators were covered with crimson cushions and yellow fringe, thus sustaining uniformity throughout. They were railed off from the line of procession.

There were but few of the nobility or officers of state who entered the Chapel by the colonnade or royal passage, but among that number were Earl Fitzwilliam and Earl Spencer, the Earl and Countess of Carlisle, the Duke and Duchess of Somerset, the Duke of Devonshire, the Marquis of Anglesey, the Marquis of Westminster, the Archbishop of Canterbury, the Archbishop of York, and the Bishop of London.

His Grace the Duke of Wellington also passed through the colonnade, and was most warmly cheered. The duke slightly acknowledged the demonstration, and wended his way onward to the place allotted for the occupation of the veteran warrior in the Chapel.

Comparatively speaking, there was a scarcity of "rank" among the company in the colonnade. The only individuals of particular note upon whom our eye alighted were Sir George Murray, Mr. Sheil, and Mr. Charles Young. To the former of these gentlemen her Royal Highness the Princess Sophia Matilda of Gloucester, from her place in the procession, spoke, while the Marquis of Anglesey stopped and shook hands most warmly with the gallant baronet. Mr. Tennyson D'Eyncourt and Sir W. Brabazon were likewise occupants of seats in the colonnade, but, like the honorable and learned member for Tipperary, their presence was allowed to pass unheeded.

Of course, anticipation long postponed, and the virtue of patience, even within the walls of a royal palace, and upon such an occasion, became exhausted, and the slightest action or movement, however trifling, which tended to create a diversion, or to shed a new feature on a scene which had grown somewhat monotonous, was hailed as a species of godsend, and accordingly the mere circumstance of the Rev. Lord Augustus Fitzclarence bringing forward one of the choir-boys, a lad apparently of some seven or eight years of age, but particularly small, and examining his uncouth dress, gave rise to considerable merriment. The occasional passing to and fro of the mace-bearers—who, from their remarkable dress, namely, black, with large gold chains tied up on the shoulders with large white favors, excited a good deal of attention—was seized as a fitting opportunity to indulge in laughter.

But, looking at the mass which paraded the colonnade, we may say that there were the burly Yeomen of the Guard with their massive halberts, and the slim gentlemen-at-arms with their lighter partisans, perpetually moving up and down the corridor, proud of the notice they excited. There were also elderly pages of state, and almost infantile pages of honor, officers of the lord chamberlain's office, and officers of the woods and forests, embroidered heralds and steel-clad cuirassiers, robed prelates, stoled priests, and surpliced singing-boys, to break the uniformity and vary the monotony of the scene.

THE CHAPEL.

The principal entrances to the Chapel Royal were from the Embassador's Court, and the color quadrangle opposite St. James's Street. The interior is oblong, standing east and west, about sixty-two feet in length and twenty-five in breadth. At the upper or eastern end is the communion-table, and at the lower end, abutting over the main entrance, is the royal gallery or closet. Two galleries supported by cast-iron pillars stretched east and west the entire length of the Chapel. On the floor, placed longitudinally, were two pews on each side of the chapel, set apart for the chief nobility, and those who took part in the procession. The galleries, east and west, from both sides of the altar to the royal closet, were occupied—the upper end, on the right, by the cabinet ministers and their ladies, on the left by the ladies and officers of her Majesty's household. Below the choir, on the right, and in the galleries opposite, usually appropriated as royal closets, the walls of the building were thrown out, and six benches on each side fitted up for the accommodation of peers, peeresses, and other distinguished spectators. The royal closet was assigned to the embassadors and their ladies, five rows of seats, elevated one above the other, having been erected for their accommodation. The whole of the seats in the chapel were stuffed, covered with crimson cloth, and elegantly ornamented with gold fringe. On the communion-table was displayed a vast quantity of golden plate, including six salvors, one of gigantic dimensions, two ponderous and rich vases, four flagons, four communion-cups, and two lofty and magnificent candelabra. The cornice above the altar, of beautifully carved oak, was richly gilt, superb crimson velvet drapery depending from it in graceful folds upon the communion-table. Within the railing, which was also covered with crimson velvet, stools were placed on the right of the altar for the Archbishops of Canterbury and York, and on the left for the Bishop of London, dean of the Chapel Royal. In front of the communion-table were placed four chairs of state, gilt, and covered with crimson silk velvet, each of different construction, and varying in elevation, according to the dignity of their intended occupants. The highest, largest in size, and most costly in workmanship, was of course appropriated to her Majesty, and was placed somewhat to the right of the centre; that on the opposite side, immediately on her Majesty's right hand, being set apart for his Royal Highness Prince Albert. Before these chairs, which were placed about six feet outside the rail, footstools were set of corresponding structure and decoration. There were also faldstools for her Majesty and Prince Albert, on which to kneel at the altar. On her Majesty's left a chair was placed for the Duchess of Kent; and at the opposite side, on Prince Albert's right, one for the queen dowager. On her Majesty's extreme left were seats for their royal highnesses the Dukes of Sussex and Cambridge; and on Prince Albert's extreme right for his serene highness the reigning Duke of Saxe-Coburg, the hereditary duke, and their royal highnesses the Duchess of Cambridge, Prince George of Cambridge, Princess Augusta and Princess Mary of Cambridge. The floor of the Chapel was covered with rich purple and gold carpeting, the prominent figure being the Norman rose. The *tout ensemble*, both as concerns the extension, decoration, and entire arrangements of the interior, completely harmonized with the original design and structure of the chapel; simplicity and elegance, not show or gaudiness, being the uniform characteristic. The ceiling is composed of antique fretwork compartments varying in size and figure, on the paneling of which are emblazoned the quarterings and heraldic distinctions of the different members of the royal family, from the time of its erection to that of his late majesty William IV. and Queen Adelaide.

About half past eleven o'clock the Archbishops of Canterbury and York and the Bishop of London took their places within the altar.

A few minutes before twelve the queen dowager entered the Chapel Royal through the dean's vestry door, and took her seat near the altar. Her Majesty was arrayed in a robe of rich silk purple velvet trimmed with ermine. The Archbishops of Canterbury and York and the Bishop of London immediately rose on the entrance of her Majesty. Her Majesty, after performing her private devotions, perceiving the most reverend prelates still standing, sent Lord Howe, who was in waiting, to desire that they might take their seats. This act of considerate courtesy created a general sensation throughout the Chapel.

A flourish of trumpets and drums at twenty-five minutes past twelve o'clock gave intimation that the procession of the royal bridegroom had commenced its movement, and shortly after, having passed through the various rooms to which we have alluded, it entered the colonnade in the following order:

THE PROCESSION OF THE BRIDEGROOM.

Drums and Trumpets.
Sergeant Trumpeter, J. Rivett, Esq.
Master of the Ceremonies, Sir Robert Chester, Knight.
The Bridegroom's Gentlemen of Honor, between two Heralds.

Vice-Chamberlain of her Majesty's Household, Earl of Belfast.	Lord Chamberlain of her Majesty's Household, Earl of Uxbridge.

THE BRIDEGROOM,
HIS ROYAL HIGHNESS FIELD-MARSHAL PRINCE ALBERT, K.G.,
wearing the Collar of the Order of the Garter,
supported by their Serene Highnesses the reigning Duke of Saxe-Coburg and Gotha,
and the Hereditary Prince of Saxe-Coburg and Gotha,
each attended by the officers of their suite, namely,
Count Kolowrath, Baron Alvensleben, and Baron de Lowenfels.

As the Prince moved along he was greeted with loud clapping of hands from the gentlemen, and enthusiastic waving of handkerchiefs from the assembled ladies. He wore the uniform of a field-marshal in the British army. Over his shoulders was hung the Collar of the Garter surmounted by two white rosettes. His appearance was attractive and much improved since his arrival on Saturday; and with his pale and pensive looks he won golden opinions from the fair coterie near which we were sitting. His father and his brother were also welcomed with the utmost cordiality. Both seemed pleased with their reception, and the hereditary prince, who has more of determination but less of good-natured complaisance in his countenance than his brother, testified his sense of it by repeatedly bowing his thanks to the fair ladies at his side.

On reaching the Chapel Royal the drums and trumpets filed off without the doors, and, the procession advancing, his Royal Highness was conducted to the seat provided for him on the left of the altar. His Royal Highness walked up the aisle, carrying a book in his right hand, and repeatedly bowed to the peers in the body of the Chapel. His form, dress, and demeanor were much admired. It might well be said of him, in the language of Scott,

> "Shaped in proportion fair,
> Hazel was his eagle eye,
> And auburn of the darkest dye
> His short mustache and hair."

Having reached the *hautpas*, his Royal Highness affectionately kissed the hand of the queen dowager, and then bowed to the archbishops and dean. Immediately on his entrance a voluntary was performed by Sir George Smart on the organ. The master of the ceremonies and the officers of the bridegroom stood near the person of his Royal Highness. The lord chamberlain and vice-chamberlain, preceded by the drums and trumpets, then returned to wait upon her Majesty.

Meanwhile his Royal Highness entered into close conversation with the queen dowager until the trumpets and drums announced the moving of the Queen's procession.

After having conducted the royal Prince to the altar, the lord steward and the lord chamberlain quitted the royal bridegroom for the purpose of conducting the Queen to the altar. In a few minutes, that which was denominated the Queen's procession was announced by a flourish of trumpets and drums as having been put in motion. The procession passed through the colonnade up to the Chapel doors in the subjoined order:

THE QUEEN'S PROCESSION.

Drums and Trumpets.
Sergeant Trumpeter, T. L. Parker, Esq.
Knight Marshal, Sir Charles Lamb, Bart.

Pursuivants.
Heralds.
Pages of Honor.

Equerry in Waiting, Hon. Charles Grey.	Clerk Marshal, Hon. H. F. Cavendish.
Groom in Waiting, Hon. Major Keppel.	Lord in Waiting, Viscount Torrington.
Controller of her Majesty's Household, Right Hon. G. Stevens Byng.	Treasurer of her Majesty's Household, Earl of Surrey.

The Lord Steward of her Majesty's Household,
Earl of Erroll.

Norroy King-of-Arms, F. Martin, Esq.	Clarencieux King-of-Arms, J. Hawker, Esq.
Lord Privy Seal, The Earl of Clarendon.	Lord President of the Council, Marquis of Lansdowne.
Two Sergeants-at-Arms.	Two Sergeants-at-Arms.

Lord High Chancellor, Lord Cottenham.
Senior Gentleman Usher Quarterly Waiter, Hon. Heneage Legge.

Gentleman Usher Daily Waiter, and to the Sword of State, W. Martin, Esq.	Gentleman Usher of the Black Rod, Sir Augustus Clifford.

Garter King-of-Arms, Sir W. Woods.
The Earl Marshal, Duke of Norfolk.
Her Highness the Princess Sophia Matilda of Gloucester.
Her Royal Highness Princess Mary of Cambridge.
Her Royal Highness Princess Augusta of Cambridge.
His Royal Highness Prince George of Cambridge.
Her Royal Highness the Duchess of Cambridge,
attended by Miss Kerr, Lady of the Bedchamber to her Royal Highness.
Her Royal Highness the Duchess of Kent,
attended by Lady Charlotte Dundas, Lady of the Bedchamber to her Royal Highness.
Her Royal Highness the Duchess of Gloucester,
attended by Lady Caroline Legge, Lady of the Bedchamber to her Royal Highness.
Her Royal Highness the Princess Augusta,
attended by Lady Mary Pelham, Lady of the Bedchamber to her Royal Highness.
His Royal Highness the Duke of Cambridge,
His Royal Highness the Duke of Sussex,
each attended by a gentleman of their Royal Highnesses' household.

Vice-Chamberlain of her Majesty's Household, Earl of Belfast.	The Sword of State, borne by Lord Viscount Melbourne.	Lord Chamberlain of her Majesty's Household, Earl of Uxbridge.

THE QUEEN,
wearing the Collars of her Orders.

Her Majesty's train borne by the following twelve unmarried ladies, viz.

Lady Adelaide Paget,
Lady Sarah Frederica Caroline Villiers,
Lady Frances Elizabeth Cowper,
Lady Elizabeth West,
Lady Mary Augusta Frederica Grimston,
Lady Eleanor Caroline Paget,
Lady Caroline Amelia Gordon Lennox,
Lady Elizabeth Anne Georgiana Dorothea Howard,
Lady Ida Hay,
Lady Catharine Lucy Wilhelmina Stanhope,
Lady Jane Harriet Bouverie,
Lady Mary Charlotte Howard,

assisted by Captain F. H. Seymour, the Groom of the Robes.

Master of the Horse, The Earl of Albemarle, G.C.H.
Mistress of the Robes, The Duchess of Sutherland.

Ladies of the Bedchamber:

The Marchioness of Normanby.
The Countess of Charlemont.
The Dowager Lady Lyttelton.
The Lady Portman.
The Duchess of Bedford.
The Countess of Sandwich.
The Countess of Burlington.
The Lady Barham.

Maids of Honor:

The Hon. Harriet Pitt.
The Hon. Amelia Murray.
The Hon. Henrietta Anson.
The Hon. Harriet Lister.
The Hon. Caroline Cocks.
The Hon. Matilda Paget.
The Hon. Sarah Mary Cavendish.

Women of the Bedchamber:

Lady Harriet Clive.
Lady Charlotte Copley.
Viscountess Forbes.
Lady Caroline Barrington.
Mrs. Brand.
The Hon. Mrs. Campbell.
Lady Gardner.

Captain of the Yeomen of the Guard, Earl of Ilchester.
Gold Stick, Lord Hill.
Captain of the Band of Gentlemen-at-Arms, Lord Foley.

Keeper of the Privy Purse, Sir Henry Wheatley.

Six Gentlemen-at-Arms.

Six Yeomen of the Guard closed the procession.

It will be seen from this official programme how the heralds had marshaled the different members of the procession. Scarcely any notice was taken of the individuals who led the way in it until the lord chancellor made his appearance. He was greeted with a few scanty cheers. Garter King-of-Arms, with all his heraldic pomp and pride, and the head of his college, the Earl Marshal the Duke of Norfolk, with all the blood of all the Howards, passed unnoticed in the throng. Her Royal Highness the Princess Sophia of Gloucester, who stopped to address Sir G. Murray as she passed, was cheered. The Princess Augusta of Cambridge excited general admiration by her affability and beauty. Her royal aunt the Princess Augusta was cheered. Her Royal Highness the Duchess of Gloucester, whose name appears in the official details of the ceremony, was prevented from being present in consequence of her having been confined by a severe cold to her house for the last fortnight, and of her not yet being sufficiently recovered to encounter the fatigue of a considerable procession at so early an hour. Her Royal Highness the Duchess of Cambridge led her young daughter the Princess Mary in her hand, and the mother of so beautiful a child was certain not to be seen without interest. Every sympathy was awakened on behalf of her Royal Highness the Duchess of Kent; but she appeared somewhat disconsolate and distressed. His Royal Highness the Duke of Sussex, who was to give away the royal bride, seemed in excellent spirits. Lord Melbourne carried the sword of state; but little attention was paid to him. Her Majesty came next, looking anxious and excited. She was paler even than usual. Her dress was a rich white satin trimmed with orange-flower-blossoms. On her head she wore a wreath of the same blossoms, over which, but not so as to conceal her face, a beautiful veil of Honiton lace was thrown. Her bridesmaids and trainbearers were similarly attired, save that they had no veils.* Her Majesty wore the collar of the Garter, but no other diamonds or jewels.† Her attendants were arrayed with similar simplicity; and ladies more beautiful never graced palace, hall, or country-green. With one exception, which we have already remarked, the praises which Dryden has ascribed to the companions of his Queen in the "Flower and the Leaf" are equally applicable to these attendants of our young and amiable sovereign:

> "A train less fair, as ancient fathers tell,
> Seduced the sons of Heaven to rebel;
> I pass their form, and every charming grace—
> Less than an angel would their worth debase;
> But their attire, like liveries of a kind,
> Simple but rich, is fresh within my mind;
> In satin white as snow the troop was gown'd,
> The seams with sparkling emeralds set around."

Every face was turned upon them and their royal mistress. Theirs was fixed upon hers, and as they moved and turned in conformity with her steps, it was evident that female vanity was for a time deadened in their bosoms, and that they were

* The bridesmaids were in white, with roses.

† Her Majesty wore a diamond necklace and earrings.

thinking, not of the impression which they themselves created, but of that which was created by the royal bride. They were followed by the Duchess of Sutherland. Of the ladies of the bedchamber and the maids of honor we have only to say that they did honor to the court and to their places in the procession. It was closed, not as the official statement announced, by six Yeomen of the Guard, but by two officers in polished cuirasses and in dirty boots, who commanded the squadron of Life Guards on duty at the Palace.

As her Majesty approached the Chapel, the national anthem was performed by the instrumental band. Her Majesty walked up the aisle, followed by her trainbearers and attendants without noticing or bowing to any of the peers. On reaching the *haut pas* her Majesty knelt on her footstool, and having performed her private devotions, sat down in her chair of state. The different officers of state having now taken their seats in the body of the Chapel, the *coup d'œil* was splendid beyond description.

> Lords, ladies, captains, councilors, and priests,
> Their choice nobility and flower; embassies
> From regions far remote
> In various habits
> Met from all parts to celebrate the day.

After the lapse of a few seconds her Majesty rose and advanced with his Royal Highness Prince Albert to the communion-table, where the Archbishop of Canterbury immediately commenced reading the service.

The rubric was rigidly adhered to throughout.

The Archbishop of Canterbury read the service with great appropriateness and much feeling, the Bishop of London repeating the responses.

When his Grace came to the words,

"Albert, wilt thou have this woman to be thy wedded wife, to live together after God's ordinance in the holy estate of matrimony? Wilt thou love her, comfort her, honor, and keep her in sickness and in health; and forsaking all other, keep thee only unto her, so long as ye both shall live?"

His Royal Highness, in a firm tone, replied "I will."

And when he said, "Victoria, wilt thou have Albert to thy wedded husband, to live together after God's ordinance in the holy estate of matrimony? Wilt thou obey him, and serve him, love, honor, and keep in sickness and in health;

and, forsaking all other, keep thee only unto him, so long as ye both shall live?"

Her Majesty, in a firm voice, and a tone audible in all parts of the Chapel, replied, "I will."

The Archbishop of Canterbury then said, "Who giveth this woman to be married to this man?"

His Royal Highness the Duke of Sussex, who occupied a seat on the left of her Majesty, now advanced, and, taking her Majesty's hand, said, "I do."

The Archbishop of Canterbury then laid hold of her Majesty's hand, and pressing it in that of Prince Albert's, pronounced these words, his Royal Highness repeating them after his Grace:

"I, Albert, take thee, Victoria, to be my wedded wife, to have and to hold, from this day forward, for better for worse, for richer for poorer, in sickness and in health, to love and to cherish, till death do us part, according to God's holy ordinance; and thereto I plight thee my troth."

Her Majesty repeated the words *mutatis mutandis*, "I, Victoria, take thee, Albert, to my wedded husband, to have and to hold, from this day forward, for better for worse, for richer for poorer, in sickness and in health, to love, cherish, and to obey, till death us do part, according to God's holy ordinance; and thereto I give thee my troth."

The Archbishop of Canterbury then took the ring, a plain gold ring, from his Royal Highness, and placing it to the fourth finger of her Majesty, returned it to his Royal Highness. Prince Albert put it on, repeating after his Grace these words: "With this ring I thee wed, with my body I thee worship, and with all my worldly goods I thee endow; in the name of the Father, and of the Son, and of the Holy Ghost. Amen."

The Archbishop then concluded the service as follows, her Majesty and Prince Albert still remaining standing at the altar:

"O Eternal God, Creator and Preserver of all mankind, Giver of all spiritual grace, the Author of everlasting life, send thy blessing upon these thy servants, Victoria and Albert, whom we bless in thy name; that as Isaac and Rebecca lived faithfully together, so these persons may surely perform and keep the vow and covenant betwixt them made (whereof this ring given and received is a token and pledge), and may ever remain in perfect love and peace together, and live according to thy laws, through Jesus Christ our Lord. Amen.

"Those whom God hath joined together let no man put asunder."

The Park and Tower guns then fired a royal salute.

The Archbishop of Canterbury then proceeded:

"Forasmuch as Albert and Victoria have consented together in holy wedlock, and have witnessed the same before God and this company, and thereto have given and pledged their troth either to other, and have declared the same by giving and receiving of a ring, and by joining of hands, I pronounce that they be man and wife together. In the name of the Father, and of the Son, and of the Holy Ghost. Amen.

"God the Father, God the Son, God the Holy Ghost, bless, preserve, and keep you; the Lord mercifully with his favor look upon you; and so fill you with all spiritual benediction and grace, that ye may so live together in this life, that in the world to come ye may have life everlasting. Amen."

The choir then performed the *Deus Misereatur* (King's in B flat), the verse parts being doubled by the choir and sung by Messrs. Knyvett, Wylde, Neil, Vaughan, Sale, and Bradbury, on the *decani* side; and on the *cantoris*, by Evans, Salmon, Horncastle, Roberts, Welsh, and Clarke.

Sir George Smart presided at the organ.

It is but justice to the gentlemen of the Chapel Royal to state that this service was executed in the most effective and spirit-stirring manner.

The Archbishop of Canterbury then proceeded:

"Our Father, which art in heaven, hallowed be thy name. Thy kingdom come. Thy will be done in earth, as it is in heaven. Give us this day our daily bread. And forgive us our trespasses, as we forgive them that trespass against us. And lead us not into temptation, but deliver us from evil. Amen.

"*Minister.* O Lord, save thy servant and thy handmaid:

"*Answer.* Who put their trust in thee.

"*Minister.* O Lord, send them help from thy holy place:

"*Answer.* And evermore defend them.

"*Minister.* Be unto them a tower of strength

"*Answer.* From the face of their enemy.

"*Minister.* O Lord, hear our prayer,

"*Answer.* And let our cry come unto thee.

"*Minister.* O God of Abraham, God of Isaac, God of Jacob, bless these thy servants, and sow the seed of eternal life in their hearts; that whatsoever in thy Holy Word they shall profitably learn, they may in deed fulfill the same. Look, O Lord, mercifully upon them from heaven and bless them. And as thou didst send thy blessing upon Abraham and Sarah, to their great comfort, so vouchsafe to send thy blessing upon these thy servants; that they, obeying thy will, and always being in safety under thy protection, may abide in thy love unto their lives' end; through Jesus Christ our Lord. Amen."

The Archbishop of Canterbury proceeded to the end with the remainder of the service as prescribed in the Book of Common Prayer, her Majesty and Prince Albert still standing before the communion-table.

The service having concluded, the several members of the royal family who had occupied places around the altar returned to take their positions in the procession. On passing her Majesty, they all paid their congratulations, and the Duke of Sussex, after shaking her by the hand in a manner which appeared to have little ceremony, but with cordiality in it, affectionately kissed her cheek. After all had passed with the exception of the royal bride and bridegroom, her Majesty stepped hastily across to the other side of the altar, where the queen dowager was standing, and kissed her.

Prince Albert then took her Majesty's hand, and the royal pair left the Chapel, all the spectators standing.

While the procession was proceeding down the aisle, her Majesty spoke frequently to the Earl of Uxbridge, who was on her right hand, apparently giving directions as to the order of the procession.

We have found it impossible, in our short description, to do justice either to the demeanor of the "happy, happy pair," which was firm, self-possessed, and dignified throughout, or to the various groups who gave interest and animation to the scene. The spectacle in the Chapel, from first to last, was gorgeous in the extreme,

Premier, prelate, potentate, and peer

giving lustre and brilliancy to the whole.

Among the various excellent arrangements connected with the celebration of her Majesty's marriage, we heard with some astonishment and regret that the gentlemen of the Chapel Royal, who were obliged to sustain no unimportant part in the solemnization, did so, for the first time on such an occasion, not only without receiving any remuneration for their trouble, but without even a pair of gloves, a rosette, or any other favor being allowed them.

RETURN FROM THE CHAPEL ROYAL.

The deep interest taken by the spectators in the colonnade in the proceedings of the day was shown by the general silence which prevailed unto the period of the Queen's approach. As soon as she had passed into the Chapel every tongue seemed set at liberty, and a confused murmur arose, which compelled the attendants to close the doors of the ante-chapel, lest it should penetrate into the Chapel where the solemn rites of religion were performing. A word, however, from one of the officers of the lord chamberlain was sufficient to put an end to this impropriety. The doors were again opened, the music of the anthem was faintly heard, the signal guns ceased to fire, and at a few minutes past one the procession began to remarshal itself for its return. The bridegroom's procession, which was, however, robbed of his presence, returned first. Again were the Duke and Hereditary Prince of Saxe-Coburg loudly cheered. The nuptial procession then returned in the same order as before. On the appearance of her Majesty hand-in-hand with her royal husband, the clapping of hands and waving of handkerchiefs were renewed time after time until they had passed out of sight. Whether by accident or design, his Royal Highness Prince Albert inclosed her Majesty's hand in his own in such a way as to display the wedding-ring, which appeared more solid than is usual in ordinary weddings. On their return, cheers were given to most, if not to all, of the ladies of royal birth who had received them on their approach. There was, however, one cheer far more long and enthusiastic than any other of the day reserved for the Duke of Wellington as he left the Chapel. He was not part of the royal procession, and it had passed to some distance before he made his appearance. As soon as he had arrived in the centre of the colonnade, spontaneously, without any signal, and yet as if by common and universal consent, the company rose and gave him three hearty cheers. The heart of the veteran appeared gladdened by it.

Lord Melbourne, who must have heard the uproar, took it as a hint that he had better return another way. At least, if he did not, his presence did not meet our view in the returning *cortège*. Her Majesty then proceeded to the throne-room, where the form of attestation took place. Her Majesty and Prince Albert signed the marriage register, which was attested by certain members of the royal family and officers of state present. A splendid table was prepared for the purpose, and this part of the ceremony, with the magnificent assemblage by which it was witnessed, presented one of the most striking spectacles of the day.

THE RETURN TO BUCKINGHAM PALACE AND THE BREAKFAST.

During the interim of the bridal procession's leaving and returning to Buckingham Palace, there was nothing of any interest that occurred in the Park, unless indeed we may mention a desperate shower of rain, which besprinkled her Majesty's subjects, but did not appear to extinguish one spark of their loyalty. At about one o'clock the firing of the guns announced that the ring had been put on the finger, the important part of the ceremony concluded.

After the ceremony, at twenty-five minutes past one, the first return reached Buckingham Palace, and consisted of the inferior officers of Prince Albert's suite, the Queen's gentlemen ushers, and a lady of her Majesty's household. At twenty minutes to two the Duchess of Kent returned; her royal highness was accompanied by her brother, the Duke of Saxe-Coburg-Gotha, and Prince Ernest. The royal duchess was loudly cheered, which she acknowledged most graciously. Viscount Melbourne and Viscount Palmerston followed soon after in full official costume, then came the Marquis of Normanby, dressed in the uniform of a colonial governor, and at ten minutes to two o'clock the royal procession returned. The Prince rode in the carriage with the Queen. His Royal Highness assisted her Majesty to alight, and led her into the Palace. The royal bride entered her own hall with an open and joyous countenance, flushed perhaps in the slightest degree, and in the most smiling and condescending manner acknowledged the loud and cordial cheers which rang through the apartment. The royal bridegroom handed her Majesty through the state rooms. The Duke of Sussex soon followed. The duke was dressed in his uniform as captain general of the Honorable Artillery Company, and wore the collars and other insignia of the Orders of the Garter, Bath, and St. Andrew. The Duke of Cambridge arrived immediately after, accompanied by the duchess, Prince George, and the two princesses. His royal highness wore the insignia of the Orders of the Garter and the Bath, and carried his baton as field-marshal. Prince George was dressed in the uniform of his regiment, and was decorated with the Order of the Garter. The duke led in the little Princess Mary. The invited guests to the *dejeûner* followed each other in rapid succession.

WEDDING BREAKFAST.

At Buckingham Palace there was a wedding repast, at which several of the illustrious participators in the previous ceremony, and the officers of the household and ministers of state, were present.

The following is the list of guests:

Her Royal Highness the Duchess of Kent.
His Serene Highness the Duke of Coburg.
Their Royal Highnesses the Duke and Duchess of Cambridge.
His Royal Highness the Duke of Sussex.
Her Royal Highness the Duchess of Gloucester.
His Royal Highness Prince George of Cambridge.
Her Royal Highness the Princess Augusta of Cambridge.
His Serene Highness Prince Ernest of Saxe-Coburg.
Her Royal Highness the Princess Sophia Matilda.
The Archbishop of Canterbury.
The Bishop of London.
Viscount Melbourne.
The Lord Chancellor.
The Lord President of the Council.
The Lord Privy Seal.
The Marquis of Normanby.
Viscount Palmerston.
Lord John Russell.
The Lord Steward.

The Lord Chamberlain.
The Master of the Horse.
The Mistress of the Robes.
The Lady in Waiting.
Maids of Honor: Hon. Miss Cocks and Miss Cavendish.
Viscount Torrington.
The Hon. Major Keppel.
Lord Alfred Paget.
Mrs. Brand.
The Lady in Waiting on her Royal Highness the Duchess of Kent.
Gentlemen of the Duke of Coburg's suite.
The Lady in Waiting on her Royal Highness the Duchess of Gloucester.
The Lady in Waiting on her Royal Highness the Duchess of Cambridge.
The Lady in Waiting on her Royal Highness the Princess Sophia Matilda.

THE DEPARTURE FOR WINDSOR.

At the conclusion of the breakfast, arrangements were made for the immediate departure of her Majesty for Windsor, and at a quarter to four the royal party left Buckingham Palace amid the cheers and festive acclamations of a vast multitude. The first carriage was occupied only by her Majesty and Prince Albert; the second and three others by the lord and lady in waiting, the groom, equerry, two maids of honor, and other attendants of her Majesty and his Royal Highness. Just before the royal *cortège* left Buckingham Palace, the sun shone forth with full brightness, the skies were cleared of their murky clouds, and all things seemed to promise that future happiness which we sincerely trust may be the lot of the illustrious pair.

The Prince was dressed in a plain dark traveling dress, and her Majesty in a white satin pelisse, trimmed with swansdown, with a white satin bonnet and feather.

CONSTITUTION HILL.

At an hour considerably before sunrise this neighborhood began to exhibit signs of preparation for the approaching spectacle, which became more evident and more bustling as the day drew on. Parties of cavalry and infantry moving to their posts, orderlies dashing to and fro, groups of sight-seers, male and female, hurrying from every quarter toward Buckingham Palace; and last, though not least, numerous swarms of persons scattered over the Green Park, laden with planks, casks, chairs, tables, and other means of elevation for the purpose of giving a sight of the procession, denoting by their wild cries and determination, and cunning in baffling the efforts of the police to prevent their ingress into the park, the origin of the majority of them from the sister island: all these gave a variety and life to the scene which almost compensated for the dullness and gloom of the morning. But, gloomy and unpromising as the morning was, the parties interested seemed determined to make the best of it, and good-humored jests circulating among the crowd, and now and then a *petite émeute*, or short-lived squabble, whiled away the damp and heavy hours. At length, however, about eight o'clock, amusement began to turn up in the arrivals of the guests invited to the royal nuptials, who, as they successively filed under the triumphal arch, were challenged by the warder, and showed the pink or white cards which gave a title to admittance, lent an air of considerable liveliness to the scene, not unmixed with something of the feudal and the romantic. First came in various flies and cabs, and vehicles of low degree, certain damsels who were pointed out to us as maids of honor, or persons otherwise appertaining to the royal household; then a strong body of the Foot Guards marched toward the position allotted to them in the immediate neighborhood of Buckingham Palace; then came a body of the Horse Guards Blue, with fifes and cymbals playing merrily, and then the general company began to make their appearance, among whom we noticed Mr. Montgomery, Lord Monteagle, the vice-chancellor, Lord and Lady Langdale, Viscount and Lady Howick, the Duke of Norfolk (in his robes and with his staff of office as earl marshal), Sir G. Grey, Lord and Lady Ashley, the Earl of Burlington, Viscount Morpeth, the chancellor of the Exchequer, Lord John Russell, Mr. Labouchere, Lord Holland, the Marquis of Normanby, Viscount Palmerston, Lord Duncannon, the lord chancellor, the Austrian and other ministers, and the Marchioness of Normanby. The ministers, with the exception of the lord chancellor, who wore his legal costume, were attired in the Windsor uniform of blue, guarded or turned up with an edging of oak-leaf in gold, but, strange to tell, they passed in every instance without the smallest notice, favorable or otherwise, on the part of the immense multitude who were congregated in this quarter. At a quarter to twelve the Duke of Cambridge and suite, in three of the royal carriages, drove through the gate, escorted by a guard of honor. The Duke of Sussex passed in a single carriage at a few minutes before twelve o'clock. The illustrious duke wore, as usual, his black silk skullcap, looked in very good health, and was very favorably received by the crowd. We should have said, however, that about a quarter to eleven the rain cleared off, and we had an opportunity to take a survey of the assembled multitude, and certainly we should say that this assemblage, though decidedly greater in numbers than any which has been collected during this reign on a like public occasion, was also decidedly inferior in the proportion of well-dressed persons, and persons carrying the air of respectability. Of these we noticed but few; at the same time there appeared to be a very much smaller display of military as well as of civil force than has formerly been usual. The police, however, in spite of the mob's restless importunity, displayed their habitual temper and firmness, and the soldiery their own unrivaled patience and good-humor. And so the day wore on, until about half past two o'clock, when, the rain and mist having cleared off, the *coup d'œil* from the triumphal arch was certainly striking, for as far as the eye could reach toward Kensington, along Hyde Park, the Green Park, and Piccadilly, the whole area was more or less thickly crowded with human beings, all anxiously expecting (though most of them at a distance disabling them from enjoying) the approach of their youthful monarch. At length, about half past two o'clock, the passage of a party of Light Dragoons, on their way to the Palace, gave people cause to think that her Majesty's appearance would not be wanting long, for it was conjectured, and rightly, that these troops were intended to form the escort of the royal pair to Windsor Castle. A few minutes past four o'clock the much-expected cavalcade drew near, a carriage with ladies of the household leading the way, a party of the cavalry following; the royal traveling chariot conveying her Majesty and Prince Albert dashed rapidly under the triumphal archway amid the warm and enthusiastic cheers of the spectators assembled around, who were manifestly much captivated by the comely appearance of the Prince, and by the affable and graceful manner in which he acknowledged their notice. Her Majesty appeared in excellent health and high spirits, and bowed in return to the cheers of her applauding subjects with much earnestness of manner.

ETON.

The preparations at Eton were on a grand scale. At the entrance of the precincts of the college, on the right-hand side of the road coming from London, and fronting the college itself, a large wooden structure, in form of a Grecian portico 60 feet in height, and of proportionate width, was erected. The whole of this erection was covered with variegated lamps; on the pediment were the royal arms. An inscription or "legend," with the words "Gratulatio Victoriæ et Alberto," surmounted the pediment. The word "Etona" was also conspicuous among the decorations. Seven large flags floated gallantly from the summit of the building, which exhibited considerable taste both in the design and embellishments. There were no less than 5000 lamps in this portico, the effect of which was at night very splendid. The interior quadrangle of the college presented a brilliant appearance. The clock-tower, on the eastern side, was illuminated by a crown, surrounded with a wreath of laurel, having the letters "V. A.," the whole in variegated lamps. Beneath were three brilliant stars. The arch of the clock-tower was surrounded by rows of lamps, and the eastern side of the quadrangle was elegantly festooned with lamps. The principal gateway into the quadrangle was also decorated with lamps, having the words "Floreat Etona" over the crown of the arch. Several thousand lamps were employed on this part of the venerable edifice. There was also a triumphal arch of laurels and lamps across the road by the Christopher Inn.

At the entrance into Eton the whole of the scholars and masters of the school were collected, to the number of 550, wearing bridal favors, and from time to time was heard the noise of maroons, fired in token of loyalty and rejoicing. Besides the preparations at the college, the main street of Eton presented a lively appearance; most of the houses were illuminated, and the principal tradesmen exhibited stars and other emblems of the joyous event. The whole place was in a state of bustle and excitement; all was felicity. At the Christopher Inn a dinner was prepared for a large party of the inhabitants, and there were private parties at most of the houses of the dames and college authorities.

WINDSOR.

In the morning the appearance of Windsor differed in no respect from its ordinary character, and scarcely a symptom was observable of an intention to make any public celebration of the royal wedding. All the shops were opened as usual; every one seemed busy in his customary avocations; no merry peal of bells welcomed in the day; and the rain, falling in torrents, made the town look very dull and miserable. By degrees this melancholy aspect of affairs wore away. The rain ceased; in the afternoon the shops were closed, and the inhabitants having now nothing to detain them at home, thronged the streets, decorated with wedding favors and dressed in the gayest possible style, and the prospect—so gloomy a short time before—became lively and charming. The sun shot forth its beams, and the bells, as if awakened from slumber, burst out in joyous chimes. As the day advanced, the weather grew more and more propitious, and numbers of strangers, anxious to see her Majesty with her illustrious Consort enter the noble palace of her ancestors at Windsor, poured into the place, conveyed in every conceivable description of vehicle. Most of these persons, after giving a hearty farewell cheer to the royal couple as they passed through the gates of the Castle, returned again to London, resolved to finish the amusement of the day by a sight of the splendid illuminations in town. About half past two o'clock considerable excitement was occasioned among the various groups of persons waiting to see the royal *cortège* pass through High Street by the appearance of the royal standard, which at that hour was raised at the Round Tower. Various were the conjectures as to the particular circumstance which the hoisting of this proud and noble banner might be intended to indicate; but, having tired themselves with explanatory suggestions, the crowd came to the conclusion that it must be the signal of her Majesty's departure from St. James's Palace after the conclusion of the nuptial ceremony. At four o'clock a troop of Life Guards left Windsor for the purpose of meeting the royal *cortège* on the road and escorting it to the castle. At this hour a dense concourse of persons had collected about the gates of the castle, which appeared to be the point of greatest attraction, and an unbroken line of spectators extended from this spot to the extremity of Eton, near to London. As always happens in cases like the present, the anxiously-expected arrival was announced about one hundred and fifty times before it actually happened, and as each successive rumor turned out to be false, it would not be easy to depict the momentary disappointment manifested by the impatient assemblage.

The evening had closed in before the arrival of the royal party. The whole town was therefore illuminated before they entered the town, and the effect produced by the glitter of the lights on the congregated multitude was exceedingly splendid. Every house in Windsor was illuminated ; many of them were handsomely decorated with flags, laurels, mottoes, and artificial bouquets. Ingenious devices and transparent representations of the Queen and Prince Albert were not few nor far between. The Town-hall, the White Hart Inn, the Castle Inn, and several houses in the neighborhood, were conspicuous for the brilliancy and beauty of their decorations.

At half past six the crowd on the castle hill had become so dense that it was with difficulty the line of road for the royal carriages was kept clear. The whole street was one living mass, while the walls of the houses glowed with crowns, stars, and all the brilliant devices which gas and oil could supply. At this moment a flight of rockets was visible in the air ; it was apparently over Eton, and it was immediately concluded that the Queen had entered Eton. The bells now rang merrily, and the shouts of the spectators were heard as the royal *cortège* approached the castle. At twenty minutes before seven the royal carriage arrived in the High Street, Windsor, preceded by the advanced-guard of the traveling escort, consisting of a body of the 2d Life Guards, commanded by Lieutenant Totenham, which relieved the 14th Dragoons at Colnbrook. The shouts were now most loud and cheering, and from the windows and balconies of the houses handkerchiefs were waved by the ladies, while the gentlemen huzzaed and waved their hats. The carriage, from the crowd, proceeded slowly, her Majesty and her royal Consort bowing to the people. Her Majesty looked remarkably well, and Prince Albert seemed in the highest spirits at the cordiality with which he was greeted. It was exactly a quarter to seven when the royal carriage drew up at the grand entrance. The Queen was handed from the carriage by the Prince; she immediately took his arm and entered the Castle. In the carriages which followed that in which the royal pair arrived were Lady Sandwich, lady in waiting; the Hon. Miss Cocks and the Hon. Miss Cavendish, maids of honor; Lord Torrington, Major Keppel, and Mr. Seymour, the groom and equerry in waiting, who formed the royal dinner-party.

In the evening the auspicious event was celebrated by a public dinner given in the Town-hall. About 100 of the inhabitants of Windsor attended, the mayor taking the chair, and being supported on either side by the members for the borough, Messrs. Ramsbottom and Gordon. At the conclusion of the dinner, "Health and Long Lives to Victoria and Albert" was proposed by the mayor, and responded to in the most enthusiastic manner, the whole company rising and cheering for several minutes. The evening's entertainment was greatly advanced by the vocal abilities of Messrs. Fitzwilliam, Jolly (senior and junior), and J. O. Atkins, who executed two or three appropriate songs written for the occasion.

Two other public dinners were given at the Castle Tavern and at the Star and Garter; and several inhabitants of the town besides had private parties in honor of the royal wedding.

We are happy to say that while the "great" feasted, the "small" were not forgotten on this joyous occasion. A substantial dinner of good old English fare was provided for the poorer inhabitants of the place and the neighboring country, the expense being defrayed by a voluntary subscription, to which fund £20 were contributed by her Majesty. Nearly 600 poor families, amounting probably to 2000 individuals, were by this considerate charity regaled at their own homes with a good dinner and some excellent beer, wherewith to do complete justice to the toast of "Health and Happiness to Victoria and Albert."

BARTH'S NORTH AND CENTRAL AFRICA. Travels and Discoveries in North and Central Africa: Being a Journal of an Expedition undertaken under the Auspices of H.B.M.'s Government, in the Years 1849-1855. By HENRY BARTH, Ph.D., D.C.L. Illustrated. Complete in 3 vols., 8vo, Cloth, $12 00; Half Calf, $18 75.

BEECHER'S AUTOBIOGRAPHY, &c. Autobiography, Correspondence, &c., of Lyman Beecher, D.D. Edited by his Son, CHARLES BEECHER. With Three Steel Portraits and Engravings on Wood. In 2 vols., 12mo, Cloth, $5 00; Half Calf, $8 50.

BRODHEAD'S HISTORY OF NEW YORK. History of the State of New York. By JOHN ROMEYN BRODHEAD. First Period, 1609-1664. 8vo, Cloth, $3 00.

CARLYLE'S FREDERICK THE GREAT. History of Friedrich II., called Frederick the Great. By THOMAS CARLYLE. Portraits, Maps, Plans, &c. 6 vols., 12mo, Cloth, $12 00; Half Calf, $22 50.

CARLYLE'S FRENCH REVOLUTION. History of the French Revolution. Newly Revised by the Author, with Index, &c. 2 vols., 12mo, Cloth, $3 50.

CARLYLE'S OLIVER CROMWELL. Letters and Speeches of Oliver Cromwell. With Elucidations and Connecting Narrative. 2 vols., 12mo, Cloth, $3 50.

CHALMERS'S POSTHUMOUS WORKS. The Posthumous Works of Dr. Chalmers. Edited by his Son-in-Law, Rev. WILLIAM HANNA, LL.D. Complete in 9 vols., 12mo, Cloth, 13 50; Half Calf, $29 25.

JOHNSON'S COMPLETE WORKS. The Works of Samuel Johnson, LL.D. With an Essay on his Life and Genius, by ARTHUR MURPHY, Esq. Portrait of Johnson. 2 vols., 8vo, Cloth, $4 00.

CLAYTON'S QUEENS OF SONG. Queens of Song: Being Memoirs of some of the most celebrated Female Vocalists who have performed on the Lyric Stage from the Earliest Days of Opera to the Present Time. To which is added a Chronological List of all the Operas that have been performed in Europe. By ELLEN CREATHORNE CLAYTON. With Portraits. 8vo, Cloth, $3 00; Half Calf, $5 25.

COLERIDGE'S COMPLETE WORKS. The Complete Works of Samuel Taylor Coleridge. With an Introductory Essay upon his Philosophical and Theological Opinions. Edited by Professor SHEDD. Complete in 7 vols. With a fine Portrait. Small 8vo, Cloth, $10 50; Half Calf, $22 75.

CURTIS'S HISTORY OF THE CONSTITUTION. History of the Origin, Formation, and Adoption of the Constitution of the United States. By GEORGE TICKNOR CURTIS. Complete in two large and handsome Octavo Volumes. Cloth, $6 00; Sheep, $7 00; Half Calf, $10 50.

DAVIS'S CARTHAGE. Carthage and her Remains: Being an Account of the Excavations and Researches on the Site of the Phœnician Metropolis in Africa and other ad jacent Places. Conducted under the Auspices of Her Majesty's Government. By Dr. DAVIS, F.R.G.S. Profusely Illustrated with Maps, Woodcuts, Chromo-Lithographs, &c. 8vo, Cloth, $4 00.

GIBBON'S ROME. History of the Decline and Fall of the Roman Empire. By EDWARD GIBBON. With Notes by Rev. H. H. MILMAN and M. GUIZOT. A new cheap Edition. To which is added a Complete Index of the whole Work, and a Portrait of the Author. 6 vols., 12mo (uniform with Hume), Cloth, $9 00; Half Calf, $19 50.

DOOLITTLE'S CHINA. Social Life of the Chinese: With some Account of their Religious, Governmental, Educational, and Business Customs and Opinions. With special but not exclusive Reference to Fuhchau. By Rev. JUSTUS DOOLITTLE, Fourteen Years Member of the Fuhchau Mission of the American Board. Illustrated with more than 150 characteristic Engravings on Wood. 2 vols., 12mo, Cloth, $5 00; Half Calf, $8 50.

DRAPER'S AMERICAN CIVIL POLICY. Thoughts on the Future Civil Policy of America. By JOHN W. DRAPER, M.D., LL.D., Professor of Chemistry and Physiology in the University of New York, Author of a "Treatise on Human Physiology," and a "History of the Intellectual Development of Europe." Crown 8vo, Cloth, $2 50.

DRAPER'S INTELLECTUAL DEVELOPMENT OF EUROPE. A History of the Intellectual Development of Europe. By JOHN W. DRAPER, M.D., LL.D., Professor of Chemistry and Physiology in the University of New York. 8vo, Cloth, $5; Half Calf, $7 25.

MISS EDGEWORTH'S NOVELS. With Engravings. 10 volsume, 12mo, Cloth, $15 00; Half Calf, $32 50.

GROTE'S HISTORY OF GREECE. 12 vols., 12mo, Cloth, $18 00; Half Calf, $39 00.

MRS. HALE'S WOMAN'S RECORD. Woman's Record; or, Biographical Sketches of all Distinguished Women, from the Creation to the Present Time. Arranged in Four Eras, with Selections from Female Writers of each Era. By Mrs. SARAH JOSEPHA HALE. Illustrated with more than 200 Portraits, 8vo, Cloth, $5 00.

HALL'S ARCTIC RESEARCHES. Arctic Researches and Life Among the Esquimaux: Being the Narrative of an Expedition in Search of Sir John Franklin, in the Years 1860, 1861, and 1862. By CHARLES FRANCIS HALL. With Maps and 100 Illustrations. The Illustrations are from Original Drawings by Charles Parsons, Henry L. Stephens, Solomon Eyting, W. S. L. Jewett, and Granville Perkins, after Sketches by Captain Hall. A new Edition. 8vo, Cloth, Beveled Edges, $5 00; Half Calf, $7 25.

HALLAM'S CONSTITUTIONAL HISTORY OF ENGLAND, from the Accession of Henry VII. to the Death of George II. 8vo, Cloth, $2 00.

HALLAM'S LITERATURE. Introduction to the Literature of Europe during the Fifteenth, Sixteenth, and Seventeenth Centuries. By HENRY HALLAM. 2 vols., 8vo, Cloth, $4 00.

HALLAM'S MIDDLE AGES. State of Europe during the Middle Ages. By HENRY HALLAM. 8vo, Cloth, $2 00.

HARPER'S NEW CLASSICAL LIBRARY. Literal Translations.
The following volumes are now ready. Portraits. 12mo, Cloth, $1 50 each.

CÆSAR.
VIRGIL.
SALLUST.
HORACE.
CICERO'S ORATIONS.
CICERO'S OFFICES, &c.
CICERO ON ORATORY AND ORATORS.
TACITUS. 2 vols.
TERENCE.
SOPHOCLES.
JUVENAL.
XENOPHON.
HOMER'S ILIAD.
HOMER'S ODYSSEY.
HERODOTUS.
DEMOSTHENES.
THUCYDIDES.
ÆSCHYLUS.
EURIPIDES. 2 vols.

HARPER'S PICTORIAL HISTORY OF THE REBELLION. Harper's Pictorial History of the Great Rebellion in the United States. Vol. I. now ready. More than 500 Illustrations. 4to, $6 00. Vol. II. is now being Published in Numbers.

HILDRETH'S HISTORY OF THE UNITED STATES. *First Series:* From the First Settlement of the Country to the Adoption of the Federal Constitution. *Second Series:* From the Adoption of the Federal Constitution to the End of the Sixteenth Congress. 6 vols., 8vo, Cloth, $18 00; Half Calf, $31 50.

HUME'S HISTORY OF ENGLAND. History of England, from the Invasion of Julius Cæsar to the Abdication of James II., 1688. By DAVID HUME. A New Edition, with the Author's last Corrections and Improvements. To which is prefixed a short Account of his Life, written by Himself. With a Portrait of the Author. 6 Vols., 12mo, Cloth, $9 00; Half Calf, $19 50.

JAY'S WORKS. Complete Works of Rev. William Jay: comprising his Sermons, Family Discourses, Morning and Evening Exercises for every Day in the Year, Family Prayers, &c. Author's enlarged Edition, revised. 3 vols., 8vo, Cloth, $6 00; Half Calf, $12 75.

KINGLAKE'S CRIMEAN WAR. The Invasion of the Crimea: Its Origin, and an Account of its Progress down to the Death of Lord Raglan. By ALEXANDER WILLIAM KINGLAKE. With Maps and Plans. 2 Vols. Vol. I. Maps. 12mo, Cloth, $2 00.

LAMB'S COMPLETE WORKS. The Works of Charles Lamb. Comprising his Letters, Poems, Essays of Elia, Essays upon Shakspeare, Hogarth, &c., and a Sketch of his Life, with the Final Memorials, by T. NOON TALFOURD. Portrait. 2 vols., 12mo, Cloth, $3 00.

DR. LIVINGSTONE'S SOUTH AFRICA. Missionary Travels and Researches in South Africa; including a Sketch of Sixteen Years' Residence in the Interior of Africa, and a Journey from the Cape of Good Hope to Loando on the West Coast; thence across the Continent, down the River Zambesi, to the Eastern Ocean. By DAVID LIVINGSTONE, LL.D., D.C.L. With Portrait, Maps by Arrowsmith, and numerous Illustrations. 8vo, Cloth, $4 50; Half Calf, $6 75.

LIVINGSTONE'S ZAMBESI. Narrative of an Expedition to the Zambesi and its Tributaries; and of the Discovery of the Lakes Shirwa and Nyassa. 1858–1864. By DAVID and CHARLES LIVINGSTONE. With Map and Illustrations. 8vo, Cloth, $5 00; Half Calf, $7 25. [*Uniform with Livingstone's "South Africa."*]

LOSSING'S FIELD-BOOK OF THE REVOLUTION. Pictorial Field-Book of the Revolution; or, Illustrations by Pen and Pencil of the History, Biography, Scenery, Relics, and Traditions of the War for Independence. By BENSON J. LOSSING. 2 vols., 8vo, Cloth, $14 00; Sheep, $15 00; Half Calf, $18 00; Full Turkey Morocco, $22 00.

MACAULAY'S HISTORY OF ENGLAND. The History of England from the Accession of James II. By THOMAS BABINGTON MACAULAY. With an original Portrait of the Author. 5 vols., 8vo, Cloth, $10 00; Half Calf, $21 25; 12mo, Cloth, $7 50; Half Calf, $16 25.

MARCY'S ARMY LIFE ON THE BORDER. Thirty Years of Army Life on the Border. Comprising Descriptions of the Indian Nomads of the Plains; Explorations of New Territory; a Trip across the Rocky Mountains in the Winter; Descriptions of the Habits of Different Animals found in the West, and the Methods of Hunting them; with Incidents in the Life of Different Frontier Men, &c., &c. By Brevet Brig.-General R. B. MARCY, U.S.A., Author of "The Prairie Traveller." With numerous Illustrations. 8vo, Cloth, Beveled Edges, $3 00.

TICKNOR'S HISTORY OF SPANISH LITERATURE. With Criticisms on the particular Works, and Biographical Notices of prominent Writers. 3 vols., 8vo, Cloth, $5 00.

THE POETS OF THE NINETEENTH CENTURY. Selected and Edited by the Rev. ROBERT ARIS WILLMOTT. With English and American Additions, arranged by EVERT A. DUYCKINCK, Editor of "Cyclopædia of American Literature." Comprising Selections from the greatest Authors of the Age. Superbly Illustrated with 132 Engravings from Designs by the most Eminent Artists. In elegant Small 4to form, printed on Superfine Tinted Paper, richly bound in extra Cloth beveled, gilt edges, $6 00; Half Calf, $6 00; Full Turkey Morocco, $10 00.

BANCROFT'S MISCELLANIES. Literary and Historical Miscellanies. By GEORGE BANCROFT. 8vo, Cloth, $3 00.

BOSWELL'S JOHNSON. The Life of Samuel Johnson, LL.D. Including a Journey to the Hebrides. By JAMES BOSWELL, Esq. A New Edition, with numerous Additions and Notes, by JOHN WILSON CROKER, LL.D., F.R.S. Portrait of Boswell. 2 vols., 8vo, Cloth, $4 00.

DR. OLIN'S LIFE AND LETTERS. 2 vols., 12mo, Cloth, $3 00.

DR. OLIN'S TRAVELS. Travels in Egypt, Arabia Petræa, and the Holy Land. Engravings. 2 vols., 8vo, Cloth, $3 00.

DR. OLIN'S WORKS. The Works of Stephen Olin, D.D., late President of the Wesleyan University. 2 vols., 12mo, Cloth, $3 00.

LAURENCE OLIPHANT'S CHINA AND JAPAN. Narrative of the Earl of Elgin's Mission to China and Japan, in the Years 1857, '58, '59. By LAURENCE OLIPHANT, Private Secretary to Lord Elgin. Illustrations. 8vo, Cloth, $3 50.

MRS. OLIPHANT'S LIFE OF EDWARD IRVING. The Life of Edward Irving, Minister of the National Scotch Church, London. Illustrated by his Journals and Correspondence. By MRS. OLIPHANT. Portrait. 8vo, Cloth, $3 50.

PAGE'S LA PLATA. La Plata: The Argentine Confederation and Paraguay. Being a Narrative of the Exploration of the Tributaries of the River La Plata and Adjacent Countries, during the Years 1853, '54, '55, and '56, under the orders of the United States Government. By THOMAS J. PAGE, U.S.N., Commander of the Expedition. With Map and numerous Engravings. 8vo, Cloth, $5 00; Half Calf, $7 25.

SHAKSPEARE. The Dramatic Works of William Shakspeare, with the Corrections and Illustrations of Dr. JOHNSON, G. STEEVENS, and others. Revised by ISAAC REED. Engravings. 6 vols., Royal 12mo, Cloth, $9 00; Half Calf, $19 50.

PRIME'S COINS, MEDALS, AND SEALS. Coins, Medals, and Seals, Ancient and Modern. Illustrated and Described. With a Sketch of the History of Coins and Coinage, Instructions for Young Collectors, Tables of Comparative Rarity, Price-Lists of English and American Coins, Medals, and Tokens, &c., &c. Edited by W. C. PRIME, Author of "Boat Life in Egypt and Nubia," "Tent Life in the Holy Land," &c., &c. 8vo, Cloth, $3 50.

RUSSELL'S MODERN EUROPE. History of Modern Europe, with a View of the Progress of Society, from the Rise of Modern Kingdoms to the Peace of Paris in 1763. By W. RUSSELL. With a Continuance of the History, by WM. JONES. Engravings. 3 vols., 8vo, Cloth, $6 00.

WILKINSON'S ANCIENT EGYPTIANS. A Popular Account of their Manners and Customs, condensed from his larger Work, with some new Matter. Illustrated with 500 Woodcuts. 2 vols., 12mo, Cloth, $3 50; Half Calf, $7 00.

SPEKE'S AFRICA. Journal of the Discovery of the Source of the Nile. By Captain JOHN HANNING SPEKE, Captain H. M. Indian Army, Fellow and Gold Medalist of the Royal Geographical Society, Hon. Corresponding Member and Gold Medalist of the French Geographical Society, &c. With Maps and Portraits and numerous Illustrations, chiefly from Drawings by Captain GRANT. 8vo, Cloth, uniform with Livingstone, Barth, Burton, &c., $4 00; Half Calf, $6 25.

SPRING'S SERMONS. Pulpit Ministrations; or, Sabbath Readings. A Series of Discourses on Christian Doctrine and Duty. By Rev. GARDINER SPRING, D.D., Pastor of the Brick Presbyterian Church in the City of New York. Portrait on Steel. 2 vols., 8vo, Cloth, $6 00.

MISS STRICKLAND'S QUEENS OF SCOTLAND. Lives of the Queens of Scotland and English Princesses connected with the regal Succession of Great Britain. By AGNES STRICKLAND. 8 vols. 12mo, Cloth, $12 00; Half Calf, $26 00.

ADDISON'S COMPLETE WORKS. The Works of Joseph Addison, embracing the whole of the "Spectator." Complete in 3 vols., 8vo, Cloth, $6 00; Half Calf, $12 75.

THE STUDENT'S HISTORIES.

France. Engravings. 12mo, Cloth, $2 00.

Gibbon. Engravings. 12mo, Cloth, $2 00.

Greece. Engravings. 12mo, Cloth, $2 00.

The same, abridged. Engravings. 16mo, Cloth, $1 00.

Hume. Engravings. 12mo, Cloth, $2 00.

Rome. By Liddell. Engravings. 12mo, Cloth, $2 00.

Smaller History of Rome. Engravings. 16mo, Cloth, $1 00.

THOMSON'S LAND AND THE BOOK; or, Biblical Illustrations drawn from the Manners and Customs, the Scenes and the Scenery of the Holy Land. By W. M. THOMSON, D.D., Twenty-five Years a Missionary of the A.B.C.F.M. in Syria and Palestine. With two elaborate Maps of Palestine, an accurate Plan of Jerusalem, and *several Hundred Engravings*, representing the Scenery, Topography, and Productions of the Holy Land, and the Costumes, Manners, and Habits of the People. 2 elegant Large 12mo Volumes, Cloth, $5 00; Half Calf, $8 50.

VÁMBÉRY'S CENTRAL ASIA. Travels in Central Asia. Being the Account of a Journey from Teheran across the Turkoman Desert, on the Eastern Shore of the Caspian, to Khiva, Bokhara, and Samarcand, performed in the Year 1863. By ARMINIUS VÁMBÉRY, Member of the Hungarian Academy of Pesth, by whom he was sent on this Scientific Mission. With Map and Woodcuts. 8vo, Cloth, $4 50; Half Calf, $6 75.

ABBOTT'S HISTORY OF THE FRENCH REVOLUTION. The French Revolution of 1789, as viewed in the Light of Republican Institutions. By JOHN S. C. ABBOTT. With 100 Engravings. 8vo, Cloth, $5 00; Half Calf, $7 25.

ABBOTT'S NAPOLEON BONAPARTE. The History of Napoleon Bonaparte. By JOHN S. C. ABBOTT. With Maps, Woodcuts, and Portraits on Steel. 2 vols., 8vo, Cloth, $10 00; Half Calf, $14 50.

ABBOTT'S NAPOLEON AT ST. HELENA; or, Interesting Anecdotes and Remarkable Conversations of the Emperor during the Five and a Half Years of his Captivity. Collected from the Memorials of Las Casas, O'Meara, Montholon, Antommarchi, and others. By JOHN S. C. ABBOTT. With Illustrations. 8vo, Cloth, $5 00; Half Calf, $7 25.

BY GEORGE ELIOT.

ADAM BEDE. 12mo, Cloth, $1 50.

FELIX HOLT, THE RADICAL. 8vo, Paper, 75 cents.
A Library Edition, 12mo, Cloth, $1 75.

THE MILL ON THE FLOSS. 12mo, Cloth, $1 50; 8vo, Paper, 75 cents.

ROMOLA. With Illustrations. 8vo, Cloth, $2 00; Paper, $1 50.

SCENES OF CLERICAL LIFE. 8vo, Paper, 75 cents.

SILAS MARNER, THE WEAVER OF RAVELOE. 12mo, Cloth, $1 50.

It was once said of a very charming and high-minded woman that to know her was in itself a liberal education; and we are inclined to set an almost equally high value on an acquaintance with the writings of "George Eliot." For those who read them aright they possess the faculty of educating in its highest sense, of invigorating the intellect, giving a healthy tone to the taste, appealing to the nobler feelings of the heart, training its impulses aright, and awakening or developing in every mind the consciousness of a craving for something higher than the pleasures and rewards of that life which only the senses realize, the belief in a destiny of a nobler nature than can be grasped by experience or demonstrated by argument. On those readers who are able to appreciate a lofty independence of thought, a rare nobility of feeling, and an exquisite sympathy with the joys and sorrows of human nature, "George Eliot's" writings can not fail to exert an invigorating and purifying influence, the good effects of which leaves behind it a lasting impression.—*London Review.*

"George Eliot," or whoever he or she may be, has a wonderful power in giving an air of intense reality to whatever scene is presented, whatever character is portrayed.—*Worcester Palladium.*

She resembles Shakspeare in her power of delineation. It is from this characteristic action on the part of each of the members of the *dramatis personæ* that we feel not only an interest, even and consistent throughout, but also an admiration for "George Eliot" above all other writers.—*Philadelphia Evening Telegraph.*

Few women—no living woman indeed—have so much strength as "George Eliot," and, more than that, she never allows it to degenerate into coarseness. With all her so-called "masculine" vigor, she has a feminine tenderness, which is nowhere shown more plainly than in her descriptions of children.—*Boston Transcript.*

She looks out upon the world with the most entire enjoyment of all the good that there is in it to enjoy, and with an enlarged compassion for all the ill that there is in it to pity. But she never either whimpers over the sorrowful lot of man, or snarls and chuckles over his follies and littlenesses and impotence.—*Saturday Review.*

Her acquaintance with different phases of outward life, and the power of analyzing feeling and the working of the mind, are alike wonderful.—*Reader.*

"George Eliot's" novels belong to the enduring literature of our country—durable, not for the fashionableness of its pattern, but for the texture of its stuff. —*Examiner.*

It is a work of real historical value, the result of accurate criticism, written in a liberal spirit, and from first to last deeply interesting.—*Athenæum.*

The style is excellent, clear, vivid, eloquent; and the industry with which original sources have been investigated, and through which new light has been shed over perplexed incidents and characters, entitles Mr. Motley to a high rank in the literature of an age peculiarly rich in history.—*North British Review.*

It abounds in new information, and, as a first work, commands a very cordial recognition, not merely of the promise it gives, but of the extent and importance of the labor actually performed on it.—*London Examiner.*

Mr. Motley's "History" is a work of which any country might be proud.—*Press* (London).

Mr. Motley's History will be a standard book of reference in historical literature.—*London Literary Gazette.*

Mr. Motley has searched the whole range of historical documents necessary to the composition of his work.—*London Leader.*

This is really a great work. It belongs to the class of books in which we range our Grotes, Milmans, Merivales, and Macaulays, as the glories of English literature in the department of history. * * * Mr. Motley's gifts as a historical writer are among the highest and rarest.—*Nonconformist* (London).

Mr. Motley's volumes will well repay perusal. * * * For his learning, his liberal tone, and his generous enthusiasm, we heartily commend him, and bid him good speed for the remainer of his interesting and heroic narrative.—*Saturday Review.*

The story is a noble one, and is worthily treated. * * * Mr. Motley has had the patience to unravel, with unfailing perseverance, the thousand intricate plots of the adversaries of the Prince of Orange; but the details and the literal extracts which he has derived from original documents, and transferred to his pages, give a truthful color and a picturesque effect, which are especially charming.—*London Daily News.*

M. Lothrop Motley dans son magnifique tableau de la formation de notre République.—G. Groen Van Prinsterer.

Our accomplished countryman, Mr. J. Lothrop Motley, who, during the last five years, for the better prosecution of his labors, has established his residence in the neighborhood of the scenes of his narrative. No one acquainted with the fine powers of mind possessed by this scholar, and the earnestness with which he has devoted himself to the task, can doubt that he will do full justice to his important but difficult subject.—W. H. Prescott.

The production of such a work as this astonishes, while it gratifies the pride of the American reader.—*N. Y. Observer.*

The "Rise of the Dutch Republic" at once, and by acclamation, takes its place by the "Decline and Fall of the Roman Empire," as a work which, whether for research, substance, or style, will never be superseded.—*N. Y. Albion.*

A work upon which all who read the English language may congratulate themselves.—*New Yorker Handels Zeitung.*

Mr. Motley's place is now (alluding to this book) with Hallam and Lord Mahon, Alison and Macaulay in the Old Country, and with Washington Irving, Prescott, and Bancroft in this.—*N. Y. Times.*

The authority, in the English tongue, for the history of the period and people to which it refers.—*N. Y. Courier and Enquirer.*

This work at once places the author on the list of American historians which has been so signally illustrated by the names of Irving, Prescott, Bancroft, and Hildreth.—*Boston Times.*

The work is a noble one, and a most desirable acquisition to our historical literature.—*Mobile Advertiser.*

Such a work is an honor to its author, to his country, and to the age in which it was written.—*Ohio Farmer.*

www.ingramcontent.com/pod-product-compliance
Lightning Source LLC
LaVergne TN
LVHW020124110826
845151LV00001B/269

9781425541538